D0205118

★★★★★★★★★★★★★★★★

TOO FUNNY TO BE PRESIDENT

★★★★★★★★★★★★★★★★★★★★★★★★★★★★★

MORRIS K. UDALL

with Bob Neuman and Randy Udall

The University of Arizona Press

Tucson

The University of Arizona Press

Copyright © 1988 by Morris K. Udall

First University of Arizona Press paperbound edition

Published by arrangement with Henry Holt and Company

All rights reserved

∞This book is printed on acid-free, archival-quality paper.

Manufactured in the United States of America

06 05 04 03 02 01 6 5 4 3 2 1

Library of Congress Cataloging-in-Publication Data

Udall, Morris K.

Too funny to be president / Morris K. Udall—

1st University of Arizona Press pbk. ed.

p. cm.

ISBN 0-8165-2175-1 (pbk. : alk. paper)

1. Udall, Morris K.—Anecdotes. 2. Udall, Morris K.—Humor.

3. Political satire, American. 4. United States—Politics and government—

1945–1989. I. Title.

E840.8.U3 A3 2001   973.925'092—dc21

00-067220

British Library Cataloguing-in-Publication Data

A catalogue record for this book is available from the British Library.

This book is dedicated to the three thousand members of Congress, living and dead, with whom I served for nearly three decades.

★★★★★★★★★★★★★★★★★★★★★★★★★★★★★★★★★★

Contents

★★★★★★★★★★★★★★★★★★★★★★★★★★★★★★★★★★

CONTENTS

★ ★

Acknowledgments

★ ★

This work is the product of a whole generation of interns, staffers, colleagues, and friends who helped collect and organize my three loose-leaf books: Larry L. King, Richard Olsen, Terry Bracy, Dee Jackson, Dean "Chuck" Ares, Bonnie Kell, Matt James, Tom Chandler, Abe Chanin, Ken Burton, to mention only a few.

Joan Shycoff deserves a great reward for her tireless efforts transcribing my scratchy tapes and old jokes.

I am indebted to my longtime friend, Art Buchwald, the author of "Buchwald's Fourth Law," which reads: "The First two times you use a joke, give your source credit. From then on, to hell with it! Be shameless—claim it as your own. After all, your source undoubtedly stole it from someone else." Another giant who honors me with a flattering foreword is Erma Bombeck, the first lady of humor, who has brought the healing power of laughter to a whole country.

Two others played critical roles in getting the project off the ground when I was discouraged and ready to abandon it: Bob Neuman, my administrative assistant, who was there at the beginning and persevered to the end. The other is James R. Udall, my second son, whose invaluable ability to put down old memories in fresh and lucid prose made him the key person in reviving the enterprise at a critical time.

His wife, Leslie, and Bob Neuman's wife, Kay, along with

ACKNOWLEDGMENTS

Ella Udall deserve thanks for their patience, understanding, and encouragement.

Finally, my thanks to Esther Newberg and Jack Macrae for sticking with us when the going was tough.

—Morris K. Udall

★ ★

Foreword

★ ★

The reason I agreed to do a foreword for Mo Udall's book is because a foreword comes at the beginning. I followed him once. I will never do it again. When he speaks, I want to be in a high-powered car, speeding through the night on my way to another country. No one needs that kind of humility.

I remember the occasion well. It was a night in 1971 in Phoenix, Arizona, when he and Senator Barry Goldwater preceded me on a program. After a half hour, they presented me with an audience who had laughed themselves into a coma.

I told myself that night that politicians had access to all the funny material: failing economy, nuclear waste dumps, vanishing natural resources to sustain life. My God, if you couldn't get a laugh out of all that, you weren't even trying.

I told myself that the audience was heeding the words of the late Fred Allen: "It's bad to suppress laughter. It goes back down and spreads to your hips."

I even rationalized that the audience was just being respectful to two politicians with handicaps: a congressman with one eye and a senator with one point of view.

The truth is, Mo Udall is one of the fastest wits in the West and shoots straight from the lips. If we traveled the same speaker's circuit, I would eventually be forced into retirement—to live out my life throwing Amway parties. From the desert of Arizona that originally laid claim to products such as copper, citrus, and cotton, Mo has given the state a new gross national product: humor. He has mined a mother lode of it for this book from the sacred halls of Congress, to the dusty campaign trails, to the pages of political history. (Of course, it's drier than most humor. What did you expect from a state with less than ten inches of rainfall a year!)

Too Funny to Be President? I don't for a minute believe that title. If a combination Will Rogers–Abraham Lincoln–Winston Churchill–Henny Youngman could represent Arizona for fourteen terms in Congress, then why not the Oval Office?

As a voter, I never take anyone seriously who takes himself seriously. I have to believe most people are like that. They trust people with a sense of humor because that's what humor is—truth—with a little exaggeration and self-effacement thrown in to make it palatable. You show me a president without a sense of humor and I'll show you a man in paper slippers sitting in cabinet meetings with his bathrobe open.

I feel cheated that Mo Udall never occupied the White House. He had the vision (20 of it). He had the experience. He had his log cabin built. He had his presidential memoirs in the hands of an agent. He would have been like a fresh breeze blowing over the stagnant rhetoric of presidents past . . . a new broom sweeping political clichés out the door . . . a new vitality to people who needed to know we're going to make it.

On the other hand, any child can grow up to be president . . . but only one person could have written *Too Funny to Be President*—Mo Udall.

—Erma Bombeck

★ ★

Preface

★ ★

> There are three things that are real: God, human folly,
> and laughter. The first two are beyond comprehension.
> So we must do what we can with the third.
> —*John F. Kennedy*

For years, friends have urged me to publish the storehouse
of jokes, tales, and quips I've collected during three decades
of public life. And for years, I hesitated, wondering whether
it might not seem immodest to do so. Then I recalled Golda
Meir's admonition, "Don't be humble, you're not that great."
I also considered the tribute Winston Churchill once paid
to his arch political foe, Labour Party chairman Clement
Atlee: "Atlee is a very modest man . . . who has much to
be modest about."

Like Atlee, I've much to be modest about. During my early
years in the House of Representatives, I tilted at the seniority
system—and got my comeuppance in contests to become
Speaker and Majority Leader. During my 1976 campaign
for the Democratic presidential nomination, I drew more
laughter than votes and placed second in seven consecutive
primaries. This prompted James J. Kilpatrick to conclude
his political obituary of me with the epitaph "Mo's too funny
to be President."

After due deliberation and two stiff drinks, I decided to
go ahead and write this book because I'm convinced that
humor is as necessary to the health of our political discourse
as it is in our private lives. Political humor leavens the public
dialogue; it invigorates the body politic; it uplifts the national

xiii

spirit. In a sprawling society where politicians often seem distant from those they represent, political humor is a bridge between the citizens and their government. In times of national strife, humor can bring a diverse society closer together. Once, while struggling to fashion a historic compromise, an exasperated Charles de Gaulle threw up his hands and said, "How can anyone govern a nation that has 246 different kinds of cheese?"

In times of national tragedy, disappointment, or defeat, political humor can assuage the nation's grief, sadness, or anger, and thus make bearable that which must be borne. At such times a joke reminds us, "And this too shall pass."

But humor is not only a tonic for the body politic, it is an elixir for the politician as well. For one thing, it helps you roll with the punches—and there are a lot of punches in politics. It was his robust sense of humor that kept Abraham Lincoln sane in the face of personal tragedy and a raging Civil War. Asked how he could tell jokes at a time when the nation was bleeding, Abe replied, "I laugh because I must not cry."

Humor is also the best antidote for the politician's occupational disease: an inflated, overweening, suffocating sense of self-importance. "A man sufficiently gifted with humor is in small danger of succumbing to flattering delusions about himself," Konrad Lorenz once observed, "because he cannot help perceiving what a pompous ass he would become if he did." Nothing deflates a pompous ass quicker than a well-placed barb; Atlee must have imploded when lampooned by Churchill.

Politics is a people business—and people crave laughter. Other things being equal, a droll politician will have an easier time than a dour one getting elected. Wit is an essential element of charisma, of leadership. "I don't care how great your ideas are or how well you can articulate them, people

Preface

must *like* you before they will vote for you," says Senator William Cohen. The fact is, people are drawn to, and reassured by, a politician who can poke fun at others and himself. It is no accident that of our last six presidents, the two most popular—John Kennedy and Ronald Reagan—have been the two most jocose. Certainly, much of the warmth people still feel for Kennedy is a result of having been charmed by his wit—more than his policies—nearly three decades ago. And much of President Reagan's popularity doubtless rests on his lively sense of humor, best demonstrated when he asked the surgeon who was preparing to remove a bullet from his chest whether he was a Republican. You can even argue that wit *won* Reagan the presidency: his timely rejoinder—"There you go again"—to a criticism leveled by Jimmy Carter in a 1980 debate might have been the margin of victory. In 1984, after stumbling in his first debate with Walter Mondale, Reagan deep-sixed the creeping-senility issue with another zinger—"I will not exploit, for political purposes, the youth and inexperience of my opponent."

Once a politician has been elected, humor becomes one of the most formidable tools he or she can wield in pursuit of legislative goals. A savvy pol can use humor to disarm his enemies, to rally his allies, to inform, rebut, educate, console, and convince. Some observers feel Senator Alan Simpson's recent success in shepherding a controversial immigration bill through Congress was a tribute as much to his wit as to his intellect. In my own career, I have used humor to help me get reelected fourteen times, and to attain passage of the 1977 strip-mining bill and the 1980 Alaska Lands bill.

Of course, there are those Scrooges who think that humor and the serious business of politics should never be mixed. One adviser of President James Garfield warned him, "Never make the people laugh. If you would succeed in life you must be solemn, solemn as an ass." Solemn as an ass he was—and somebody shot him three months into his term. It is true, however, that the business of government is serious business, and in politics, as in any other endeavor, wisecracks are no substitute for substance. But, used adroitly, wit is something more than oratorical ornament; rather, it is a gentle pry bar with which to open the minds of your constituents and colleagues. If your speeches have a humorous slant it is less likely that their substance will be rejected out of hand. In the same way that wit strengthens politicians, a total absence of it can wound. If President Nixon had had a sense of humor, would he have countenanced the Watergate burglary at a time when his reelection seemed assured? I doubt it. One of the reasons Jimmy Carter wore out his welcome with some Americans was that, for all his intelligence, he came to be viewed as humorless. If Gary Hart had been able to parry Mondale's "Where's the beef?" jab with a witty rejoinder he might have won the Democratic presidential nomination in 1984.

I first learned that humor pays nearly forty years ago, when I began practicing law. Ever since, I've been collecting legal and political jokes, yarns, and saws. I've got jokes my granddad used in frontier Arizona in the late 1800s. I've got jokes that Ben Franklin used in the late 1700s. I've got jokes about bureaucrats, voters, Yasir Arafat, Jesus Christ, Calvin Coolidge, Republicans, Democrats, Indians, animals, Mormons, Jews, blacks, whites, politicians, polygamists, and polygamist politicians . . . thousands of them.

Some jokes I've heard in the courtroom or on the floor of the House. Others I've found in old speeches and newspaper articles. Still others I've kidnapped on the rubber-chicken circuit. Many of my best quips have come from constituents, supporters, fan mail, even questionnaires: *Question:* "Do you support spending $20 billion to put a man on the moon?"

Answer: "Yes—if you go." In the last chapter you'll find my favorites. If you like them, feel free to use them. After all, I stole them "fair and square," just as that great semanticist and inveterate napper, Senator S. I. Hayakawa, said we did the Panama Canal.

This book is dedicated to the proposition that humor is the *saving grace*—in our own lives, and in our political life as a great country. It is one politician's view of the human condition and the role humor has played in his career. Join me as we stroll the halls of Congress and trek the campaign trail. We'll meet and swap yarns with all kinds of people.

Because it's virtually impossible to index the jokes that run through practically every paragraph of this book (the index would soon match the text in length), I suggest that those who want to remember a favorite line for future use make a note or two as they read the book. To make joke-telling somewhat easier, I've included, in Chapter 14, some of my favorite jokes under a half dozen or so categories.

Having read the book, I hope you will feel you've gotten your money's worth. Which reminds me of something Adlai Stevenson once said to an audience of lobbyists: "Now, as I understand our respective roles, I am to contribute a speech—and you are to contribute something more tangible. This is a nice division of labor, much like the relationship of Big Ben to the Leaning Tower of Pisa. That is to say, I've got the time, if you've got the inclination."

—Morris K. Udall
Washington, D.C.

Too Funny To Be President

★★★★★★★★★★★★ **1** ★★★★★★★★★★★★

The United States of Laughter

★★★★★★★★★★★★★★★★★★★★★★★★★★★★

Oh, yes, and they even accuse us of having a sense of humor.

—*Adlai Stevenson*

I'm not sure most Americans realize how lucky they are to live in one of precious few nations on earth where laughter of, by, and for the people is not regarded as a dangerous and subversive force. In my view, what's most remarkable about America is not that any child can grow up to be president, but rather that any child or adult can safely make jokes *about* the president—and not just in the privacy of his or her home. Try that in Chile, Iran, or pre-glasnost Russia.

Ronald Reagan is the maximum leader of the free world, the Supremely Addled Commander, some would say, of a military force on which we lavish $300 billion per year. And yet, if you wake up one morning with the urge, you can, in complete safety, place a full-page ad in your local paper saying, "IMPEACH BONZO!" Alternatively, you can go down to your neighborhood shopping mall and don a signboard stating, "REAGAN HAS QUAKER OATS FOR BRAINS." If this entails some risk, it's because you're maligning a brand-name product, not the president.

Not only can Americans freely poke fun at the president (it goes without saying that such piddling potentates as congressmen, governors, et cetera are fair game, too), more than a few humorists have become rich and famous for doing

1

so. Think of Johnny Carson, Art Buchwald, Russell Baker, Garry Trudeau, and Pat Oliphant as just a few examples. Of course, bumbling statesmen aren't their only targets, but when all else fails, well, the foibles and follies of politicians are always good for a few laughs. Easy targets, no doubt about it.

For more than two hundred years our robust tradition of political humor has been a reflection of our occasionally robust democracy. "Democracy," one philosopher said, "is like sex. When it is good, it is very, very good. And when it is bad, it is still pretty good." So is much of our humorous political folklore. Throughout our history political jokes have served to humanize our democratic process and to reaffirm our common heritage. The schoolchild who is taught all about American history, names and dates and places, but who does not learn that the founding fathers were gifted with humor as well as wisdom, has been done a disservice. Humor is one form of history, and helps bring it alive.

One of our first political humorists was Ben Franklin. Picture him hunched over a desk, chuckling to himself while writing a tongue-in-cheek article about the marvels of America for the unwitting readers of a London newspaper: "The grand leap of the whale up the Fall of Niagara is esteemed, by all who have seen it, as one of the finest spectacles in nature."

In the first years after America won her independence, she was regarded as a brash newcomer abroad, and her envoys were held in the lowest possible esteem. At one diplomatic affair in Versailles, a group of dignitaries were offering toasts to their respective sovereigns. The British ambassador toasted King George III and likened him to the sun. The French foreign minister then proposed a toast to King Louis XVI and compared him to the moon. One-upping them, Franklin raised his glass and proposed a toast to "George Washington, commander of the American armies, who, like Joshua of old, commanded the sun and the moon to stand still, and they obeyed him."

Franklin's wit spanned the spectrum from lighthearted jests—"The noble turkey rather than the thievish bald eagle should be our national bird"—to pithy aphorisms, such as his remark to John Hancock at the signing of the Declaration of Independence: "We must indeed all hang together, or, most assuredly, we shall all hang separately." Franklin even found time, amid his other duties, to write a tract enumerating reasons for selecting an elderly mistress, which concluded: "Eighth and lastly, they are so grateful."

An examination of quips from the eighteenth and nineteenth centuries reveals that the basic themes of political humor—politicians, Congress, presidents, Democrats, Republicans, controversial issues, scandals—have remained the same. These are rich veins, and although they have been mined by a long line of political humorists for more than two centuries, they show no sign of depletion.

More than two hundred years ago, Franklin drew laughs when he said of one bombastic politician: "Here comes the orator, with his flood of words and his drop of wisdom." A few decades later, Ralph Waldo Emerson mocked another sententious politician, saying, "The louder he talked of his honor, the faster we counted our spoons." Abraham Lincoln shook his head over another long-winded orator and remarked, "He can compress the most words into the smallest idea of any man I ever met."

Presidents always make jokes about Congress but it's hard to beat Lincoln's jest: "I have been told I was on the road to hell, but I had no idea it was just a mile down the road with a Dome on it." The real essence of the institution may have been captured by a baffled foreign observer, Boris

Marshalov, who reported: "Congress is so strange. A man gets up to speak and says nothing. Nobody listens—and then everybody disagrees."

One famous humorist who lived during Lincoln's day was Charles Farrar Browne, who wrote political satire under the pseudonym Artemus Ward. Ward was one of the first to discover that a man could make a good living by roasting politicians. "I am not a politician," Ward once said, "and my other habits are good also." Ward typically looked at government with a twinkle in his eye—while writing in a tortured vernacular meant to represent the common man. "My pollertics," Ward exclaimed, "like my religion, is of an exceedin' accommodatin' character." Surveying the political scene, Ward found that "The prevailin' weakness of most public men is to slop over"; they would do better to follow the example of "G. Washington, who never slopt over."

Either by coincidence or reincarnation, in 1867, the same year that Browne died, Finley Peter Dunne was born. Speaking through a character he created, an Irish bartender named Mr. Dooley, Dunne was to become the most popular political humorist of the late nineteenth century. Of American justice and corrupt politicians Dooley said, "This is the home iv opporchunity where ivry man is th' equal iv ivry other man befure th' law if he isn't careful." The best political humor packs a hidden punch—you couldn't find a more apt moral for Watergate.

Mr. Dooley had a good grasp of the role of the vice president: "It is his jooty to rigorously enforce th' rules iv th' Sinit. There ar-re none. Th' Sinit is ruled by courtesy, like th' Longshoreman's Union."

Dooley was not the first or last to discover that "Th' dimmycratic party ain't on speaking terms with itself." Of political idealists, Dooley remarked, "A man that'd expict to thrain lobsters to fly in a year is called a loonytic; but a man that thinks men can be tu-rrned into angels be an iliction is called a rayformer an' remans at large."

As our political parties evolved—if that's the right word—into their current forms during the second half of the last century and the first half of this one, political humorists, led by Will Rogers, began to take aim at Republicans and Democrats.

"The 1928 Republican convention opened with a prayer," Rogers reported. "If the Lord can see his way clear to bless the Republican Party the way it's been carrying on, then the rest of us ought to get it without even asking." Rogers was a populist and his aim was completely bipartisan: no politician was safe from his zingers. "I generally give the Party in Power, whether Republican or Democrat, the more digs because they are generally doing the Country the most damage, and besides I don't think it is fair to jump too much on the fellow who is down. He is not working, he is only living in hopes of getting back in on the graft in another four years."

Clare Boothe Luce, the sharp-tongued former congresswoman and widow of *Time* magazine publisher Henry R. Luce, said of the Democratic party: "Its leaders are always troubadours of trouble; crooners of catastrophe. . . . A Democratic president is doomed to proceed to his goals like a squid, squirting darkness all around him." Is *that* why we've only had one Democratic president in the last twenty years?

Come presidential election time, Democrats, like so many blind pigs looking for acorns, begin snuffling about the political landscape vainly searching for unity. Inspired by some convention donnybrook, one reporter quipped, "When Democrats form a firing squad they probably arrange themselves in a circle."

Of course, these intraparty feuds never prevent Democrats

from sniping at Republicans. Adlai Stevenson proposed a cease-fire: "If the Republicans will stop telling lies about Democrats, we'll stop telling the truth about them." Harry Truman had a slightly different formulation: "I don't give 'em [Republicans] hell; I just tell the truth and they think it's hell."

Political humor is also spawned by controversial social issues. During the great debate over repealing Prohibition, one wit criticized the Prohibitionists for advocating "the reckless use of water." W. C. Fields, renowned for his fondness for spirits, complained that Prohibition had forced him to live "for days on nothing but food and water." As the debate raged, and state after state voted on the issue, Will Rogers predicted, "Oklahoma will remain a dry state as long as the voters can stagger to the polls." In 1928, the Democrats straddled the fence by nominating Governor Alfred Smith, who favored repeal, for president, and Senator Joseph Robinson, who favored Prohibition, for vice president. Will thought they should reverse the ticket: "They got a wet head and a dry tail. It's better to have your feet wet than your head."

Taxes are a perennial target, proof again that laughter can triumph over any adversity. "If Patrick Henry thought taxation without representation was bad," an anonymous wit once said, "he should see it *with* representation."

Political scandals, too, are guaranteed to tickle the national funny bone. Meg Greenfield, editorial page editor of the *Washington Post,* likes to tell this story: The late Joe Staszek was a Baltimore tavern owner and state senator who worked tirelessly for legislation that would help his own liquor business. When asked whether such efforts did not constitute a conflict of interest, Staszek replied in wonderment: "How does this conflict with my 'interest'?"

During the Iran-contra scandal, when it was first revealed that National Security Council "cowboys" working out of the basement of the White House had run amok, trading a cake, Bible, and one thousand TOW antitank missiles to "Iranian moderates" in return for kidnapped American hostages, one wag asked, "How does the NSC staff differ from kids in a day-care center?" The answer: "The kids have adult supervision."

"What's the definition of an Iranian moderate?" comic Mark Shields was soon asking. Answer: "A graduate student who's run out of ammunition." "Husbands don't listen to their wives enough," gag writer Bob Orben wrote. "All this could have been avoided if Ronnie had cleaned out the basement like Nancy kept telling him to." As the White House kept insisting that the whole idea had been Oliver North's, somebody quipped, "Oliver North. The first lieutenant colonel in the history of the Marine Corps who believed that the chain of command started at the bottom." Asked if we were contemplating making more shipments to Iran, President Reagan answered, "We were considering one final shipment, but no one could figure out how to get Sam Donaldson in a crate."

Although such jokes offer a cutting commentary on current events, it would be wrong to conclude that our rich tradition of political humor demeans political institutions or politicians. Of course, humor can be, and from time to time has been, used for this purpose. But the motives behind it are usually transparent and the "jokes" fall with a dull thud. Political humorists always walk a fine line—and even the best of them sometimes fall off.

For example, Mark Twain seemed to become less and less funny to the people of his time as he grew older and more irascible, railing against all institutions, politicians, and religions. "Reader," began one article, "suppose you were an idiot. And suppose you were a member of Congress. But I repeat myself." That's a funny gibe, and one can momentarily enjoy the play on words, yet it ultimately fails to illuminate or persuade. "Wit has truth in it," said *The New Yorker*'s Dorothy Parker, drawing a crucial distinction. "Wisecracking is simply calisthenics with words." In his later years, many of Twain's fulminations were seen as dyspeptic rather than humorous. Even his classic zinger—"A dead politician is the noblest work of God"—was about as unfunny as saying, "The only good Indian is a dead Indian." I think you'll find that most politicians and Indians concur.

Don't get me wrong—I don't believe that politicians or any other area of political life should be off limits. But in my opinion, the best political humor, however sharp or pointed, has a little love behind it. It's the spirit of the humor that counts, and that's why Will Rogers was the best and most popular political humorist this country has ever produced.

Will loved America, was a friend of many politicians, and, of course, "never met a man I didn't like." People always understood this—which is why politicians found it easy to forgive him when they were the butt of one of his jokes. Rogers was a prolific gag writer, but as he once remarked, "There's no trick to being a humorist when you have the whole government working for you." One of his favorite targets was Congress: "When the Congress makes a law, it's a joke; and when the Congress makes a joke, it's the law."

Presidents, of course, have never been spared as objects of humor, with the exception of George Washington, probably because he never "slopt over." In fact, some presidents have been closet humorists themselves. Why, even Gerald Ford told jokes. I mean, *on purpose.* Asked by reporters to comment on the earthshaking controversy raging a few years ago as to whether Ronald Reagan dyed his hair, Ford replied that he didn't think he did. "It's just prematurely orange."

Calvin Coolidge, President Reagan's favorite president (he

said it, I didn't), was a man of few words and even fewer actions. Coolidge explained his terseness, "If you don't say anything, you won't be called on to repeat it." Years earlier at a dinner party in Boston a woman gushed, "Oh, Mr. Coolidge, what do you do?" "I'm the Lieutenant Governor," he replied. "How interesting, you must tell me all about it." Said Coolidge, "I just did." He later remarked, "I should like to be known as a former President who minded his own business." Asked once what direction the economy was headed, he boldly predicted, "Business will be better or worse." On hearing that "Silent Cal" had died, Dorothy Parker asked, "How could they tell?"

Although Coolidge was taciturn in public, around the White House he was an inveterate practical joker. One night a group of guests arrived for dinner. Inquiring about the proper table manners in such an elegant setting, they were advised to simply do whatever the president did. After sitting down, Coolidge called for a glass of milk. All the guests did the same. When his milk arrived, Coolidge poured some of it in a saucer. The guests did likewise. Then, without a word, Coolidge put his saucer down on the floor for the cat. The embarrassed guests, not knowing what else to do, followed suit. On Coolidge's sealed lips there was just a faint flicker of a smile as he continued eating.

On another occasion a woman accosted the president and gushed that she had bet a friend that she could get him to say more than two words. "You lose," Coolidge replied.

Another low-profile chief executive was Millard Fillmore. Fillmore was acutely self-conscious about his impoverished background and borderline literacy. After leaving the White House, Fillmore toured Europe. Offered an honorary degree by Oxford University, he declined to accept, for fear that the students would make fun of him: "They would probably ask, 'Who's Fillmore? What's he done? Where did he come from?' My name would, I fear, give them an excellent opportunity to make jokes at my expense." Besides, he added, "no man should, in my judgment, accept a degree he cannot read."

President Herbert Hoover was a dour man, not much given to mirth. But he did have the capacity for an occasional wry observation. In retirement he said, "Once upon a time my political opponents honored me as possessing the fabulous intellectual and economic power by which I created a worldwide depression all by myself." Hoover also said something that is becoming more apropos all the time: "Blessed are the young, for they shall inherit the national debt." Sounds like David Stockman.

Lyndon Johnson was a humorous braggart in the swaggering Texas style. When West German chancellor Ludwig Erhard met LBJ for the first time, he said, "I understand you were born in a log cabin, Mr. President." Johnson replied, "No, Mr. Chancellor, I was born in a manger."

On another occasion, as a fleet of helicopters sat waiting at an air base in Vietnam to whisk the presidential party away, LBJ got out of his limousine and began walking toward one of the helicopters. A young military attaché ran up and tried to redirect the president. "Sir, your helicopter is over there." LBJ fixed him with a baleful eye and drawled, "Son, they're all my helicopters."

The types of jokes a president tells offer insights into his personality. LBJ liked to tell the story of a boy who showed up late for work one day. When his boss asked why, the boy explained, "Well, I listened to a United States senator make a speech." The boss said, "Well, the senator didn't speak all day, did he?" The boy said, "Mighty near, mighty near." The boss then asked, "Who was the senator and what did he speak about?" "Well," said the boy, "boss, his name was Senator Joseph Weldon Bailey from Texas, and I don't recall all the senator talked about, but the general impression I got was that he was recommending himself most highly." After telling the story, LBJ would purr, "It is naturally to be assumed that I would recommend myself most highly."

American government offers a wide playing field for the political comedian. One can make jokes about politicians running for office, politicians *in* office, presidential appointees, even bureaucrats. Asked to define a bureaucrat, the late vice president Alben Barkley replied, "A bureaucrat is a Democrat who has a job some Republican wants."

There's another joke that is applicable to any administration simply by inserting the correct names. As the story goes, the president is deeply troubled by the difficulty he is having with leaks to the press and constant squabbling among the cabinet members. Sound familiar? Seeking relief, the president evades his Secret Service at Camp David and walks deep into the woods. As dusk falls, the president notices a small cave. On coming closer, he sees a white-bearded man dressed in robes huddled in the cave's entrance. There is an aura of mysticism about the old fellow.

"I need a sign," the president says. "Can you give me your wise counsel?"

"Ask me any question," the old man replies, "and by my answer you will have your sign."

"I need to know if my secretary of state, secretary of defense, and secretary of the treasury all climbed to the top of the Washington Monument and jumped at the same instant, which would land first?"

The sage bows his head in contemplation. When he finally looks up, he says, "That is not important. What is important is that they should jump."

But of course it is when election time draws near that our body politic is most likely to break out in a rash of jests, gibes, and tales. That is when the fur and words fly.

11

The rash can appear in a lot of different places, from comic strips like *Doonesbury* to campaign buttons. (When Barry Goldwater declared at the 1964 GOP convention that "extremism in the defense of liberty is no vice and moderation in the pursuit of justice is no virtue," buttons immediately appeared that said, "I'm a moderate extremist.") Oftentimes, the humor that endures is not that manufactured by the gag writers and clever columnists; instead, it is the humor that springs from the people themselves that proves to be the wisest and wittiest.

During the 1976 Wisconsin presidential primary campaign I found myself talking to a bright-eyed seventy-year-old farmer in a small upstate town.

"Where you from, son?" he asked.

"Washington, D.C.," I replied.

"You've got some pretty smart fellas back there, ain't ya?" he asked.

"Yes, sir, I guess we do."

"Got some that ain't so smart, too, ain't ya?" he said.

"Well," I replied, "I guess that's true too."

"Damn hard to tell the difference, ain't it," the old-timer concluded with a chuckle.

In a democracy, you see, the people always have the last laugh.

★★★★★★★★★★★★ **2** ★★★★★★★★★★★★★

Fire in the Belly: On the Campaign Trail

★★★★★★★★★★★★★★★★★★★★★★★★★★★★★

> Lawd, give us Mistah Roo-se-velt ag'in. Fer he knows
> that [breaks into song] Where the coyotes howl/and
> the wind blows free/He'll bury them thar' on the lone
> prai-rreeeee . . . [wild cheering]
> —*Senator Tom Heflin of Missouri*
> *seconding FDR's nomination at*
> *the Democratic National Convention*

In November 1974 then-senator Walter Mondale aborted
his exploratory campaign for the presidency. "After spending
a year pounding the campaign trail," he said, "I found I
did not have the overwhelming desire to be president which
is essential for the kind of campaign that is required. . . .
For one thing, I have no desire to spend the next two years
sleeping in a different Holiday Inn each night." This lighthearted comment alarmed scores of solemn pundits, who
wrote long belabored columns wondering whether Fritz had
the right stuff, specifically, enough "fire in the belly" to become president. At the time I thought it peculiar that a perfectly understandable reluctance to sleep in Holiday Inns
should be a touchstone for evaluating a candidate's man-
hood, fortitude, and presidential qualifications. You might
as well have him run a gauntlet of room clerks and hotel
maids while being struck with credit card vouchers and fresh
linens.

If the ability of a candidate to stomach roadside lodgings

13

determines whether he or she has fire in the belly, I must have had a raging inferno in mine, and not just because of the kielbasa in Detroit. During my 1976 quest for the Democratic nomination my impoverished campaign was often forced to bunk in quaint but crumbling hotels with turn-of-the-century ambience and plumbing to match. Holiday Inns? Hell, we felt grateful when we found a hotel with a pop machine and functional switchboard so that reporters accompanying us could file their stories. One night veteran reporter Jack Germond was awakened by high-pitched squealing sounds. Lifting his head off the pillow to look bleary-eyed toward the window, Germond espied a pair of rats enjoying conjugal relations on the radiator. The next day Germond went around snorting, "Traveling with Udall is a good way to get acquainted with the third world."

There are several important lessons for presidential contenders in all of this. First, you may discover that having fire in the belly sufficient to satisfy the pundits is a lot like finding yourself dressed up with no place to go. Second, a presidential campaign is flat-out *guaranteed* to test your stamina, health, marriage, and, not least, sense of humor (you would do well to cultivate a robust one—you'll need it). Third, never, ever, joke about Holiday Inns—especially if you hope to end up sleeping in the White House. Last, no candidate, no matter how high-minded or principled, should be so naïve as to think he can enter the political arena while remaining above the fray. Woe unto the politician who jumps into a race with the attitude of Henry VI, who said, "Pray that I take but two shirts out with me and I mean not to sweat extraordinarily."

Oftentimes, when an unsuspecting politician does come to the tardy and startling conclusion that he is in a real dogfight, he will react like Count Rostov in *War and Peace*, whose departure for the battlefront is preceded by weeks of elegant farewell parties. When the noble count finally gallops off on his first cavalry charge and finds real bullets snapping at his ears, he is shocked: "Why, why, they're shooting at me! Me, whom everyone loves!"

Once you've thrown your hat in the ring—it's not called that for nothing—there is no easy retreat. A candidate can't be like the cowardly fellow who got drunk one night, and, after getting in an argument, rashly agreed to a duel at sunrise. By the fateful hour, he'd sobered up and come to dread the appointment. When courage failed him he dispatched his second with a note: "I am going to be late; go ahead and shoot."

For his part, Mondale believes that running for president is an undertaking so outsized it's difficult to describe: "It's physically, emotionally, mentally, and spiritually the most demanding single undertaking I can envisage unless it's World War III." The major difference between World War III and a presidential campaign is that in the former you can only die once.

The truth is that the campaign trail is a rough one—bandits, ambushes, and pitfalls abound. Whatever your political persuasion, there are a lot of brigands out there who'd love to count coup on you. Presidential politics is also unlike any other battle in that, if you're not careful, a single misstep on the part of your tongue can cost you your scalp. Here lies George Romney, who got "brainwashed"; here lies Jerry Ford, "There is no Soviet domination of Eastern Europe"; here lies Jimmy Carter, "I've committed adultery in my heart many times"; here lies Ronald "We start bombing in five minutes" Reagan. Of the hundreds of hurdles on the road to the White House, you're bound to trip over a few. And when you do, the hyenas will rush in from the sidelines eager for the kill. By the end of the campaign you're likely to find yourself nodding as you hear those famous words of the late mayor Richard J. Daley of Chicago: "They have slandered me, they have castigated me, they have vilified me, yes, they have even criticized me."

But the fact that political campaigns can be rough-and-tumble doesn't mean they can't be conducted with decency and good humor by candidates who strive to keep the political dialogue on a high plane. True, that kind of campaign is becoming more of an endangered species every year. Nonetheless, I still believe that we as a people are best served when our political discourse rises above the shoot-'em-up *High Noon* rhetoric of a dirty campaign. Granted, there will always be those cynics who snicker at candidates who travel the high road, particularly those commentators of the "let's you and him fight" variety. Such people think that the only real politics is akin to bare-knuckles brawling, and that the only thing that matters is winning or losing. The last time they had their way, we got Watergate. I rest my case.

In 1972, when he sought the Democratic presidential nomination, frontrunner Ed Muskie was criticized for sashaying along the high road and not being vicious enough in attacking his opponents. Wrote one wag: "Some politicians have an instinct for the jugular. Muskie has an instinct for the capillaries."

The gibe is funny, even though I disagree with the implied premise. During my own campaign, columnist Robert Novak thought I, too, lacked the requisite savagery. After observing a press conference in which I flayed Scoop Jackson, Novak wrote, "Mo Udall attempted to do a hatchet job on Sen. Henry Jackson, a task to which he is spectacularly unsuited. . . ."

But it has ever been thus. Adlai Stevenson was continuously faulted in 1952 and 1956 for his lofty, witty style and his painstakingly responsible rhetoric. His response to these attacks was, typically, to deflect them with humor: "I have tried to talk about the issues in this campaign . . . and this has sometimes been a lonely road, because I never meet anybody coming the other way." When he was criticized for not doing a better job exploiting popular passions, Stevenson, always a diffident candidate, retorted, "It's hard to lead a cavalry charge if you think you look funny on a horse." On another occasion, Stevenson, who suspected he was doomed to lose in the face of General Eisenhower's overwhelming popularity, delivered a particularly eloquent, well-crafted speech. It was a tour de force that included a near-poetic recitation of the current issues, the various policy options, and his personal prescription. Afterward, a woman came up to him and gushed, "Governor, your speech was magnificent. You'll get the vote of every thinking person." Stevenson replied, "It's not enough. I need a majority."

The process by which we nominate and then elect our presidents has been called "the longest folk festival in the world" by Charlie McDowell, veteran Washington correspondent for the Richmond, Virginia, *Times-Dispatch*. Folk festival, circus, comic opera, farce—call it what you will, nothing beats the campaign trail for the spontaneous generation of humor.

There was humor in the unabashed enthusiasm of Hubert Humphrey as he practiced his "politics of joy," and there was humor in that famous photograph of a prim Herbert Hoover staring unhappily from beneath an Indian war bonnet, trying desperately to look as if he was enjoying himself. And there was humor in 1948 when Harry Truman, attacking Republican Thomas E. Dewey, said, "Dewey opened his mouth—and he closed his eyes—[pause] and he *swallowed* the whole record of that good-for-nothin' Republican Eightieth Congress!"

Dewey's campaign got off to a shaky—but humorous—

17

start. After a long day on a cross-country whistle-stop train trip designed to woo some of the labor vote away from the Democrats, Dewey criticized the engineer for being late in leaving the station. This proved to be a major embarrassment and created a furor over his position on labor relations. It also allowed James Reston of *The New York Times* to conclude his dispatch about the incident by writing: ". . . and the train pulled off with a jerk."

One story from FDR's 1944 reelection campaign provides an excellent illustration of how a candidate can use humor to deflect an attack. It had been charged, spuriously, that millions of dollars had been spent to send a U.S. destroyer back to the scene of a presidential visit in the Aleutian Islands to pick up the Roosevelts' Scottish terrier, Fala, who'd somehow been forgotten. I can still remember seeing newsreel footage showing a most solemn and grave FDR, speaking in the saddest possible voice, telling a labor audience: "These Republican leaders have not been content with attacks on me, or my wife, or on my sons. No, not content with that, they now include my little dog, Fala. Well, of course, I don't resent the attacks, and my family doesn't resent the attacks— but Fala *does* resent them! His Scotch soul was furious. He has not been the same dog since." The audience howled with laughter, and so did the rest of the country, including, no doubt, a few Republicans.

When Calvin Coolidge announced, "I do not choose to run for President in 1928," it was widely assumed that he was simply being modest, as was the custom in those times, and that secretly, in his heart of hearts, he yearned to be drafted for another term. This led Will Rogers to declare that not only did he, himself, choose not to run for president, but that he actually wouldn't run under any circumstances, "no matter how bad the country will need a comedian by that time."

Fire in the Belly: On the Campaign Trail

Any recounting of classic presidential campaign gibes would be incomplete if it failed to recall the spectacle of a dozen manifestly pregnant women trooping through the lobby of the hotel in Miami where Richard Nixon's convention headquarters was located. Hired by the inveterate political prankster Dick Tuck, the women carried placards emblazoned with Nixon's campaign slogan: "NIXON'S THE ONE!"

Nixon was never a scintillating conversationalist. During a campaign appearance in Florida, Nixon stopped his motorcade after he observed a member of the motorcycle escort lying in the street after being struck by a car. Nixon left his limo and approached the downed policeman. He knelt by him and there was an embarrassing silence until the president said, "Tell me, sir, how do you like your job?"

Nor can I forget the time NBC's John Chancellor was arrested on the floor of the 1964 GOP Convention: "Well, there's a policeman here, badge number thirty-eight, who's got a hand on my elbow and there is a sheriff coming forward. . . . I beg your pardon. . . . Here we go down the middle aisle. . . . You'll have to assist me, is that right? Walk? Uh. It's hard to be dignified at a time like this. . . . What do you say, I'm in custody. . . . I have been promised bail, ladies and gentlemen, by my office. . . . This way, officer? . . . This is a disgrace. . . . This is John Chancellor, somewhere in custody."

Of all recent presidential candidates, perhaps the wittiest was Gene McCarthy. McCarthy always maintained that he'd never specifically expressed a desire for the job, only that he'd be willing to take it: "I could not say that I ever looked at the White House and said, 'I want to live there sometime.' In fact, I thought it should have been made into a museum the first time I saw it. . . . The seeking of me as a candidate came like a dew in the night. It was rather gentle, I must say, and soft, but there were signs in the morning that something happened during the night, and so here we are." Most presidential candidates, of course, have more robust motives; some believe they have been summoned to lead a great crusade. "We stand at Armageddon," Teddy Roosevelt bellowed, "and battle for the Lord!" (Come to think of it, that wouldn't be a bad slogan for Pat Robertson.) Running as a third-party "Bull Moose" candidate that year, Teddy, and presumably the Lord, lost to Woodrow Wilson. It must have been quite galling to Teddy that the country and the Lord survived his loss, apparently without ill effect.

Throughout his campaign, McCarthy kept up a wry running commentary. He had no illusions about how much intelligence politics required. "Being in politics," he said, "is like being a football coach. You have to be smart enough to understand the game—and dumb enough to think it is important."

Other candidates might talk about staff problems, the need to do TV spots in a certain media market, how to counter an attack by an opponent, or how to deal with an image problem. But McCarthy got to the essence of the thing: "The real problem in a political campaign is to get a good man to drive your car."

McCarthy also was one of the first to notice that campaigning had changed in modern times. "You can't campaign in a drugstore anymore. People don't want you to see what they're buying." Besides, he added, "It's a little embarrassing to go up to someone and say, 'Hello. I'm Senator McCarthy. How are your corns?'"

Speaking of Republican liberals, McCarthy said, "Their function is to shoot the wounded after battle." He described the atmosphere at meetings of liberal Democrats as resembling "the atmosphere in a restaurant after there's been a small grease fire." Of those seeking the highest office in the land he said, "No man could be equipped for the presidency if he has never been tempted by one of the seven cardinal sins." Asked to comment on President John F. Kennedy's performance during the frantic first hundred days of the New Frontier, McCarthy recalled something a music critic once said about Liberace: "The critic said that he didn't know whether Liberace played well . . . but that he surely played fast." More recently, McCarthy warned, "You really have to be careful of politicians who have 'no further ambitions': they may run for the presidency."

Some of the humor one sees on the campaign trail results from the incongruity of men and women behaving in ways they ordinarily wouldn't because they've been caught up in the political drama: the hoopla, the music, the merriment, the fury and furor, all of it culminating on election night with the exhilarating thrill of victory or the agony of defeat. Yes, you *can* live for weeks on nothing but coffee, Coke, and donuts, but scientists have proved that it's guaranteed to addle your brains and warp your morals. At home you might be the most circumspect, virtuous person in your parish, but after a few weeks on the campaign trail you're liable to find yourself staying up all night to howl at the moon, treat jet lag with hard liquor, and lust after some charming reporter (an oxymoron, for sure) or lithe staffer caught on the same relentless treadmill. In general, the comportment of reporters and staffers (not to mention candidates) on the campaign trail leaves something to be desired; some take a perverse delight in making a mockery of the Ten Commandments.

As Fritz Mondale observed, in some ways a presidential campaign resembles a military campaign. But where, as Napoleon said, "An army travels on its stomach," modern presidential candidates limp forward on their polls. Recently, someone had the temerity to observe, "I think the only reason we still have elections in this country is to find out how accurate the polls were." The pollsters won't be able

21

to completely subvert the electoral process as long as there are enough mulish and apathetic voters around. Imagine how dumbfounded one pollster was when he asked a sweet little old lady in New Hampshire who she favored, only to be told, "Oh, I never vote. It only encourages them."

Presidential candidates will go anywhere in search of votes, which often creates comic scenes. Charlie McDowell, in his first-rate book, *Campaign Fever*, reported one foray into New Hampshire:

> In Claremont, a little city of 13,000 at the foot of a swooping ski slope, the Hotel Moody gives a birthday party for its oldest resident, Miss Milly Avery, who is 90. As her eyes shine in the glow of the candles, who comes in to wish her a happy birthday but Barry Goldwater, all the way from Arizona. He is followed into the dining room by a large troop of newsmen. Microphones are hooked up. Blinding floodlights illuminate the scene. Three television networks and two wire services begin to photograph the old lady's birthday party. A score of expert political reporters crowd in close to catch every quote. Miss Avery, as it turns out, is not at all sure who Goldwater is but says he looks like a nice young man. A public relations man from Chicago assures the press, however, that Miss Avery is for Goldwater.

The people of New Hampshire have gotten used to being invaded every four years. "Oh, nobody minds," said one voter. "At this time of year we are glad to have any kind of entertainment we can get." After I had tramped through the living rooms of Nashua for the second time, a reporter asked a jaded homeowner what he thought of candidate Udall. "Well, I don't know, I've only met him two or three times."

Presidential campaigns are a time when rhetoric is guaranteed to fill the air, especially if there is a candidate running as prolix as Hubert Humphrey. Groucho Marx once said of Hubert: "I don't know what sort of a president he'd make. He talks and talks and talks. He'd make a helluva wife." To which Hubert responded: "I've never thought my speeches were too long—I've enjoyed all of them."

Another day, two Yankees, one of whom was hard of hearing, were standing on the edge of a crowd listening to a candidate make his spiel. The slightly deaf one nudged the other and asked him what the politician was talking about. After listening closely for another moment or two, the other replied, "He don't say."

During the 1976 Democratic presidential primary race *nine* Democrats descended on New Hampshire. We had a number of debates—all of us lined up onstage to be questioned and poked and prodded as if we were so many cattle. I used to joke that these cattle shows were a kind of foreplay in which, in a five-minute speech, you tried to stroke all the erogenous zones in the political body. And God help you if you overlooked the Navaho Gay-Lesbian Alliance.

Primary elections are the one time when politicians of the same party routinely criticize each other. When the race is crowded, the sniping can get fierce. As election day approached after a particularly bitter primary battle some decades ago, Chauncey DePew, a Republican leader from New York, observed: "The only question now is which corpse gets the most flowers." In another primary, one candidate was forced grudgingly to admit that his opponent bore a strong resemblance to Abraham Lincoln, "If you can imagine a short, fat, dishonest Abraham Lincoln."

Running a modern presidential campaign has become so logistically and politically complex, it would take an Einstein to figure out the relativity of it all. And, in fact, Einstein

23

once visited FDR in the White House and sat enthralled as FDR worked the phones, cajoling feuding members of his campaign staff. Einstein came away murmuring, "I didn't realize that politics was so much more complicated than physics."

Over fifty years ago, Will Rogers observed of the 1928 presidential campaign, "So much money is being spent that I doubt if either man, as good as they are, are worth what it will cost to elect them." Afterward Rogers would add, "Politics has got so expensive that it takes a lot of money even to get beat with."

Amen. The Udall campaign spent nearly $5 million to get beat in 1976. It might sound like a lot, even today, but to run against Jimmy Carter, it was just peanuts. [*Editor's note:* Ow, Mo!]

The candidates' families pay a price, too. Once in New Hampshire Ed Muskie's shy wife, Jane, nervously clutched a microphone in front of a big crowd: "Oh, I think I'm going to faint. But before I do, I'd like to say a few words about my husband. . . ." The taciturn Yankees ate it up.

Jokes play a crucial role in enlivening the deadly grind, and the press corps can be depended upon to ferret out the hidden humor that resides within every campaign. Press anecdotes, sometimes humorous, sometimes dripping with cynicism, are among the most irreverent and hilarious in existence, though their shelf life is often short.

Perhaps no candidate took the roasting of reporters better than Robert F. Kennedy. In 1968 the press was merciless in mimicking RFK's speech mannerisms, including his constant repetition of the theme, "I think we can do better, I think we can turn this [city, town, or industry] around. . . ." When reporters traveling with RFK were lodged at what they regarded as an intolerable dive in Indianapolis, David Halberstam declared, "I think we can do better, I think

24

we can turn the Indiana hotel industry around." If RFK's reporters encountered a lazy waitress they would declare, "The service is unacceptable. I think we can do better. I think we can turn this restaurant around." There is no record of what bewildered waitresses, restaurant managers, or hotel clerks may have thought about all of this.

Newspeople also teased RFK about his habit of closing his stump speech with a favorite quotation: "As George Bernard Shaw once said. . . ." After they had heard it a few dozen times, the quote became the press's cue to run for the bus or train or plane scheduled to carry them to the next stop. Once, Kennedy inadvertently omitted the quote and his campaign train chugged off, leaving the entire press corps stranded on the platform. When they finally caught up, the press asked Kennedy to be sure to always include the cue. At the next stop, to the confusion of the locals, RFK ended his speech: "As George Bernard Shaw once said, run for the bus."

Behind his back, reporters compared Bobby to Bugs Bunny and tried to create lyrics for a song titled, "I Don't Want a Wabbit in the White House." Characteristically, RFK knew all about it—and took it in stride.

Knowing that Bobby was sensitive to charges that he was ruthless, during a whistle-stop train trip through Indiana the press corps composed a ditty, "The Ruthless Cannonball," sung, of course, to the tune of "The Wabash Cannonball." When they summoned Bobby and Ethel to the club car to hear a rendition, Jules Witcover was there to record the lyrics:

Oh listen to the speeches that baffle, beef and bore
As he waffles through woodlands, and slides along the shore.

He's the politician who'd be touched by one and all.
He's the demon driver of the Ruthless Cannonball.

25

So here's to Ruthless Robert, may his name forever stand,
To be feared and genuflected at polls across the land.

Old Ho Chi Minh is cheering, and though it may appall,
He's whizzing to the White House on the Ruthless
Cannonball.

The Kennedys, according to Witcover, took it in good spirits
and applauded at the end. When reporters called, "Speech!
Speech!" Kennedy replied, "As George Bernard Shaw once
said, the same to you—sideways." The lesson for politicians
was that Robert Kennedy was one of those rare candidates
who could poke fun at himself and enjoy a joke—even when
the laugh was on him—and for this he was much admired
by the press.

RFK, however, never forgot that charming a crowd was
more important than joshing with reporters. And he was
one of the best at using humor to achieve that goal. Frequently,
RFK would tell an audience that all his life he'd wanted to
visit their little out-of-the-way burg and that he hoped that
someday he and Ethel and their eleven children could move
there to live. Then he'd smile and say, "All of you who
believe that please raise your hands." The response he got
was tremendous.

Thankfully, reporters don't play favorites—their darts
aren't always intended for Democrats. In 1964 reporters ridi-
culed Barry Goldwater for what they saw as a tendency to
shoot from the hip. Barry was a marksman; according to
one jokester, his motto was, "Ready! Fire! Aim!" Being teased
didn't faze Barry—he played right along. Asked by a reporter
how he would respond to a Russian nuclear strike, Barry
said the first thing he would do would be to circle the wagons.
On another occasion Barry called a press conference to announce that there would be a movie made about his life.

The producer? "18th Century–Fox." Yes, Barry is a true conservative—he's never seen *anything* happen for the first time.

Finally, Barry decided to confront the "trigger happy" issue head-on. He challenged a couple of reporters to come to his Phoenix home and compete with target pistols. After thoroughly humiliating them, he lectured them on the art of shooting—from the hip and otherwise.

Reporters also kidded Goldwater about his tendency to misspeak. One reporter said that he had had a special typewriter key installed that, when pushed, printed out, "Goldwater's staff later issued a clarification saying that what the senator really meant was . . ."

While reporters may be responsible for discovering many of the jokes that surface during a campaign, they are sometimes their butt as well. Probably the most memorable comment made about political reporters during the past several decades was Gene McCarthy's. Remarking on the phenomenon of pack journalism, McCarthy compared reporters to blackbirds sitting on a telephone wire: "One flies off and they all fly off. One flies back and they all fly back." The remark's been repeated and revered by campaign staffers ever since.

Once again, though, the best campaign humor isn't spawned by reporters *or* politicians, but rather by the voters themselves. In 1980 Ronald Reagan was quoted as saying that trees, which give off nitrogen, caused more air pollution than factories. A few weeks later when he arrived on the campus of Claremont College in the southern California "Smog Belt," Reagan discovered that students had draped all the trees on campus with placards pleading, "STOP ME BEFORE I KILL AGAIN."

Kiss My Donkey: Election Night '76

★ ★

. . . and in Wisconsin, ABC-TV predicts Mo Udall will
defeat Jimmy Carter . . .

. . . the people have spoken—the bastards.
—*State Senate candidate Dick Tuck*

A funny thing happened to me on my way to the White
House. On election night of the crucial, make-or-break 1976
Wisconsin primary, I responded to the pleas of my staff and
the press and went down to the hotel ballroom to claim
victory. The race was close, but both ABC and NBC had
predicted a Udall win—our first after eighteen months of
campaigning. In the rosy glow of victory, it was clear that
this was a pivotal night, my first giant step toward the White
House. Surely, our newfound momentum would lead to other
triumphs—in upcoming primaries, at the convention in July,
and in the general election in November. Finally, after so
many heartbreaking losses, I was firmly on the road to the
White House.

"How sweet it is!" I told the press, smiling and waving
to my cheering supporters. After the applause had finally
died down, I said that after all those close second-place fin-
ishes, I was reminded of the Rockefeller who said, "I've been
rich and I've been poor, and believe me, rich is best." "Well,"

28

I said, "I've been a winner and I've been a loser, and believe me, winning is best." The crowd burst into cheers.

Mellowed by the heady nectar of sweet success, I went to bed and slept better than I had in weeks. When my 6:00 A.M. wake-up call came, I discovered that someone had misplaced my triumph during the night. A few votes, dribbling in from the northwestern dairy counties after midnight, had enabled Jimmy Carter to edge me—by a freckle and a hair. It was a narrow loss, yes, but a loss nonetheless—and its narrowness made it all the more crushing.

Three weeks earlier my pollster, Peter Hart, had shown me losing to Carter in Wisconsin by two to one. But in the interim my campaign had come on strong. Ten days before the election Hart's new poll showed it Carter 34 percent, Udall 30 percent. By election night it was a dead heat. As it turned out, I lost by 5,000 votes out of 670,000 cast. Five thousand votes—less than one *percent*! Hell, Fred Harris and Sargent Shriver, liberals whose rigor mortis candidacies had gone belly-up weeks earlier but who were still on the ballot, received 13,000 votes between them. If either man had thrown his support my way I probably would have won.

My bitter remorse was compounded when I turned on the news and saw Jimmy grinning his one-hundred-watt smile, proudly waving the early edition of the Milwaukee *Sentinel* over his head, flaunting its premature headline: "CARTER UPSET BY UDALL." I've believed in ghosts ever since. This was Tom Dewey's revenge. In my mind's eye, I could picture that famous old photo of a joyous Harry Truman holding up a copy of the Chicago *Tribune* with its bold headline: "DEWEY DEFEATS TRUMAN." And I could hear the echoes of that famous speech in which Truman described how he had awakened during the night and turned on his bedside radio to hear H. V. Kaltenborn smugly assert, "I am confident that when the country vote comes in Mr. Truman will be defeated by an overwhelming majority. . . ." *That fool,* Truman thought, switching off the radio. *He'll be sorry he ever opened his mouth.* After drinking a glass of milk, Truman went back to bed and slept soundly the rest of the night. Republicans have never been allowed to forget it.

As I crawled out of bed that morning in Milwaukee, I braced myself for what was guaranteed to be a bad day. As I was pulling on my pants, one of my assistants came to the door and called, "Mo, the press is clamoring for a statement." After retrieving from memory a couple of relevant jokes, I went downstairs. My campaign was badly wounded, and the scent of blood had sent the media into a feeding frenzy. Humor would have to be my shield. I swallowed my sorrow, cleared my throat, pointed to a reporter's notebook, and said, "I'd like to ask each of you to take those statements I made last night and every instance where you find the word 'win' strike it and insert the word 'lose.' "

"How does it feel to come in second *again?*" someone asked.

"In the grand scheme of things," I said, "not everyone can be first. As you may recall, even George Washington, the father of our country, married a widow."

To this day, I keep a framed copy of that Milwaukee *Sentinel* on my wall as a warning never to take anything for granted—especially if it's in the early edition. I think it was Adlai Stevenson who said, "Accuracy is to a newspaper what virtue is to a lady, but a newspaper can always print a retraction."

I can laugh about it today, but at the time my loss in Wisconsin was devastating. For a year and a half I had trudged through the cornfields of Iowa, the snowdrifts of New Hampshire, the suburbs of Massachusetts, the sidewalks of New York, the bowling alleys of Wisconsin. For eighteen hours a day, day after day after day, I had given it my all. I had pleaded, cajoled, preached, and pressed the flesh. Lots of it: each day I had shaken hands with at least two thousand strangers. Try that sometime—it's exhausting. And yet, no matter how hard I worked, it seemed as though I was doomed to come in second to that g'damned peanut plowman from Plains. After my loss in Wisconsin I felt like the missionary in one of Mark Twain's stories who set out to convert the cannibals: "They listened with the greatest of interest to everything that he had to say," Twain wrote. "Then they ate him."

Being boiled alive probably hurts more than losing a close election, but at least you aren't tortured by the what-ifs. What *if* I had spent one more week in Wisconsin? What *if* Shriver or Harris had dropped out and urged their supporters to vote for me? What *if* I had taken a mortgage on my house to fund a few last-minute TV ads? What *if* we had spent more money in Wisconsin and less in Pennsylvania where I would never be a factor? What *if* we had gone ahead with a last-minute mailing of 100,000 letters we had prepared? Even Carter's chief aide, Hamilton Jordan, would later concede, "A weekend of television has to be good for five thousand or more votes easily. It had to make the difference. That's how they lost it. That's how we won." Which only raises another if—*if* we *had* won in Wisconsin . . . well, there's no telling for sure, but a Udall victory there might have led to a dramatically different outcome in 1976. But it was not to be, and, instead of savoring a victory, I was left saddled with remorse and regrets.

In truth, political campaigns are *battles*—battles it's excruciatingly painful to lose. If you're a fighter—and most politicians are—you will be loath to concede a race into which you have poured weeks if not months of effort. When the returns start coming in and it becomes clear that you've lost, your instincts are to curse or kick the dog, not go down and gracefully fall on your sword. A few years ago there was a Broadway musical that included an election-night scene in which a defeated candidate sent a wire to the winner: "Heartily congratulate you on your splendid victory—Stop— And I charge vote fraud in Indiana, Illinois, Nebraska, Montana, Washington, Ohio and Massachusetts." That, oftentimes, is how a politician feels.

Nevertheless, the sore loser is surprisingly rare in American politics. Richard Nixon—"You won't have Nixon to kick around anymore"—is the exception that proves the rule. Another especially bitter loser was Al Smith after his 1928 election loss to Herbert Hoover. After hearing the Unhappy Warrior pour out his inner thoughts, an observer concluded, "Smith lacks, in age and defeat, that inner equilibrium which alone can save a disappointed man."

Inner equilibrium. That's what a loser needs, in spades. Hubert Humphrey, whose "politics of joy" sometimes invited ridicule from jaded copractitioners of politics, once spoke of his painful loss in the 1968 presidential election. "It's not what they take away from you that counts," Hubert said, "It's what you do with what you have left. Never give up and never give in."

When Senator Bob Dole lost his race for vice president on the ticket with Gerald Ford in 1976, he arrived at the postelection news conference to set the record straight. "Contrary to reports that I took the loss badly, I want to say that I went home last night and slept like a baby—every two hours I woke up and cried."

In Arizona there was a Democratic politician who fancied himself something of a poet. After losing a close race to become mayor of Tombstone, he walked up to his Republican opponent and said:

Kiss My Donkey: Election Night '76

The election is now over.
Let all this bitterness pass.
I will hug your elephant
and you can kiss my . . . donkey.

A loss is particularly shocking—and hard to stomach—when the preelection polls have shown you winning. UPI reporter Dick West recalls an upset in which former senator Thomas J. McIntyre of New Hampshire lost his reelection bid. As West tells it, "McIntyre was dumbfounded: his polls had shown him well ahead. Curious to see what could have gone wrong, McIntyre commissioned a postelection survey. That poll showed him winning, too."

Candidates who believe they have something worthwhile to contribute often risk much in order to run for office. Oftentimes, a challenger will take an unpaid leave from his job and dip into his savings to run for office. If he loses, well, he can return to work a bit poorer perhaps but no worse for wear. If, though, the losing candidate is an incumbent, he's lost not just an election but also his job. This can be a cause for some concern. "Big Jim" Folsom, former governor of Alabama, was asked by a reporter: "Governor, what are you going to do if elected to a third term?" Replied Big Jim, "Son, that's not what is bothering me. What is bothering me is what I'm going to do if I'm *not* elected to a third term."

"In our system," says Fritz Mondale, "at about eleven-thirty on election night, they push the loser off the edge of the cliff—and that's it. You might scream on the way down, but you're going to hit the bottom, and you're not going to be in elective office. It's so abrupt."

Does losing have a silver lining? I think the answer is yes. For a politician, losing is the ultimate test. A crucible for character. I'd bet that Bob Dole is today a better candidate, a more mature person, than he was in 1976 or 1980. And, if he does win in 1988, I think his earlier losses to Ford and Reagan will have made him a wiser president than he would have been. Losing an election is guaranteed to broaden your perspective—the first prerequisite for a statesman. Losing can also help clarify why you were running—or should have been running—in the first place. In the wise words of TV commentator Eric Sevareid: "The difference between the men and the boys in politics is, and always has been, that the boys want to *be* something, while the men want to *do* something." Losing's bottom line? Well, as the late labor leader Walter Reuther once said, "If you're not big enough to lose, you're not big enough to win."

By that standard, I was BIG. The discouraging thing about the Udall campaign was the long string of primaries—seven in a row—where we almost won, primary after primary, coming within a hairsbreadth of victory, where just a few hundred or a few thousand more votes would have given us a magic *win*, the key to more money and more television and more wins. The Udall campaign was like the cartoon-strip character Pogo, who said, "We are confronted by insurmountable opportunities."

Well, I can't complain: I knew from the outset that a run for the presidency would be no bed of roses. Shortly after I declared my candidacy I received a note from a supporter quoting that great German political humorist—no, not Henry Kissinger—Konrad Adenauer, who once said, "A thick skin is a gift from God."

I soon found out *how* thick a skin I would need. The Sperling Breakfast is a Washington institution named for its founder, Godfrey "Budge" Sperling, the veteran political writer for the *Christian Science Monitor*. Twice a week some twenty to thirty bureau chiefs, reporters, and columnists gather at the Sheraton Carlton Hotel in downtown Washington for breakfast, on the record, with a current political celebrity.

Soon after announcing my candidacy, I was invited to appear at the Sperling Breakfast. After the niceties had been exchanged and I had managed to gulp down some orange juice and a shred of bacon, John Pierson of the *Wall Street Journal* asked the first question: "Congressman, you are known to be a bright and witty man, an innovative and resourceful legislator, and an astute student of the Congress and the way government works. My question is this: Are you prick enough to be president?"

I was momentarily speechless. Granted, that's rare for a politician, but I challenge anybody to come up with a snappy rejoinder to that question. Smart enough? Tough enough? Rich enough? Crazy enough? Those questions are relatively easy to answer. But "prick enough"? That gave me pause.

After the laughter died down, I told this story: In 1971, during a contest for Majority Leader of the House, I had confidently counted on receiving a certain number of votes, based on firm assurances from my colleagues that they were in my corner. Once in the caucus, however, I discovered how flimsy "firm assurances" could be. After being trounced by the late Hale Boggs, I exited the caucus room to face a horde of reporters all asking: What happened to your campaign, a campaign you said was in good shape? "I have learned the difference between a cactus and a caucus," I replied. "On a cactus, the pricks are on the outside."

The reporters at the Sperling Breakfast laughed, but the question nagged them, and me, in the months ahead. Later in the campaign, during a period when my campaign staff were bickering among themselves, another reporter asked

35

me the prick-enough question. I told him this story: A stuffy old senator goes to an Indian village for a Fourth of July parade. The chief asks the senator if he would like to ride in the parade. "Okay," says the senator, "if I can ride that big white stallion I rode last year." "I'm sorry," says the chief, "we don't have a white stallion." "Sure you do," says the senator, "I can see him over there in the corral." The two go over to look. Reaching the fence, the senator points to a big white horse and says, "There he is, that's the same one I rode last year." "But that's not a stallion, it's a mare," says the chief. "She's one of our best horses." "Well, okay," says the senator. "Throw a saddle on her and I'll ride her. But I know there's some mistake. I can distinctly remember riding through the streets and hearing people say, 'Look at that big prick on that white horse.' "

Campaigning for a presidential nomination is a marathon ordeal—a death march consisting of a series of lightning-quick, mind-numbing visits to states like Iowa and New Hampshire, which vote early on the primary calendar. Both the timetable and the scheduling are relentless. In each twenty-four- or forty-eight-hour trip you try to cram in as many appearances as possible. Ideally, you want to get on TV, meet with the press, garner endorsements, hobnob with local bigwigs, raise money . . . the list is endless. From the time I decided to run in early 1975 until the convention eighteen months later, I rarely slept in the same bed—even my own—more than three nights in a row.

During the early primaries the press could care less what you, the "dark horse," have to say. But if you're still a contender after New Hampshire, their attention span increases dramatically and their ears perk up, alert for some awful gaffe that might torpedo your campaign.

My biggest boner occurred when I tried to coin a new term to describe my politics. At a press conference following the Massachusetts primary, I said, " 'Liberal' is just a buzz word. I don't mind answering to it, but by my standards I think it's more accurate to call me a 'progressive' in the tradition of Woodrow Wilson, Franklin Roosevelt, and John F. Kennedy." In retrospect, this was a bit too ingenuous, but at the time it seemed a perfectly innocuous—and strategically crucial—distinction to make.

At various times, there were eleven candidates, most of them "liberals," wrestling for the Democratic nomination in 1976. The primary fights were big dog piles, free-for-alls. The goal of the Udall campaign in the early primaries was just to finish in the upper half—to stay alive—and this we accomplished. As the primaries continued, the "winnowing-out process" took its toll. (After the New Hampshire primary, when Fred Harris finished fifth of nine candidates, he crowed to the press, "I've been winnowed in.") But Birch Bayh, Milton Shapp, Sarge Shriver, George Wallace, and even Harris soon bit the dust.

Following our surprisingly strong showing in the Massachusetts primary, where we came second to Senator Scoop Jackson, with Carter fourth, the Udall campaign was sitting pretty. We were just where we wanted to be. There was only one problem: As the last remaining liberal, I was emerging as heir-apparent to the still-fresh memories of George McGovern's crushing defeat in 1972. Faced with a choice between Udall, Wallace, Jackson, and Carter, many of McGovern's supporters were choosing to back me. As they did, my campaign began to be tainted with the perception that I was the candidate of draft dodgers, dopers, and daisy-picking radical environmentalists. Well, notwithstanding the fact that I *was* their candidate, I knew that to win the nomination I needed to do something to alter this portrayal of me as a "flaming liberal." I didn't want to change my positions—I was proud to be the candidate attacking the big oil companies, calling for national health insurance and the Humphrey-Hawkins jobs bill, etc.—but I knew I needed to moderate my image to be elected in a national race. And so it was that I told the press that I was not a "liberal" but a "progressive." Of course, I was a damn fool for believing the press would fall for that maladroit ruse.

Liberal? Progressive? The press wasn't having any. They think it's their prerogative to pin the tail on the donkey, so to speak, and they don't want you trying to change your stripes once they've gone to the trouble of painting them on. For the next few weeks, more was written about this tomfoolery than what I was saying I stood for. My campaign began to lose momentum, and soon we were bogged down like a dinosaur in a tar pit.

To demonstrate how silly I thought this tempest in a teapot was, I started telling this story: A law professor is quizzing his class about the differences between various improprieties. "Johnson," he says, "please tell the class the difference between adultery and fornication." Johnson thought and thought, but for the life of him he couldn't remember that adultery occurs when one of the two partners is married, whereas in fornication neither is. So, finally he says, "Well, to be honest, Professor, I've tried them both, and I can't tell any difference."

Meanwhile, as I wallowed in my semantical swamp, Carter was escaping virtually untouched on the issues. Perhaps blinded by his smile, the reporters traveling with him wrote mostly positive stories about his do-good, feel-good quest for a renewal of trust, goodness, and godliness in Washington. Throw the rascals out and let the Saints Come Marching In. Carter was the first politician in memory to come complete with halo. This strategy, conceived by Jody Powell, Hamilton Jordan, and Pat Caddell, was brilliant—and brilliantly executed. By the time my campaign got tough on Carter, he was so far ahead that my accusations that he was waffling on the issues only served to make me look shrill. In the aftermath of Wisconsin my campaign headed downhill. I got clobbered in Pennsylvania by Scoop Jackson. Carter beat me soundly in the District of Columbia, and then nipped me again—by three-tenths of a percentage point: 1,000 votes out of 659,000—in Michigan. Despite these recurring disappointments, we kept plugging away. At times I wanted to quit. My back was aching, my wife was tired, most of my kids had bailed out for school or other activities, money was tight, and the pressures to raise more were excruciating. I was now into my fourth or fifth campaign manager, American Express had repossessed my credit card, and my campaign plane—"the Basler Bomber"—was grounded because we couldn't pay to gas it up. Finally, we had to surrender the plane and fly commercial, which meant terrible connections and wasteful waits in airports from Sioux City to Dayton.

Charles Mohr of *The New York Times* was following me at this point and he later told me that he didn't understand how we could continue to compete in states where we knew we were going to get scalped, or how we managed to get up each morning and confront the world with a brave, even happy, face. Mohr didn't know the half of it. At one point, I had to spend more than two hours in a hotel room near LaGuardia Airport as Representative Bella Abzug, a putative supporter, howled, shrieked, and cursed me for what she saw as inequities in the delegate selection process in New York. This was vintage Bella: pure bedlam.

Bella's harangue didn't end when I pledged to get more of her supporters on the ballot. A few days later she called me when I was in the midst of a critical meeting with the editorial board of the Green Bay *Press-Gazette*. I never got a word in edgewise until she ran out of breath after a twenty-minute diatribe. Before hanging up, I was tempted to suggest she get a rabies booster and call me back when it had taken effect. (As it turned out, Bella's support was evanescent. After the last primaries, my New York delegates pledged to stay with me through the first ballot. Most did, but Bella jumped ship and dog-paddled toward Carter at the first opportunity.)

Toward the end of May, my spirits and endurance began to flag. Even my sense of humor was deserting me. I found myself becoming angry about Jimmy Carter and the latecomers, Frank Church and Jerry Brown. I began to brood, and my dark inner feelings bubbled to the surface in private conversations and at news conferences. In Ohio I was gently interrogated during a few long car rides by the *The New Yorker*'s Elizabeth Drew. In her story, published a few weeks later, she commented on my bitterness. (This was, as far as I know, the only instance where my irritation and frustration were seen in print.)

Thank God I had a few staffers who refused to let me feel sorry for myself, especially Mark Shields, now a newspaper columnist and political humorist. Shields was in charge of my Ohio effort, lame as it was. Riding on the press bus, Shields once loudly proclaimed, "You can put your ear to the ground and hear the movement to Udall as sure as you can hear elephants making love." The reality was that you couldn't hear anything, not even butterflies in foreplay.

Nevertheless, we trudged on. From state to state, the faces varied, but the questions remained the same:

"Will you drop out if you don't win?" Answer: "No, I'm in for the duration, blah, blah, blah . . ."

"Will you accept the vice-presidential nomination if you don't make it?"

"I'm against all vice—including the vice presidency."

"What separates you from Jimmy Carter?"

"About seven hundred delegates."

By June, my great adventure was coming to a fitful end. I was hopelessly out of it in Ohio and not even seriously contesting New Jersey and California, the big prizes on Super Tuesday. Although it was clear to everyone that the good ship Udall was foundering, I was determined that the entire crew—staff, friends, family, and candidate—go down with heads held high.

In any struggling campaign there's a temptation to scapegoat the press, but despite their lavish coverage of my shooting myself in my "progressive" foot, all of us had grown close to the reporters who had traveled with us from Iowa to South Dakota. After our surprisingly strong showing in New Hampshire, each of the networks had assigned a camera crew, producer, and correspondent to the Udall campaign. Though the networks rotated the reporters, my most constant companions were Bill Plante and Ike Pappas of CBS, Don Farmer and Charles Gibson of ABC, and Chuck Quinn of NBC. Luckily, each was blessed with good humor, for our schedules were chaotic, our meals sporadic, and our accommodations, well, as Plante once put it, "they reminded us of our humble origins."

Now, on the night before the Ohio primary (my dismal showing was a foregone conclusion), the press and my staff arranged a surprise party for me featuring songs and skits depicting the highs and lows of the Udall campaign. Although I was in no mood to celebrate, I fell for my wife's ruse that she wanted to go out for some fresh air. Grudgingly, I left the hotel room and stalked down to the lobby, only to be met by my staff, who escorted me to the ballroom of the Lakefront Holiday Inn.

What ensued was a bittersweet evening of unusual conviviality and warmth. For openers, the press presented me with a canvas straitjacket emblazoned with the Udall for President logo and a picture of me nude with my head backward, or was it ass backward, my memory fails. There were two other highlights: The first was the swift delivery of a cream pie into the unsuspecting face of Chuck Quinn by one of my female staffers who had been offended by his blatant sexism during the campaign. The second highlight was the singing of a song written by the press and sung to the tune of "Second Hand Rose":

Still running win, place, or show—still on the go,
That's why they call me "Second Place Mo."

Seems to me they want a liberal starter,
But the bastards were seduced by Carter!

Second Place Mo, I'm just Second Place Mo,
I never seem to get a first, that's true.

Even Lady Tiger, she's the gal I adore.
She had the nerve to tell me she's been married before.

Now they all know that I'm just Second Place Mo,
From Ari-zo-na too.

We call you Second Place Mo, yes, Second Place Mo,
The voters have dealt you a terrible blow.

You got rid of Scoop and Birch and Freddee—
In Wisconsin, thought you toppled Jimmmeee—

Second place there, just didn't seem fair,
It really was a disappointment, that is true.

Now when Frank Church tells you to get out of the race,
You thumb your nose and tell him, "For you—it's third place!"

You are second it's true,
When will you say that you're through!

Kiss My Donkey: Election Night '76

You are progressive, that's so,
But you're Second Place Mo,

And we keep on asking why should it be so—

Like some ancient classic Grecian chorus,
Arrogant and always lead with Moorrisss.

Pains in the ass and devoid of class,
We have just one more question, then we're through.

In our hearts we know that you are ethnically pure—
But can a man named Morris be a Mormon for sure?

Though while we know that you are Second Place Mo

We—all—love you so.

I was moved. My wife, aka the "Tiger," who never allows me to wallow in sentimentality or shows much sympathy for my physical handicap, a glass eye, went to the podium and said, "Look at Mo. He's got a tear in his *good* eye."

I stood up before this gaggle of press, staff, and friends and said, "I'm reminded of a story about this old boy in Georgia," at which point everyone who had heard me say "I'm reminded . . ." thousands of times, interrupted with plaintive cries, "We've heard it!"

"No, you didn't, goddammit! I just remembered it. This Georgia preacher took this fellow out to the stream to baptize him. He put him under the water and said a mighty prayer, and allowed the man to surface, where he was asked, 'Do you believe?' The man gave a gasp, said he believed, and down he went again while the minister gave another mighty prayer and then brought him up again. The minister said, 'Johnson, do you believe?' And Johnson sputtered, 'I do believe,' whereupon the minister put him under the water again.

After another long-winded prayer, the minister brought Johnson up and said, 'Brother Johnson, what do you believe?' And Johnson said, 'I believe you bastards are trying to drown me!'

"Well," I said, "if, by exceedingly slim chance, this campaign should endure for yet another thousand weeks, it will be said that, surely, *this* was its finest hour.

"You know, there was a moment during this campaign, as we passed Mount Rushmore, when I imagined my face up there with Roosevelt, Washington, and Lincoln. Alas, it was not to be," I continued, glancing at the press corps so they would know I was joking, "due to the inadequate press coverage . . . and faulty camerawork.

"But in times of disappointment I think not of Adlai Stevenson but of the great thinkers of all time, the classic Greeks like Thucydides, Aristotle, Spiro Agnew, and Ike Pappas. I don't know where the hell we're going to be tomorrow night," I rambled on, "or next week at this time. Maybe something positive will develop . . . although it sure as hell doesn't look that way. Tonight, though, I'm reminded of that great poet who said,

> Some men are rather superior,
> and others have plenty of class,
> but the man who is worthwhile,
> is the man who can smile,
> when he gets a big kick in the ass.

"Well," I concluded, "I suppose I've had more kicks in the ass, more practice at coming in second, and been the subject of more political obituaries than any other candidate in modern times, but all that has just taught me the wisdom of what Will Rogers once said: 'Live your life so that whenever you lose, you are ahead.'

"And I am ahead. I'm ahead in staff people who loved

me and believed in me. And I'm ahead because I have love, respect, and admiration for all of you in this room.

"I'm sorry to end this on a somber note, so I think I'll have a drink. . . ."

Ten years later when my campaign staff and members of the press—in all, some three hundred strong—gathered for a reunion in Washington, appropriately at a Holiday Inn, the talk was largely about the fun we had had together, not our mistakes. Columnist David Broder recalled the 1976 campaign in this way: "Mo Udall wanted to run for president in the worst way . . . and did."

Flooding the Sistine Chapel: A Grand Canyon Debacle

★ ★

> Leave it as it is. You cannot improve on it. The ages
> have been at work on it and man can only mar it.
> What you can do is keep it for your children, your
> children's children, and for all who come after you.
> —*Teddy Roosevelt, speaking at*
> *the rim of the Grand Canyon in 1903*

Being in Congress during the decade of the 1960s allowed
me to watch and participate in the flowering of the environmental movement, a truly historic, some say revolutionary,
sea change in the way Americans viewed the land, air, and
water that surrounds and sustains us.

Looking back, I am amazed at how much progress was
made in only ten short years. In 1960, the word *ecology*
was used only by scientists; to the rest of us the word's
meaning was a mystery. At that time, the environmental
movement consisted of a ragtag band of bird-watchers
and backpackers and a handful of well-intentioned, relatively
impoverished organizations whose grasp of lobbying and public relations skills was unremarkable and whose political clout
was, with rare exceptions, negligible. It is true that only a
few years previous, the Wilderness Society, the Sierra Club,
and other conservation organizations had combined to halt
a proposed dam on the Green River at Echo Park in Dinosaur

National Monument—but only by accepting a "compromise" dam (which they later were to rue as equally if not more catastrophic) at Glen Canyon on the Colorado River. In 1960, most politicians paid little heed to environmentalists. It was usually safe to ignore them, for as the decade dawned environmental concerns were a growing but still minor cloud at the far horizon of the national agenda.

How things had changed only ten years later! By 1970 *ecology* was a buzz word, and environmentalism was one of the most powerful forces at play in American politics. Between them, the major groups—the Sierra Club, the Audubon Society, the National Wildlife Association, the Wilderness Society, the Environmental Defense Fund, Greenpeace, and many, many others—had hundreds of thousands of new members. Capitol Hill swarmed with dozens of environmental lobbyists whose youth and energy belied the cunning and experience they had gained while racking up a surprisingly large number of legislative victories. Now the environmental concerns they articulated were something no politician could afford to ignore.

A recounting of some of the significant milestones of that momentous decade reveals how fast history was being made. Rachel Carson's portentous *Silent Spring* was published in 1962. The Wilderness Act was passed in 1964, the Endangered Species Act in 1966. In 1968 the National Wild and Scenic Rivers Act was approved, and in 1969 the National Environmental Protection Act brought the "environmental impact statement" into the national jargon. In that same year, Apollo 11 landed on the moon. There, Neil Armstrong found an inhospitable world whose barren harshness only accentuated the verdant beauty of our planet. The contrast was underscored by those breathtaking photos of a cloud-draped blue orb drifting alone in space. The decade was capped with

47

Earth Day in 1970, when hundreds of thousands of Americans took to the streets in an outpouring of concern for man's impact on what was now being called "Spaceship Earth."

I have always considered myself an environmentalist and I am proud to have participated in many of the great battles fought during that decade (and since). How sweet our victories were! What a joy it was to have been on the winning side as the forces of preservation took on some of the largest, toughest, best-funded lobbies in Washington—and whipped them.

But being on the right side depends on whose ox is being gored. Yes, I was on the right side in expanding the national seashores from one in 1960 to nearly a dozen now. Yes, I was on the right side in greatly expanding wildernesses and national parks. But there was one major battle in my own backyard—over two proposed dams on the Colorado River in Grand Canyon National Park—in which, to my friends in the conservation movement, I was one of the bad guys, specifically, the tall, lanky fellow in the black hat.

This was one of the major environmental battles fought during the 1960s—and, in retrospect, I was on the wrong side. I can only thank God that the growing environmental movement outgunned those of us—including my brother Stewart, then secretary of the interior, Senator Barry Goldwater, the rest of the Arizona congressional delegation, and most other western congressmen—who favored the dams.

As proposed, the dams were to sandwich Grand Canyon National Park, one upstream, one down. The upstream dam was to be located at Marble Canyon, 60 miles below Glen Canyon Dam. The second dam was to be built 200 miles downstream at Bridge Canyon, close to where the Colorado flows into Lake Mead. If they had been built, the dams would

48

have flooded 146 miles of the Colorado River—and the bottom 600 feet of much of the Grand Canyon.

The Grand Canyon is one of the great wonders of the world, but it's also a dam builder's fantasy: Those looming walls. That powerful river. Those exquisite dam sites. Engineers had surveyed the Marble Canyon and Bridge Canyon sites back in the 1920s, and the dams had been a gleam in Arizona's eye ever since. The primary justification for building the dams was that they could provide the vast quantities of power needed to pump water into the parched lands of central Arizona. "Making the desert bloom" had been a dream for generations of Arizonans, and dams in the Grand Canyon seemed a small price to pay to achieve it.

At first glance the idea had a lot going for it. Some of the electricity the dams would generate could be used to pump water from a site lower on the Colorado through a proposed system of canals—the Central Arizona Project (CAP)—which would wind across the desert for nearly three hundred miles to Phoenix and Tucson. The excess power could be sold to help finance both the CAP and other mammoth reclamation projects in California, Utah, and Nevada contemplated in the Pacific Southwest Water Plan (PSWP), of which the CAP was part.

The PSWP was a billion-dollar plan, unveiled by the Bureau of Reclamation in 1963, designed to slake forever the booming Southwest's apparently unquenchable thirst. The bureau's rationale went like this: There was plenty of water in the West—it just wasn't properly *distributed*. If, as everyone agreed, the Colorado is overworked and overallocated, why don't we "augment" it with water from northern California? If that's not enough, let's go farther north and tap the Columbia. And, if *that's* not enough, we'll stick a straw in the Yukon. (Think of PSWP as the reclamationary equivalent of Star Wars. Ronald Reagan wants to unfurl a peace-shield umbrella over North America; the bureau wanted to unroll a hose three thousand miles long.)

Although the idea seems farfetched, even chimerical, today, so does the idea of putting a man on the moon. The sixties were a different era, a time when what we could accomplish seemed to be limited only by the scope of our dreams. Viewed through that lens, the Pacific Southwest Water Plan appeared ambitious rather than outlandish. After all, wasn't it true that each year more than 100 million acre-feet of the Columbia River flowed unused, and therefore "wasted," into the Pacific? (By contrast, the annual volume of the Colorado is about 15 million acre-feet.) Surely, Washington and Oregon could spare a tenth for the greening of Arizona.

If the plan had been announced fifteen years earlier it might have been greeted with universal acclamation. As it was, however, the bureau's timing could not have been worse. In January 1963, the floodgates on Glen Canyon Dam, which had been under construction for seven years, had been shut. As Lake Powell began to rise, drowning willows, then cottonwoods along 180 miles of the Colorado, conservationists were heart-stricken. As they mourned the loss of Glen Canyon, they had plenty of time to reevaluate what it meant to "compromise"—particularly where free-flowing rivers were concerned.

Glen Canyon—"the place no one knew"—wasn't as big as the Grand Canyon, but its spectacular sandstone cliffs beautifully streaked with "desert varnish" and its sinuous side canyons, some so narrow that a man could hold his arms outstretched and touch walls soaring eight hundred feet into the sky, made it one of the most sublime canyons on earth. I was not in Congress when Glen Canyon Dam was approved, but Stewart was and he voted for it, as did almost every other western senator and representative. Some grew to regret it. Barry Goldwater recently said that if he had any vote that he could change, it would be his vote on Glen Canyon Dam. (In the early 1940s, Barry took a river trip down the length of the Colorado. This made him one of only a few hundred people lucky enough to see Glen Canyon before it vanished forever beneath the murky waters of Lake Powell.)

For environmentalists, particularly those who had seen it, the loss of Glen Canyon was tremendously galling. The depth of the anguish can be illustrated by two passages from a book the Sierra Club published as an elegy, *The Place No One Knew*. In the foreword, David Brower wrote,

Glen Canyon died in 1963 and I was partly responsible for its needless death. So were you. Neither you nor I, nor anyone else, knew it well enough to insist that at all costs it should endure.

Eliot Porter added:

Nowhere in the world are these drowned canyons duplicated. In place of infinite variety, awesome convolutions, mysterious and secret recesses, glowing painted walls and golden streams, we have received in exchange a featureless sheet of water, a dead basin into which all the flotsam from the surrounding land accumulates. . . . The exchange [of Glen Canyon for Lake Powell] is one of the greatest frauds ever perpetrated by responsible government on an unsuspecting people. They have been cheated out of a birthright without ever knowing they possessed it.

Having been an unwitting party to the loss of Glen Canyon, Brower and the Sierra Club were bound and determined to see that no more dams were built on the Colorado, particularly in the Grand Canyon. As Brower put it, "If we can't save the Grand Canyon, what the hell can we save?"

Deciding whether to support the construction of Marble Canyon and Bridge Canyon dams was one of the most wrenching decisions I've faced during twenty-six years in the Congress. Philosophically, I was committed to preservation of the environment, but I was equally if not more committed to the orderly development of natural resources in the best interest of my state. Getting the CAP authorized had been the paramount issue in Arizona politics since I was a boy, and more than 90 percent of my constituents favored the dams. Grappling with the pros and cons brought me face to face with my heritage.

It may be an exaggeration, but only a slight one, to say that the Colorado River is in my blood. I was born just a few hundred yards from the Little Colorado, and as a boy I played along its banks and drank its waters. But there are other binding ties between the river and me, and some go back more than a century.

My Mormon ancestors were among the first whites since the Spanish conquistadors to explore southern Utah and northern Arizona, whose tortured "canyonlands" have been cleaved by the Colorado and its tributaries. As recently as 1850, this region was a blank spot on the map, a sprawl of wilderness over which a playful cartographer conceivably could have written: "Here Be Dragons—Thirsty Ones." The Escalante River, named by explorer John Wesley Powell on his 1869 trip down the Colorado River, was the last major river to be discovered in the lower forty-eight; the Henry Mountains just to the north, the last-named mountain range. On Powell's second trip down the river two years later, he stopped and had dinner with a man who had just begun operating a ferry at the mouth of Glen Canyon. Powell's host was John D. Lee—my great-grandfather.

Lee's Ferry is near the center of the Colorado Plateau, but in those days it was a tremendously isolated spot. Until Lee began his ferry there was no place you could get a wagon across the Colorado between Moab, 300 miles to the northeast, and Pierce's Ferry, nearly 300 miles to the southwest. For 100 miles in any direction, and farther in some, the surrounding area was a true wilderness, a paradoxical landscape whose most striking features had been carved by rivers but whose dominant characteristic was aridity.

In Lee's footsteps came wagon trains of other Mormon pioneers, dispatched by Brigham Young to colonize the outer margins of the Mormon Empire. Their courage goes unquestioned. If the Saints (as they called themselves) had not been so headstrong, determined, and well organized they would not have even considered settling this region, much less succeeded.

The secret to their success was their skill at reclamation— ditch-and-dam building. The Mormons were farmers, and in this arid region a bountiful harvest could be reaped only by supplementing the sparse rainfall—irrigation was absolutely essential to their survival.

The Mormon fervor for reclamation can best be illustrated by an anecdote: An honest taxpayer dies and goes to heaven. Admitted with no problems, he settles in to enjoy the hereafter. But after a few months he gets a bit bored. Finding St. Peter, he tells him that he'd heard a lot about hell and wondered if he could see it. Of course, says St. Peter, follow me. They went out a back door, down many flights of stairs, and finally came out in a broad valley, dappled with lush green fields bordered by beautiful cottonwood trees. "Why, this doesn't seem so bad," the taxpayer exclaims. "It's actually quite nice. Has hell always looked like this?" "No," says St. Peter. "It's those damn Mormons. They've been irrigating again." The Mormons were devout reclamationists, yes, but in their way they were also environmentalists. They understood the critical importance of taking care of the land that sustained them. They rotated their crops to protect the soil's fertility. They guarded against soil erosion. Even then, nothing was guaranteed. A sudden hailstorm or a freeze in late May could destroy the fruit trees and crops so laboriously planted.

Although it was vastly different from what many of them had known as children, the Mormons gradually developed an aesthetic appreciation for the strange, in places unworldly, scenery that bracketed their lives. You could not drive a wagon along the base of a flaming red, sheer sandstone cliff one thousand feet high and not recognize that the Colorado Plateau was unique. Intuitively, the Saints knew that these land forms were not duplicated anywhere else on the planet. As they moved, dwarfed and antlike, among the great red canyons and brilliant cliffs, they carried their awe with them.

When it came time to take a stand on the dams in the Grand Canyon, I found myself in a bind. I was caught between my Mormon upbringing, my environmentalist leanings, and my constituents' near unanimous support for the dams. My decision finally turned on one irrefutable fact: water is life in the desert. Since the dams were presented as an absolutely essential component of the CAP, on which the future of Arizona hinged, I came out in favor of the dams, and threw my whole energies into getting them approved.

In retrospect (and this is something I wish I had understood then), two deeply rooted but antithetical American traditions—development of our natural resources and preservation of our wild landscapes—were about to collide. After two hundred years, the balance was about to shift. The wheel of history was turning—and I was in the way.

In 1965 and 1966 the House held its initial hearings on the Central Arizona Project, which included the two dams. From the start it was clear that the dams would be the most controversial part of the bill, and that we faced a stiff fight to get them approved.

The environmentalists' opening shot was not long in coming. On June 9, 1966, a now-famous full-page ad appeared in *The New York Times* and *Washington Post*. "NOW ONLY YOU CAN SAVE GRAND CANYON FROM BEING FLOODED—FOR PROFIT," the headline blared. The ad concluded with this message:

> Remember, with all the complexities of Washington politics and Arizona politics, the ins and outs of committees and procedures, there is only one simple, incredible issue here: This time it's the Grand Canyon they want to flood. *The Grand Canyon.*

The ads, which cost $15,000, proclaimed the opening of an unprecedented and innovative lobbying campaign orchestrated by David Brower and funded by the Sierra Club and other conservation groups. The ad caused a stir, but it might have been short-lived had the government not made a monumental blunder. A day later the Internal Revenue Service notified the Sierra Club that it might lose its tax-exempt status if it continued lobbying against the dams. This heavy-handed maneuver only served to add a David-versus-Goliath theme to the conflict. When dozens of newspapers ran editorials ripping the IRS for trying to stifle the Sierra Club, thousands of people who might not otherwise have heard about the dams were alerted that something was afoot: What are those politicians up to now? They can't seriously be thinking of flooding the Grand Canyon . . . can they?

Striking while the iron was hot, Brower placed another ad. Under a headline, "SHOULD WE ALSO FLOOD THE SISTINE

CHAPEL SO TOURISTS CAN GET NEARER THE CEILING?" ran this copy:

> There is a bill in Congress to "improve" Grand Canyon. Two dams will back up artificial lakes in 148 miles of canyon gorge. This will benefit tourists in power boats, it is argued, who will enjoy viewing the canyon wall more closely. (See headline.) Submerged under the tourists will be part of the most revealing single page of earth's history. . . .
> There is no part of the wild Colorado River, the Grand Canyon's sculptor, that will not be maimed. . . .
> *This* generation will decide if something untrammeled and free remains . . . help fight a mentality that may decide Man no longer needs nature.

Together, the two ads and the IRS's blatant attempt to muzzle the Sierra Club sparked a firestorm of protest. It was phenomenal. The republic was nearly two hundred years old and we had finally found something everybody could agree about. As near as I could tell, when it came to dams in the Grand Canyon every American was a radical environmentalist.

When Aunt Mabel in Omaha, who had visited the Grand Canyon on her honeymoon thirty years earlier, got wind of what was up, she did two things. First, she sat down and sent the Sierra Club a contribution. Next, she took pen in hand to write her congressman, ol' what's-his-name. *I'll give him a piece of my mind,* she thought. And she did. Congressmen were deluged with mail, nearly all of it against the dams. I came under heavy fire myself, as this letter attests:

Flooding the Sistine Chapel

Dear Mr. Udall:

Damn it, what do you mean, saying there's "justification" for damming up the Grand Canyon and the Colorado River?

Don't you realize that you have responsibilities transcending the here and now, that you are, as an elected official, a caretaker of the public trust, and that the public has few greater possessions than the natural wonders of the Grand Canyon?

And here you are, taking seriously the claims that the Southwest needs drinking and industrial water more than the world needs that beautiful Canyon.

What shortsighted stupid *crap* that is.

Let's get our water for human use from the ocean or somewhere. That's all trivial, incidental stuff. Technology could achieve that in ten years.

It's taken a billion years to give us the Grand Canyon. It is not replaceable. Yet, here *you* are, ready to flood it.

Gurney Norman

Whew. When Gurney gets the bit in his teeth he does not let go.

Shortly thereafter, I received another letter that illustrates the passions aroused by western water fights. In 1967, an eighty-seven-year-old man—one Jose "Joe" Chavez—lying ill on his deathbed but still possessed of unfailing memory and rare eloquence, dictated a letter to his granddaughter with instructions to mail it to the governor of Colorado, the state's two senators, and then chairman of the House Interior Committee (on which I sat), crusty, irascible Wayne Aspinall.

57

Dear Sirs:

I am an old man and I know a lot about . . . this Udall outfit. My father had a ranch on the Little Colorado River when I was a boy. We had cattle, sheep and goats and horses. In the bottom land we raised our corn and beans and chile and we were contented and happy. Then David K. Udall [my grandfather] moved down to St. Johns . . . and he and some other men like him [Mormons, no doubt] put in a dam across the Little Colorado. We objected because it was a dangerous place to put in a dirt dam but they went right ahead and put it in anyway.

When it broke, it ruined our land and drowned our cattle and goats and . . . I have been poor ever since. They never paid us a cent for the damages. [The dam broke any number of times; everyone suffered when it did; the Mormons always rebuilt it. As for damages, it's unclear whether Mr. Chavez was due any. He may have been.] I confess I do not like the Udalls and this is one reason.

Another reason is that you cannot trust any of them. The whole tribe were Republicans and David K. Udall and his brother Joe Udall tried for years to get the Mexicans, who were then all Republicans, to give them a public office. But . . . Don Lorenzo Hubbell, who was a great leader, saw through this scheme and never would let them get on the Republican ticket. And the Mormons, who were nearly all Democrats, would have none of them. But when Franklin Roosevelt came in, some of the Mexicans switched to him and the Udalls went along, or most of them did.

However, David K. Udall, the big shot, had a second wife hid out down the river at a place called Hunt and this wife had some boys who stayed Republican and one of them got to be mayor of Phoenix. In this way the Udall family can now work both sides of the street. I want you to check up on this because I am an old man and I want to be sure of my facts. But my granddaughter tells me this Stewart Udall is trying to steal the water from Colorado and I can believe it. Because this is the way it happened fifty and sixty years ago. The Udalls have been at this business a long time.

Respectfully yours,

Jose (Joe) Chavez
(X) His Mark

Aspinall gave me a copy of the letter and I showed it to Stewart. We both got a chuckle out of it. The letter was, however, another niggling reminder that dams were not always unalloyed blessings. (Since Stew held a national office, he was freer than I to entertain misgivings about the dams. These were reinforced when, in the summer of 1967, he took his kids on a raft trip through the Grand Canyon. Afterward, he would say that he erred in making an "armchair" judgment. "The burden of proof," he declared, "rests on the dam builders.")

As the debate raged, it became increasingly apparent that the bureau's rationale for the dams was flawed on the merits, even if one completely disregarded the larger question of whether dams belonged in the Grand Canyon. The weakness of the arguments in favor of the dams was borne home to me the day I had to debate David Brower—as clever, tough, and tenacious an opponent as you could want—in front of a gaggle of national press at the worst possible venue: the *rim of the Grand Canyon*. This was a tough assignment—comparable to debating the merits of chastity in Hugh Hefner's hot tub in front of an audience of centerfold models, and me being on the side of abstinence. Brower raised three formidable objections: First, the dams would not provide any irrigation water—they were too deep in the Canyon and too far removed from arable land. Second, rather than conserve water, the dams would lose hundreds of thousands of acre-feet each year through evaporation and seepage. Finally, like all dams, these would eventually silt in and become useless. I sputtered and fumed, doing my best to refute Brower's allegations, but for much of the debate I was, in the immortal words of George Bush, "in deep doo-doo."

Later, when Brower came to Washington to testify before my committee, I queried him about the Sierra Club's uncompromising stand. "Suppose," I asked, "we have a low, low, low Bridge Canyon Dam, maybe 100 feet high, is that too much? Is there any point at which you compromise here?"

Brower responded, "You are not giving us anything that God didn't put there in the first place. . . . We have no choice. There have to be groups who will hold for these things that are not replaceable. If we stop doing that, we might as well . . . throw in the towel."

By late 1967, it was painfully obvious that we would never get the Central Arizona Project passed as long as it included dams in the Grand Canyon. Since the CAP was our foremost objective, we struck an agreement with Brower and the conservationists, agreeing to forego the dams and instead build a huge power plant at Page, Arizona, to provide the electricity to operate the CAP's pumps. (As it turned out, this solution was not environmentally benign, either: air pollution from the coal-fired plant has helped reduce visibility throughout the Southwest. But that's another story.)

Once we had shucked the albatross, the Arizona congressional delegation was finally able to get the CAP bill passed in 1968. By that time, however, Washington and Oregon had discovered that they really didn't have any water they wanted to share. To make sure Arizona got the message, Senator Henry "Scoop" Jackson inserted an amendment into the CAP bill prohibiting the Bureau of Reclamation from even studying the possibility of diverting water from the Columbia River for ten years. I used to tease Scoop, telling him that I knew I wasn't permitted to *study* the idea, but what if, early one morning lying in bed, I dreamily *contemplated* how nice 10 million acre-feet of the Columbia flowing south toward Arizona would look. Would that be a violation? His answer was, "No, Mo. According to my reading of the law, you can't *study* it, *contemplate* it, or even *dream* about it. The only thing you are permitted to do is to *forget* about it!" And I almost have.

The conservationists' victory in stopping the Grand Canyon dams marked a turning point in American history. From this time on, large reclamation and public works projects would be subject to much closer scrutiny. Hereafter, the value of preserving free-flowing rivers and wild landscapes would be factored into any project's "cost-benefit analysis." And, from now on, half-baked schemes—visions in search of reality—cooked up by an obtuse engineer or greedy developer would be met with greater skepticism. Stewart was right: the burden of proof *had* shifted. Within a few years, courts and legislatures would begin to recognize that plants and animals and free-flowing rivers and wilderness areas had *standing*—a value in their own right, and a right to belong.

In hindsight, what amazes me most about the dams we nearly built in the Grand Canyon (and the one we *did* build at Glen Canyon) was how cavalier the process was. Here were congressmen nonchalantly contemplating the drowning of hundreds of miles of free-flowing rivers—rivers that most of us had *never seen*, except perhaps from a plane. The Bureau of Reclamation's engineers didn't "waste a lot of time" studying the environmental impacts of Glen Canyon Dam. They just *built* it. That seems incredible to me today.

But it would be wrong to scapegoat the bureau. After all, the agency is simply the embodiment of our long-standing American belief that the good Lord put natural resources on the earth for us to develop. A perspective often lacking among today's younger environmentalists was that when the government first got into the dam-and-ditch business, the motivation was to *enhance*, not destroy, the natural environment. The Bureau of Reclamation was founded in 1902, and throughout the next five decades its mission—to bring water to the land—was universally regarded by westerners as good, even noble. Dams could, with a single stroke, provide a region with irrigation and drinking water, electricity, recreation, industry, and jobs. In this context, *dam* was a good word, a hopeful word, a word to be savored. When Hoover (1936) and Grand Coulee (1942) dams were completed, they were touted as the "eighth and ninth wonders of the world," and their engineers were feted and lauded as great heroes.

Today, the pendulum has swung. It's now fashionable among environmentalists to say that the "Big Dam Era is dead." What some fail to recognize, however, is that the bureau's successes, rather than its excesses, are primarily responsible for its demise. The reason I can't foresee any more sizable dams being built on any major western river is simply that the big dam sites are nearly all gone. Before consigning the bureau to the trash can of history it's worth taking a look at what the agency accomplished.

In the last fifty years, the West has become as well plumbed as any region on Earth. By 1980 the Bureau of Reclamation had built and was operating 345 dams, 14,590 miles of canals, and 50 power plants in the eleven western states. More than 16 million westerners benefited from federal irrigation water, spread upon 9 million acres of farmland. None of this came cheap—the total bill was $8 billion—but by the time the bureau was finished the desert *had* bloomed.

The big dams of the West—Hoover, Glen Canyon, Grand Coulee, Blue Mesa, Flaming Gorge, and many, many others—have changed the face of the region. It's only been a bit more than one hundred years since John D. Lee started his ferry, but he'd hardly recognize today's Colorado. The river is now less a watershed than a delivery system in which the Grand Canyon is just the biggest ditch. Water that begins as snowmelt in the Rocky Mountains flows, not to the Sea of Cortez, but to houses and condominiums in Denver, Colorado Springs, Los Angeles, San Diego, Tijuana, Albuquerque, Phoenix, and, shortly, Tucson. A great deal of ingenuity, imagination, money, and labor have been expended in the construction of this "modern miracle."

For the short term, these reclamation projects have enabled the West to prosper. But how about the long term? What will our great-great-great-grandchildren do once Lake Mead and Lake Powell fill with silt—as they are predicted to do within a few centuries? How will they judge us? Have we robbed their future to succor our present? We can measure the economic impacts, but the environmental ones are more difficult to judge. What have been reclamation's *real* impacts, its *true* costs?

No one really knows. But one can safely say that the environmental impacts of our reworking of western rivers have been staggering. For plants and animals that live in arid lands, water is energy, their form of wealth. It is a wealth that we have wantonly usurped and sometimes squandered for more than a century. We have used that water to construct a glorious civilization in the desert—a civilization many experts believe is not sustainable.

When I moved to Tucson in 1950 there were fifty thousand

people living there; there are now half a million. The trend has been the same in Phoenix. Both cities are losing the pristine qualities that made them so attractive; today, they are all too often wrapped in smog. This does not please me. But I am realistic enough to know that, for a politician at least, it is futile to fight all development. One can argue ad nauseam that it is not in nature's plan for man to inhabit the deserts, but the fact is, he does.

Arizona is here to stay. So, fortunately, is the Colorado River and the Grand Canyon. For the moment at least it seems to me that we've struck a balance where man can use some of the river's water without killing all of its beauty. As Rod Nash puts it in his book, *Wilderness and the American Mind,* "the Colorado . . . has been stretched to its limits in the service of man's body. Yet it still retains the capacity to satisfy his spirit. In this standoff, perhaps, is the final lesson of conservation's civil war over the river: both development and preservation can exist on one waterway, and both are necessary."

Saving the Crown Jewels: The Fight for Alaska Wilderness

★★★★★★★★★★★★★★★★★★★★★★★★★★★★★★

> Imagine, anyway, going from New York to Chicago—
> or, more accurately, from the one position to the other—
> in the year 1500. Such journeys, no less wild, are possible,
> and then some, over mountains, through forests, down
> the streams of Alaska. Alaska is a fifth as large as the
> contiguous forty-eight states. The question now is, what
> is to be the fate of all this land?
> —*John McPhee, in his 1975 book,*
> Coming into the Country

In 1972 I introduced a bill to put more than 100 million acres of federal land scattered throughout Alaska into more than a dozen new national parks, wildlife refuges, and national forests. My aim was to protect what are sometimes called the "Crown Jewels"—the most spectacular of the many large tracts of pristine wilderness in Alaska— from despoilment by natural-resource developers and exploiters of the native Eskimo. Thus began an epic fight, which soon came to be dubbed "the conservation battle of the century."

In retrospect, the Alaska Lands bill would never have gone anywhere had it not been for the yeoman efforts of literally thousands of conservationists, who donated their time, money, and labor to mount an unprecedented lobbying campaign in support of wilderness areas most of them will never have an opportunity to see. But the forces arrayed against the bill were equally formidable, and there were many times when I doubted it would pass. But finally, after eight long years, the bill was passed and on December 2, 1980, President Jimmy Carter signed it into law. With one stroke of his pen, Carter doubled the size of the national park system, doubled the size of the national wildlife refuge system, and tripled the size of the national wilderness system. This was the greatest single act in the history of wilderness preservation, a magnificent, historic moment, one I'll always treasure.

If there had been vigorous dissension and bitter discord over whether to build dams in the Grand Canyon, it was akin to the Oxford debates when compared to the controversy sparked by the Alaska Lands bill. What made the dispute particularly fierce was that most of the people who wanted to preserve Alaskan wilderness lived in the lower forty-eight—while most Alaskans favored leaving essentially their entire state open for development.

In this corner, you had the Alaska Coalition representing the Wilderness Society, the Sierra Club, Friends of the Earth, the Audubon Society, the National Parks and Conservation Organization, and a host of lesser-known groups, including the LOLITAS (Little Old Ladies in Tennis Shoes) and the THUPPS (Tree-Hugging Posy-Pickers). In the other corner, you had the state of Alaska and the Citizens for Management of Alaska's Lands (CMAL), a coalition of large corporations—what the environmentalists called the "five-star greed merchants," "the rape, ruin, and run crowd"—representing oil, timber, and mining interests. The two sides were about evenly matched. CMAL may have had more money, but wilderness had more friends: in time the Alaska Coalition grew to include fifteen hundred national, state, and local associations with more than ten million members.

The stakes were immense and both sides mounted frenzied lobbying campaigns—campaigns that were adroit at getting headlines while obscuring the real issues (in particular, CMAL's arguments were often unfettered by the truth). Although neither coalition liked to acknowledge the fact, there *was* a middle ground between saving the most spectacular scenery in the western hemisphere for future generations to enjoy, and blocking all future development of natural resources in Alaska. It was my task to find this *terra incognita*.

Now, I've been lambasted in print by some pretty ornery and miserable people, but the Alaska Lands bill spawned more inflamed rhetoric and scathing editorials than all of my other legislative endeavors put together. Consider, for example, the following two quotations. Can they be about the same fellow?

From an article in *Audubon* magazine:
Representative Morris King Udall of Arizona climbed out of the Army helicopter, took a long look at the Nizina and Chitina canyons below him, gazed at the snowcapped peaks of 16,000-foot mountains above him, spread out his arms in ecstasy, and said: "I want it all!" The occasion was Udall's first extensive trip to Alaska, two weeks that represent what he says were some of the "most exciting" days of his life. The visit led, ultimately, to Udall's proudest achievement, passage of the Alaska Lands bill that set aside 104.3 million acres with some of the most spectacular scenery in the world for the benefit of all of us, forever. . . .

Compare that with this, from an article entitled "Udall Treachery" in *The Arctic Sun,* published in Anchorage, Alaska:

And treachery it is. Suckled on the same teat, these two. . . . Stewart and Morris Udall are working for the good of, Lord knows whom. Not the American people, that is for sure. Stewart, a onetime Secretary of the Interior, is now pimping for a foreign country in an effort to deprive the American people of over 12,000 jobs and nearly $10 billion in taxes . . . using his influence, from his past position with the American Government, he has sold out to Canada . . . and his brother, Morris, as bad, if not worse than Stewart, is trying to block all future development of energy resources in Alaska. . . . Can we sue, can we take these monsters to court, or are our courts only for the criminal?

"Suckled on the same teat"—my mom got a chuckle out of that one. To explain why emotions were running so high requires a brief digression. By 1975, development in Alaska had been essentially halted for more than a decade because of legislative and legal battles over the distribution of the state's lands. Actually, the fight to pass the Alaska Lands bill was just the third and final chapter in a saga that began more than thirty years ago, at a time when Alaska was still a territory.

During the 1950s, I was not in Congress, but my brother Stewart was. Throughout much of that decade, Stew held a seat on the Interior and Insular Affairs Committee, which played a major role in drafting the bill, passed in 1959, granting Alaska statehood. Of the roughly 370 million acres in the new state, the bill gave the people of Alaska more than 100 million acres for themselves. This was a California-sized chunk of unbelievable beauty and wealth—a generous settlement by any standard.

Chapter two began in the early 1960s, when the native Alaskans—the Aleuts, Indians, and Eskimos—who had been living in this vast and wonderful place for fifteen thousand years before the white man arrived, said, in effect, "What the hell's going on here? What about us? We were here first, and we want some land, too!" Stew was sympathetic to this claim, and he helped draft a bill, the Alaska Native Claims Settlement Act (ANCSA), to redress this inequity.

Under the terms of ANCSA, Alaska would be divided between the state, the natives, and the federal government. Each of the parties could do as they saw fit with their lands. The state of Alaska could sell, lease, or develop its land; the natives likewise; and the federal lands were to be managed by the Bureau of Land Management, the Forest Service, the Fish and Wildlife Service, or the National Park Service, depending upon how they were eventually designated. ANCSA gave the state first crack at choosing the lands it wished to have; the natives got second pick; and the Feds came last.

ANCSA was a fair and reasonable approach to a thorny problem. But when the state of Alaska attempted to block ANCSA in Congress, Stew, who by now had been appointed Secretary of the Interior, issued an administrative edict "freezing" *all* Alaskan lands, until the state reached an acceptable settlement with the natives.

This "Udall freeze" was hardball politics and it caused a great deal of bitterness on the part of non-native Alaskans whose hopes of buying or developing some of their state land were stalled. Understandably enough, many Alaskans came to hate the federal government with a passion. As for the name Udall, well, from this time on most Alaskans held it in "minimum high regard"—a term former Speaker John McCormack once used to describe the status of a ne'er-do-well congressman. In Alaska, where conservationists are the only endangered species, "Udall" became a slur, an epithet. I have it on good authority that of the thousands of babies born in Alaska during the past two decades not one has been named Stew or Mo.

In any event, the "freeze" eventually did force the state to negotiate a generous settlement with the natives, a settlement ratified by Congress in the 1971 Alaska Native Claims Settlement Act, which gave the natives 44 million acres of land and $962 million. Thus ended chapter two.

Chapter three was triggered by an amendment the late, great Republican congressman John Saylor and I inserted into ANCSA. That 130-word amendment, "section d-2," said, in effect, "All right, the state got its land, the natives got their land, now how about the people of the United States?" D-2, which was destined to become one of the most famous amendments in environmental history, instructed the Secretary of the Interior to compile a list of lands, a total of 80 million acres, which met the criteria for, and should be considered as, potential new national parks, wildlife refuges, and national forests. Shortly thereafter, the members of the House Interior Committee went to Alaska for two weeks to see for ourselves what lands should be preserved.

When we arrived in Alaska we were met by an exceedingly frosty reception—and I'm not talking about the weather. Alaska has always attracted individuals fleeing the regimentation and, to them, stifling rules of the lower forty-eight. Here, in this huge state, they have a chance to seek near-total freedom in a vast expanse of tundra, forest, remote islands, and towering mountains as lovely as they are lonely. It is a mad eugenicist's dream: take a few hundred thousand hardy, indomitable people; scatter them lightly over half a million square miles of frozen wilderness; subject them to mosquitoes the size of meadowlarks and temperatures of 50 below and 100 above; succor them with kegs of liquor; supply them ample gunpowder and guns—and see what happens. It's not particularly surprising that you end up with a citizenry—to use the term broadly—composed in large part of wild characters who have in common only their disdain for sissified city folk and pompous politicians.

Before I left for Anchorage, friends had warned me that I might need Secret Service protection. "There are more nuts and more nuts with guns there than in any other single place in the world!" I was told. It did not reassure me to learn that one rabid hunting guide had vowed, "If the feds come up here, they'd better bring bulletproof vests and a priest!" When our party arrived in Alaska, we were met by a full-fledged "welcoming" committee, which I at first mistook for a lynch mob. These outspoken men—in their eyes, latter-day Paul Bunyans—were not at all reticent about registering their choice opinions of our attempt to "lock up" some of the most spectacular lands in their state. They jeered at us, waved hostile signs, and repeatedly saluted us with their uplifted middle fingers. We were touched. Not to be outdone, the local papers kept up a steady drumbeat of vitriolic editorials throughout our stay. In what we took to be a signal honor, the people of Sitka hung Representative John Seiberling and me in effigy.

Despite the hostility, the trip was one of the best of my life. I had not been to Alaska before and thus was totally unprepared for how majestic it truly is. The state just grabs you; it's a stunning piece of real estate. Both the beauty and the *scale* of the beauty are overwhelming. Alaska is twice the size of Texas; in two weeks we traveled seven thousand miles, and still only sampled the state's grandeur. At one stop, I remember meeting a group of scientists who talked rhapsodically about a place called the Noatak—an entire river basin, an entire *ecosystem,* absolutely untouched by man. And we had an opportunity to preserve the whole thing.

Our junket was a fabulous experience for all of us, particularly the foot soldiers—those government experts whose task it would be, on returning to Washington, to pore over stacks of maps deciding just where the lines should be drawn. One of the staffers, a favorite of the group, was a brash and talkative New Yorker by the name of Dora Trapkin. Dora, a self-described "Jewish-American princess," had never been closer to a wilderness than the basement of Bloomingdale's; not surprisingly, the wardrobe she had brought was more suited for a Caribbean cruise than for camping out by a glacial lake (still, it was more appropriate than that of the wife of Representative Tony Won Pat, the delegate from Guam, who had brought a muumuu and open-toed sandals for trekking across the Arctic tundra). One chilly morning we disembarked from our Twin-Otter, which had just landed on a gravel riverbed shorter and more crooked than a Tip O'Neill golf shot, near the Kobuk Sand Dunes, north of the Arctic Circle. After summoning the staff, press, and congressmen to a spot overlooking the desolate terrain, I put my arm around the dazed Miss Trapkin and said, "I hereby declare this the Dora Trapkin Memorial Sand Dune." It is perhaps the only dedicated sand dune in the national park system.

Another highlight was a visit to the windswept Eskimo village of Shishkameet on the Bering Sea. One staffer gave me the translation as, roughly, "the place where the walrus breaks wind causing the seal to turn its head." The residents of Shishkameet had gone out of their way to make us comfortable. They entertained us with tribal dances and displays of folk art, and feted us with traditional food. Touring the area where the villagers kept their umiaks, the boats in which they hunt walrus, we came upon racks of drying salmon and seal. Our guide selected a particularly ripe strip of seal meat, apparently in the process of becoming a fragrant delicacy, and offered it to me. This posed a difficult question of protocol for me, the chairman of the committee, a member of Congress, veteran, father of six, and, at this moment, possessor of a queasy stomach. I feigned a nibble, then called for my press secretary to taste the meat, then commanded, "When Udall eats, everybody eats."

By the time we returned to Washington, Seiberling and I were more convinced than ever that we needed to preserve much of the landscape we had seen. We drafted a bill to set aside more than 100 million acres of Alaska wilderness and introduced it in the House. Then we began what was to be an eight-year fight to get it passed.

Understandably enough, the Alaska congressional delegation—Senators Mike Gravel and Ted Stevens, and Representative Don Young—hoped to substantially amend, if not completely torpedo, our bill. But the delegation was riven by personality conflicts and, although each member individually wanted to be hailed as the man who stopped the "Great Lockup," they never managed to form a unified front.

Young was a former trapper, a cunning man well versed in bushcraft, and from day one we had to contend with his indefatigable efforts to weaken the bill. His strategy was to offer literally hundreds of "minor" amendments, each slicing off a few thousand acres here, a few hundred thousand there. This was a legislative war of attrition—the bill was in danger of bleeding to death before it could be approved. Young did, however, have a welcome sense of humor. During a debate over the future of the Chandalar Mountains, a question arose: Were both polar bears and brown bears found there? Young's reply: "There are no polar bears that far from shore. With all of the progress [we have made] in the area of integration, the polar bear does not mix with the brown bear and the brown bear does not mix with the polar bear. Perhaps we could work on that and it will come about, but I am not sure."

Over in the Senate, Senator Stevens followed the same

delaying strategy. Senator Gravel, however, was even worse. Gravel, who lost his reelection bid in 1980, was an erratic legislator possessing a volatile temper and a mercurial personality. He first gained widespread notoriety during the Vietnam era by attempting to have the *Pentagon Papers* report—all *eleven volumes* of it—entered in the *Congressional Record.* When his effort failed, he held a tearful press conference that raised a few questions about his emotional stability. Later, at the 1972 Democratic Convention, Gravel requested permission to bring a guest up to the podium. Once there, Gravel seized the microphone and put his own name in nomination for vice president. This forever ensured his reputation for unpredictability.

On most issues Gravel was a liberal, but when it came to the disposition of Alaska lands, he continually tried to upstage Young and Stevens, despite the fact that he had made little substantive contribution to drafting the Alaska Lands bill. Gravel employed every possible tactic to delay the bill; most notable was his attempt to have the complete text of a two-volume biography of Gerry Ford inserted as an amendment. Even I got a chuckle out of that. Through a whole series of shenanigans like that, Gravel successfully killed the bill the first time we had a chance to get it passed.

In 1978, after the House and Senate had passed different versions of the bill, we convened an ad hoc conference committee to write a compromise bill, which would then be resubmitted for final approval to both chambers. After nearly a week of toil, it appeared as if all sides were in substantial agreement and that we could wrap up our deliberations. I said, "Gentlemen, I think we've made history here tonight. Let's get out of the way and let the staff put this in final form." Just as we were to adjourn, Gravel, who had sat for six days without saying a word, said, "Mr. Chairman, I have just a few changes I want in the bill." Feeling magnanimous,

I said, "All right, what are they?" Gravel then handed me his list, headed by a proposal for a $5-billion hydroelectric project to dam the Susitna River. This would have been the single most costly public works project since the Panama Canal. It was Mike's way of trying to kill the bill. All of us, Democrats and Republicans alike, could have strangled him.

Over Gravel's objection the conference committee passed the compromise bill and reported it back to the full House and Senate. It passed easily in the House, but in the Senate Gravel succeeded in filibustering the bill to death because other senators were anxious to go home and campaign in the fall. This was a Pyrrhic victory, because it allowed President Carter and his great Interior Secretary, Cecil Andrus, to outflank Gravel and the prodevelopment interests by issuing an administrative edict that locked up more land than the bill would have. Alaskans were outraged.

When Congress recessed, Gravel and Stevens flew back to Alaska to regroup their forces. Here their long-running feud turned tragic. On a trip to Anchorage, Stevens's plane crashed on landing, killing his wife and injuring him. Later, Stevens would say, and with no little bitterness, that the trip would not have been necessary had Gravel not filibustered the compromise bill. He never forgave Gravel for forcing the fatal flight.

Throughout this entire period, my popularity in Alaska was plummeting ever lower, as this anecdote illustrates: Each summer, service organizations sponsor booths, featuring games of chance, at the Fairbanks County Fair. In 1979, at the height of Jimmy Carter's unpopularity due to the gasoline shortage and the hostage crisis in Iran, the Jaycees came up with a foolproof scheme for raising money. They constructed a backdrop with three faces emblazoned on it: Ayatollah Khomeini, Carter, and Morris Udall. For a dollar, you got three chances to throw a long-necked beer bottle into a hole below one of the three faces. By the time the fair ended, the heap of broken shards beneath my face, much higher than that below the Ayatollah or J.C., irrefutably demonstrated that I was the chief villain in Alaska that summer. The fact that this was the first time I had bested Carter in any political contest (to say nothing of the Ayatollah) was small consolation.

Throughout the seventies, I occasionally went to Alaska for yet more hearings. On one trip one of our hosts suggested that the congressional party take some time off and fly to a remote wilderness lake to go fishing overnight. We landed, pitched our tents, and went to bed. Early the next morning I was awakened by a small float plane that landed and taxied to shore about five hundred yards away. Two men got out, assembled a canoe, and came paddling past. They said hello, identified themselves as "Anchorage businessmen," and paddled away. I thought nothing more of it. A few hours later they came back, dressed as game wardens. Paddling up to where I was casting, they flashed their badges and asked to see my nonresident fishing license. Luckily, I actually *had* a license—I had bought it the afternoon we arrived in Alaska— and thus this elaborate attempt to frame me failed. It was a headline that never was, but how some Alaskans would have loved it: "UDALL NABBED POACHING TROUT—PROSECUTOR ASKS DEATH PENALTY."

In Dirty Tricks, Part II, Langhorne A. "Tony" Motley, a former Alaska Commissioner of Commerce who had been hired as the chief lobbyist for CMAL, the umbrella organization leading the fight against our bill, flew to Arizona for the express purpose of riling up the independent miners in my congressional district. In his role as *agent provocateur,* Motley told the crusty miners, "Udall is locking up Alaska"— implying, Arizona is next. The gullible miners, ever suspicious of any attempt to regulate their freedom to explore the barren deserts and rocky mountains, went through the roof. Their recall campaign never got off the ground, but during my 1978 reelection campaign they caused me no end of grief. The tactic backfired, however, because it just gave me additional opportunities to explain that we hoped to do in Alaska what earlier conservationists such as John Muir and Teddy Roosevelt had done in the lower forty-eight when they established Grand Canyon, Yosemite, and Yellowstone national parks. "Not in our generation, nor ever again, will we have a land and wildlife opportunity approaching the scope and importance of this one," I told my constituents. "In terms of wilderness preservation, Alaska is the last frontier. This time, given one great final chance, let us strive to do it right." Soon my polls showed that my efforts on behalf of Alaska wilderness were a big political plus for me in Arizona.

By 1980 it looked like all the pieces were finally coming together. After endless testimony, debate, hearings, and inspection trips, the Alaska Lands bill was coming to a head. For eight long years I had been pilloried in print, hung in effigy, threatened with fillet of seal, but at last we were going to vote: yea or nay; up or down. In Alaska the outcome was of such compelling interest that the proceedings were televised and beamed north by satellite. Thousands of Alaskans dropped whatever they were doing to watch the closing arguments. At the end of my speech, I advised the good people of Alaska that someday they would appreciate what was being done in Congress. "I've been through legislation creating a dozen national parks," I said, "and there's always the same pattern. When you first propose a park, and you visit the area and present the case to the local people, they threaten to hang you. You go back in five years and they think it's the greatest thing that ever happened. You go back

77

in twenty years and they'll probably name a mountain after you."

In the House, the final tally was 360 in favor, 65 opposed. In a single vote we had doubled the size of the national park system and preserved the "Crown Jewels" for posterity, in large measure because of the dedication of John Seiberling. (In hindsight, I can only thank God that we passed the bill before Ronald Reagan and Jim Watt took office. Watt's failure, as secretary of the interior, to enforce laws governing strip mining and his attempts to sell oil leases for cut-rate prices will not earn him high marks in the hereafter. Likewise for Reagan, who, for all his professed love of the outdoors, his *wood chopping* and *horseback riding,* has been the most environmentally destructive president in this century.) A few days after the vote, I got a letter in the mail from an irate Alaskan who said he had viewed my televised remarks and had concluded that I was a blockhead. Enclosed with his letter was a beautiful photo of a lofty, snowcapped mountain, below which he had written, "With regard to your comments about our naming a mountain after you—you asked for it, you've got it. MOUNT BULLSHIT—named in honor of Morris Udall, and his programs which so well reflect the name of this mountain."

You just can't please all the people all the time.

Postscript: As this book goes to press, there is a move afoot to open 1.5 million acres of the Arctic National Wildlife Refuge for oil exploration. The Department of the Interior predicts there is only a 19 percent chance of oil being found, but it also says there *may* be 9 billion barrels there. If so, that would make it the nation's largest remaining oil reserve. (Which isn't saying much, when you consider how much oil we Americans burn. Nine billion barrels is less than a six-hundred-day supply at current rates of usage. That's right:

it may not exist, but even if it does, our largest remaining oil reserve would last us less than *two years* if it were our only supply.) The fact that even now, in the midst of an oil glut, with gasoline cheaper in real terms than in 1950, there is a push to explore that wildlife refuge does not leave me sanguine about the chances of protecting it in perpetuity. Is this a bleak harbinger of what the future holds?

Today the environmental movement has never been stronger, but I sometimes worry that the pendulum may swing back—if it hasn't already begun to. As America's finite resources and fossil fuels begin to run out, will ecologically aware legislators be able to resist the pressures of a voting public that may well be willing to exchange open space and free-flowing rivers, even the "Crown Jewels" of Alaska, for jobs and highways and gasoline? I hope so, but it saddens me to say: I wouldn't bet on it.

6

A Boy for All Seasons: Origins of a Politician

During his run for the White House, Jimmy Carter often cited his small-town origins as the signal difference between him and the rest of us "big-city highfalutin politicians." Jimmy gave the impression that growing up in Plains, Georgia, had given him some special character qualities; the not-so-subtle implication was that he was better qualified to represent the common man. I found that I could deflate this argument and get a laugh in the process by doing a "little hometown" routine of my own. To counter Carter's lascivious fans following the legendary *Playboy* interview I'd say, "You think Plains, Georgia, is small; my hometown of St. Johns, Arizona, was so small you couldn't even 'lust in your heart.' "

In New Hampshire it became, "St. Johns was so tiny that they put the ENTERING and LEAVING signs on the same post."

And finally in the rural Midwest, the words became, "I had a friend who was nine years old before he found out that our town was not named 'Resume Speed.' "

Of all the places that the Mormons picked to settle, St. Johns was as harsh and stubbornly unproductive as any. Some early settlers were disheartened by the hellishly hot summers, spotty rainfall, frigid winters, and obdurate soil found along the Little Colorado River in northeastern Arizona; they referred to the region as "the land God forgot." St. Johns, now known as "The Gateway to Concho and

80

Show Low," may not be the end of the earth—but you sure as hell can see it from there.

My grandfather, David King Udall, founded St. Johns in the 1880s. Leaving Kanab, Utah, he led fifty families on a three-hundred-mile trek across a stretch of barren desert where even today few people live. Arriving in St. Johns the clannish Mormons settled in an area sparsely populated by Mexican and Anglo ranchers and farmers. Given the cultural and religious differences, strife was probably inevitable; in any event, the animosity of their neighbors was soon added to the other hardships the settlers faced.

While I have been the focus of scathing editorials during my career, they pale in comparison to what my grandfather faced; the editorial writers of the Old West knew not the meaning of restraint. This is how the *Apache County Chief* welcomed the Mormons: "How did Missouri and Illinois get rid of the Mormons? By use of the shotgun and rope. Apache County can get rid herself [*sic*] of them also. . . . He [the Mormon] has no rights and should be allowed none. Down with them. Grind out their very existence."

And that's what they set out to do, economically, socially, and legally. The locals trumped up some charges against David King Udall, convicted him of perjury, and packed him off to prison. After he had served six months in a federal prison in Detroit, evidence vindicating my grandfather was discovered. The judge and prosecutor appealed to President Grover Cleveland to grant a pardon. He did and my grandfather was freed.

At that time, the most controversial practice of the Mormon church was polygamy or "plural marriage." My grandfather Udall had two wives, but my maternal grandfather, John D. Lee, had seventeen. Only a small percentage of Mormon men practiced polygamy, and those who did required church approval. The practice lasted three or four decades; it ended for all intents and purposes in 1896 when Utah gained statehood.

Shortly thereafter, one of Utah's first senators, Reed Smoot, traveled to Washington to take his place in the U.S. Senate. His swearing-in was delayed by a filibuster fueled by rumors that he practiced polygamy. The truth was that Smoot was not a polygamist, although as a loyal Mormon he had supported the practice when it was church doctrine. As the filibuster droned on, an old senator, looking around the chamber at the many philanderers among his colleagues, said, "Gentlemen, I would rather have a polygamist who does not polyg, than a monogamist who does not monog." Smoot was seated.

During the 1968 presidential campaign, when George Romney was a leading Republican candidate, I told this story: Romney's grandfather was a Mormon, too; in fact, he was my grandfather's second-in-command on the journey from Utah to St. Johns. Romney's grandfather, like mine, was a polygamist and when the heat from federal marshals turned torrid, he moved his families to Chihuahua, Mexico, where he helped found a Mormon settlement that exists to this day.

When my grandfather, David King Udall, was arrested, he was hauled off to the territorial prison in Prescott. A local merchant, learning that my grandfather could not make bail, signed the bond that allowed him to return home to await trial. The merchant's name was Baron Goldwater—and he was the uncle of Barry Goldwater. Here was my grandfather, Barry Goldwater's uncle, and George Romney's grandfather all involved in this intertwined tale of the Old West. How about that for a "small world" story?

That relationship between the Goldwaters and the Udalls has endured for a full century. Barry and I have had our public differences during our years together in Congress, but I don't have a better friend, nor is there a public official I admire more for his conviction, candor, and honesty. Although Barry and I reside at different ends of the political spectrum—on his car he has a bumper sticker with a picture of an American flag that reads, "I Support the Right to Bear Arms"; on my car I have a bumper sticker with a picture of Smokey the Bear that reads, "I Support the Right to Arm Bears"—we do have at least one thing in common: we've both gotten clobbered in presidential elections. In 1964 Barry lost the presidential election to LBJ by 17 million votes; in 1976 I lost fourteen primaries to Jimmy Carter. I often joke that between the two of us we've made Arizona the only state in the union where mothers don't tell their children they can grow up to be president.

My father, Levi Udall, was a correspondence-school lawyer who eventually became Chief Justice of the Arizona Supreme Court. Never a superb spinner of yarns, he did have an appreciation for the role of humor in human affairs. His courtroom stories and tales of early St. Johns fascinated me and inspired me to follow in his footsteps.

The area around St. Johns was thinly populated, and Levi served concurrently as judge, church leader, and prominent citizen. He was often called upon to speak at funerals, Fourth of July celebrations, and other commemorative occasions. Levi liked to begin his talks with a joke, and he kept a collection of them suitable for every type of event in a musty, yellowing file. After Levi died, my brother Burr went through the file and found entries for "Funerals (stock)" and "Funerals (special)." That tells something about my father's organizational abilities and dry sense of humor.

The Mormons were an agricultural people, and like their neighbors to the northeast, the Hopi Indians, they often found themselves praying for rain. Jokes about aridity have always been a conversational staple in the high desert around St. Johns, where it's so dry that trees sometimes chase dogs.

Levi used to tell the story about the tourist driving through the Arizona desert during a 110-degree-in-the-shade day and stopping at a service station. Mopping his sweaty brow, the tourist asked the operator, "Say, mister, it's hot as the hinges of hell here and I don't see a cloud in the sky. Do you ever get any rain?"

The old fellow replied, "Yeah, we get some."

"How much?"

"Oh, about four inches."

"In a whole year you get four inches of rain? That ain't very much, is it?"

"Nope," said the Arizonan. "But you ought to be here the day we get it."

Later, on a rare cloudy day, a tourist came to the same service station and encountered the old man with his grandson.

"Looks like a little rain," the visitor said.

"Well, I sure hope so. Not so much for myself as for the boy."

"For the boy? Why's that?"

"Well," the old-timer said, "I've *seen* it rain."

My mother, Louise Lee, in addition to raising six devilish children, with all that entails, found time to pursue a number of religious, intellectual, and artistic interests. During her last twenty years, she developed an intimate relationship with Helen Sekaquaptewa, wife of a Hopi leader from Oraibi, the oldest continuously occupied settlement in North America. The Hopis are a gentle people who have not always received gentle treatment at the hands of the federal government. Over the years, Helen told Louise stories about the mesas on which the Hopis lived, and what it was like to be a young girl in this ancient culture. The result of this unusual collaboration was a widely praised book, *Me and Mine: The Life Story of Helen Sekaquaptewa as Told to Louise Udall.*

A Boy for All Seasons: Origins of a Politician

By the time I was a teenager I had developed a passionate interest in history, politics, and international affairs. With typical teenage arrogance, I considered myself an expert in all three fields; after all, wasn't I a regular reader of *Time,* even *Reader's Digest?* I would soon discover that I had a lot to learn.

I began loitering around the offices of the *Apache County Independent News,* the local weekly. When I turned seventeen, I approached the owner, who served as editor, printer, publisher, and advertising manager, about writing a weekly column on foreign affairs. I argued that in these years of cataclysmic events overseas, an insightful and informed column would be invaluable to his readers. He must have been dubious, but for some unknown reason—perhaps he thought my "serious" column would give a light touch to his paper (and, as it turned out, it did)—the editor gave me the go-ahead to launch my journalism career.

It did not take long for my faintly isolationist views to nettle Columbus Giragi, the volcanic-tempered editor of a newspaper in the neighboring town of Holbrook and a man who was staunchly supportive of FDR and the British. A lively newspaper war was soon under way. In columns of growing stridency—strident enough to embarrass my father, who knew Giragi and was seeking his support in his reelection campaign—I took on my Holbrook rival. Giragi was "nothing short of a warmonger," I declaimed, "and was clearly out of touch with international events in the *real* world."

In August 1939 I concluded a piece with these words: "I can safely predict that there will be no general war in Europe for at least ten years." I turned in the copy to the editor on Monday. On Tuesday, it was set in type. On Wednesday, the German Army launched its Blitzkrieg. On Thursday, as the people of St. Johns listened to radio accounts of Hitler's murderous thrust into Poland, the newspaper containing my column was delivered. Soon my confident prediction of a decade without war (Ten years? Hell, I was lucky to get ten hours!) was getting laughs in every home in the county.

Many years later, when I first ran for Congress, Giragi decided I had sufficiently moderated my views so that he could see fit to endorse me. After I was elected, I dropped by his office and we had a good laugh about the old days and my abortive career as newspaper pundit. Four years ago I went back to Apache County to find the old newspaper file with my famous blunder. Unfortunately, a fire in the 1970s had destroyed the building and there were no copies of the article to be found anywhere. But the lesson remains indelible. As Yogi Berra put it in his fourth law of prudence, "A guy ought to be very careful in making predictions . . . especially about the future."

My initial foray into politics came about a year after my journalism career ended. My friends and I were too young to vote, so we thought we would have some fun with a quixotic campaign caper. We put the name of a local bum, Crawford "Lantern" Maybin, in nomination for town constable. Lantern's nickname came from his fondness for spirits: he was always "lit." Thanks to the voters' sense of humor we almost elected Lantern, a gentle soul whose habit of wobbling around town at night peering in windows came to an untimely end—one night ol' Lantern was permanently unplugged by a round from a frightened widow's rifle.

The St. Johns High School had a student body of sixty boys and sixty girls in 1940. It was the size of school where you could do just about anything you wanted to do, and I was the kind of kid who wanted to do it all. A pale kid, six feet, five inches and 165 pounds—my football coach once said, "Morris, if you drink red soda pop you'll look like a thermometer"—I quarterbacked the football team, played center on the basketball team, acted the lead in the school play, edited the yearbook, played trumpet in the school band, was student body president and valedictorian. On the seventh day I rested.

For many years our community was blessed with an energetic and cosmopolitan music teacher, who delighted in broadening the cultural horizons of her students. As soon as she had taught my class to perform light opera and drama, she began scheming to achieve her dream of launching an honest-to-goodness uniformed marching band. This proved to be an ambitious and expensive undertaking, and her initial proposal was greeted with little enthusiasm by the principal. But after a determined lobbying campaign, a little intimidation, and considerable harassment she was given permission to start her band. At the last football game of the season, the traditional Thanksgiving Day grudge battle with Round Valley, she choreographed the first performance of the St. Johns High School Marching Band—all twenty of us, including the quarterback, two guards, and a halfback. At halftime I took off my leather football helmet, picked up my trumpet, put my band cap on my head, and marched up and down the field tooting Sousa as assiduously as I had carried the ball moments before. Halftime over, the four of us who were "going both ways," so to speak, donned our helmets and lined up for the kickoff—boys for all seasons. We really thought we were hot stuff.

For spirited teenagers, St. Johns could be humdrum, and, in pursuit of excitement, my friends and I sometimes strayed onto the wrong side of the law. Before I graduated from high school, my honor-studded résumé came to include a few petty misdemeanors.

One night a friend and I decided to go for a joyride in Brother Lillywhite's new flivver. Lillywhite was a stuffy, sanctimonious type and our plan was to spirit his car away while he was in church. Since Lillywhite's car had no battery, he customarily parked it on a hill so that he could jumpstart it. After watching Lillywhite enter the church, I crept behind the wheel and instructed my accomplice to remove the chocks. Down the hill we went, picking up speed. I popped the clutch and away we roared. All was going according to plan until I failed to negotiate the turn at the bottom of the hill and we ran smack into an irrigation ditch. Water began to pour in, and as we leapt out and started running, a baby began to cry in the backseat. Lillywhite had left his eighteen-month-old daughter asleep in the car! Now we were in trouble. The noise of the crash attracted a crowd, who quickly rescued the baby. A short time later the long arm of the law—in the form of my dad, the judge—had picked us up by the scruffs of our necks.

I toiled for two long summers in the fields to pay off my fine.

On another occasion, the circus rolled into St. Johns, complete with wagons and bears and clowns and the canvas big top. My gang was especially fascinated by the steam calliope, the big organ mounted on a wagon that went up and down Main Street tooting up a storm. Displaying a scientific curiosity we rarely evinced in school, we decided to conduct an experiment: What would be the effect on the tone and volume of the organ if rotten eggs were inserted in its pipes? The result was an incredibly noxious odor that cast a pall over the proceedings—and a visibly enraged calliope player who had no trouble identifying me as one of the culprits.

I guess I could say that these diverse experiences taught me the joys and rewards of being a generalist, but I only recently learned the meaning of the word. Later in life, as a trial lawyer, I needed to master enough math and engineering to try a construction case on Monday, enough knowledge of medicine to cross-examine an orthopedic surgeon on Tuesday. Knowing a *little* about a lot of things also helped me as a young congressman. I remember arriving one morning to dedicate a post office at Naco, a tiny town on the Mexican border. The postmaster, a nervous sort, wouldn't start the ceremony because the local minister wasn't on hand to give the invocation. This made *me* nervous, since I had another dedication to make that same morning in another town, fifty miles away. Rather than wait, I told the beleaguered postmaster that I could offer the prayer. After my invocation, they had trouble with the halyards, so, ever confident, I went over and raised the flag, upside down as I remember. Then I was introduced and gave my speech. As I was leaving, I told the postmaster that I was seeking to be not just a triple threat but Congress's first quadruple threat: I could pray, raise the flag, sing "The Star-Spangled Banner," and give the main address. He was not amused.

I can't talk about my boyhood without mentioning one incident that has had a profound effect on my life, my sense of self, and my dealings with people. When I was six years old my right eye was punctured by a playmate's rusty pocket knife as I held a string for him to cut. An alcoholic physician botched the injury, and six months later the optic nerve got infected. When another doctor, a specialist, discovered that the infection was spreading to my good eye, he hastily performed an emergency operation to remove the bad one. He told my mother that I came within twenty-four hours of going blind. Kids can be cruel, and the inevitable jokes about "Cyclops" and "here comes Ol' One Eye" hit hard. My glass eye, coupled with my gawky frame and lack of confidence, made me an extremely self-conscious boy. Fortunately, the "up" side was also present, in the form of a loving family who inspired me to compensate by excelling in athletics and academics.

In her journal, my mother wrote with anguish about the

89

loss of my eye, directing her anger against the inept local doctor whose judgment was apparently clouded by demon rum. She noted with resignation my stubbornness through the discomfort of the operation and the fitting of a glass eye:

> Morris wouldn't wear the sun glasses we had made and I could hardly stand him out of my sight for fear something would happen to his remaining eye. The fear of blindness was with me for a long time. I felt so grateful to the Lord. Had things not happened just as they did and when they did, we would have lost the light from both blue eyes without any warning. All my life I must do all I can to show my gratitude.

In later years, the family, especially my mother, used to jokingly reminisce about the process of getting new artificial eyes to replace the ones I would lose or break. When I needed a new eye, my mother would send a money order to the Denver Optical Company; a few weeks later they would send back thirty-six fragile eyes, wrapped in cotton. Then the whole family would spend an evening trying to determine which eye fit best. The one that was the right size would usually look off to the left or right, giving me a demented stare. The one that looked straight ahead was invariably the wrong color. And so forth. Now you can get a custom-made eye that even members of my family can't tell from the good one.

I was healthy for two years after losing my eye, but then I contracted a nearly fatal case of spinal meningitis. I can still remember Mormon elders coming to put their hands on me and pray for my recovery. The pressure of increased spinal fluid would bend me over, and, at times, it would take three grown men sitting on me to hold me still while the doctor administered an excruciatingly painful spinal tap. I remember when the county health department put a quarantine sign on our door to prevent people from coming in and us from going out of the house. It was a miracle that I survived.

During the next forty years I enjoyed the gift of robust health. In fact, I didn't see the inside of a hospital until 1976, when I broke both arms in a fall off a ladder, caught viral pneumonia, had my appendix burst, got peritonitis, and contracted Parkinson's disease—all within eight months. This last illness I'm still battling today.

Parkinson's is an incurable disease—although there have been some exciting new treatments developed recently—caused by a shortage of dopamine in the brain. It does not affect your mental capacity, but it does affect your ability to perform fine motor skills. I don't feel lucky in having gotten the damn thing, but I do feel lucky that it is not as disabling for me as it is for many. If not medicated correctly, those afflicted with Parkinson's may appear "too loose"; sometimes the head can loll from side to side, and the limbs may shake with faint tremors. Similar symptoms are sometimes seen in drunks, and from time to time I've been accused of being an alcoholic, but believe me, drink isn't the cause.

One way to deal with a disability is by making light of it. Shortly after I was first diagnosed as having Parkinson's, there was a scandal involving Paula Parkinson, a blonde lobbyist who kissed and told about her affairs with several congressmen. I used to joke that there were two kinds of Parkinson's disease: the kind discovered by an English doctor, and the kind that you get when you go to Florida with a blonde lobbyist. There are no similarities between the two afflictions, except that they both cause you to lose sleep—and they both give you the shakes.

I also have a list of one-eyed jokes I've used down the

years. Sammy Davis, Jr., the famous entertainer, lost an eye in an auto accident and converted to Judaism. One time he went golfing, and someone asked him, "Sammy, what is your handicap?" Said Sammy, "Handicap? Man, I'm a one-eyed Negro Jew, do I need one?" During my presidential campaign, I would add, "Handicap? I'm a one-eyed Mormon Democrat from conservative Arizona . . . you can't find a higher handicap than that."

Several of my one-eyed stories have to do with flying, which I was able to enjoy for twenty years, passing the pilot's test despite the loss of one eye. With training, I was able to develop pretty good depth perception and after several months could grease a landing as well as anyone else. Others, though, had doubts, as I learned when I asked former Arizona governor Bruce Babbitt, now running for the presidency, if he wanted to catch a ride to Tucson in my single-engine airplane. I was wearing an eye patch at the time. He looked at my patch and then at the plane. "Mo," he said, "I don't fly in single-engine airplanes with one-eyed pilots on account of my back." I told him that I didn't know he had a back problem. "It's not that," he said, "it's that I have a yellow stripe down the middle of it."

When I graduated from high school I followed my brother Stew's lead and enrolled at the University of Arizona in Tucson. There I shared a basement apartment in the university infirmary with two other students attending school, as I was, on a basketball scholarship. We took meals to the patients and cleaned up the dispensary to earn extra money. To earn some more, I started a barbershop to trim the heads of my fellow jocks. On December 7, 1941, I was setting up my chair for the brisk Sunday afternoon trade when I heard that the Japanese had attacked Pearl Harbor.

Seven Good Eyes on the Starting Five: My Formative Years

★ ★

> It is important for a man to be a part of the action and the passion of his times, at the risk of being judged not to have lived.
>
> —*Judge Oliver Wendell Holmes*

Certainly, that is the way I felt about World War II; it was the most important event of my young life and I longed to be a part of it.

And so, though I knew that a one-eyed volunteer stood little chance of being accepted, the next morning I joined my fellow patriots in rushing to the recruitment offices. But my pessimistic expectations were realized as the Navy, Army, Marine Corps, and Coast Guard all said, Thanks, but no thanks.

Next, I attempted to join the university's advanced ROTC program. I passed the written test, but then came the physical exam, which I knew included a vision test. In anticipation, I had devised and practiced a clever subterfuge. When the doctor began the test, he asked me to cover my right, or blind, eye and read the chart. "Top row: 'A, G, X'; middle row: 'C, M, O'; bottom row: 'I, B, H' "—that was a snap. Then he asked me to cover my other eye. With my right hand I removed the piece of cardboard covering my right eye, shifted it to my left hand, and once again covered my blind eye. This sleight of hand went undetected and I passed!

All was well until another disgruntled applicant complained bitterly to the examiners: "You are rejecting me for flat feet and you are accepting Udall with his glass eye? That's a hell of a way to run an army."

The embarrassed examiners collared me and forced me to take a second and more closely observed test. I tried to fake it, but it was no good. With the card over my good eye, I couldn't see a thing. They gave me an A for effort and a 4-F for the record, and sent me home.

My hopes of bringing down the Third Reich and the Imperial Japanese Army were dashed. But, as it turned out, I didn't have enough faith in the vagaries of the government. Six months later, with the Japanese running wild in the Pacific and the Germans on the move in Europe, the Apache County Selective Service Board began drafting anybody who was "warm and moved." By that standard I qualified, and soon I was in the Army.

To ease the boredom at my first duty station at Fort Douglas, Utah, I formed a basketball team composed entirely of men on noncombatant status due to various handicaps. Our starting five had a grand total of seven good eyes. We played small college teams and squads from other military bases. In time, we got to be pretty good and soon found ourselves playing preliminary games before sizable crowds at the University of Utah.

This pleasant interlude ended when our commanding officer was ordered to send six enlisted men to Officer Candidate School to be molded into "Ninety-day Wonders." The first generation of Wonders was shipped off to the Pacific and Africa. Those of us with "limited service" ratings went off to battle red tape and Army brass. Our survival rate was higher, but almost all of us would rather have been where the action was. The one exception was a bunk mate of mine who confided that he aspired to be a personal aide to a cowardly general.

I was assigned to the Army Air Force, the forerunner of the U.S. Air Force, and sent to a base near Tampa, Florida, which afforded about all the cultural and climatic advantages a young single man from arid Arizona could want. Of course, it was too good to be true. Only a few weeks later I was posted to a B-26 training facility at Lake Charles, Louisiana, deep in redneck country. The difference in cultures, from Arizona Mormon to Old Deep South, was alarming, and events would make it difficult for me to adapt.

My first superior was a bigoted major whose primary pleasure in life seemed to be abusing anyone who was black or Jewish. When I introduced myself, the major scowled as he looked me up and down. " 'Morris'? What kind of a name is that?" he asked. His worst suspicions were confirmed at mail call when he saw a letter to me from one "Judge Levi Udall." For six long months he treated me as he did his Jewish officers—badly. It proved a painful but eye-opening experience.

I was to spend two years at Lake Charles. In time I grew to love the Cajun country, but I never grew accustomed to the segregation of the Deep South. While the Mormon religion also discriminated against blacks, at home I had rarely seen a black person. In Louisiana, however, I dealt with racial conflict on a daily basis as the commander of a segregated squadron—one with all black enlisted men and all white officers, a situation identical to that which was later depicted in the popular Broadway play and the motion picture, *A Soldier's Story*.

Later, when I left Louisiana, I wrote a letter to Franklin Roosevelt recounting my experiences during four years in the service and pleading for an end to military segregation. I said that the races could live and fight together, and that the military should establish integrated units. Several years later, to my pleasant surprise, Harry Truman mandated this with an executive decree. It was one of his most courageous acts, and certainly one of the most important human rights advances in United States history.

For the next few months, my unit, Squadron C ("C" for colored, another subtle military touch), waged war against an insidious foe: venereal disease. In the immortal words of Pogo, "we had met the enemy and he was us." Eventually, through great sacrifice, Squadron C was honored for having achieved the largest reduction in VD of any unit in the Third Air Force. This was accomplished by a combination of intimidation and, as some of you will remember, endless screenings of graphic VD films showing the grisly effects of gonorrhea and syphilis on one's most private parts.

The army was dead earnest about its assault on VD (one wit suggested a slogan: "Beat the Axis with Prophylaxis"). The most efficacious tactic was to deploy mobile PRO stations (that's right, "PRO" for prophylactics) in close proximity to nearby red-light districts. The PRO stations offered both before and after services: outbound into the battle zone one could get a brace of condoms; inbound, a dose of antibiotics. On returning to base following a weekend leave, every soldier would be interrogated: had he visited a PRO station for a checkup? If the answer was no, the soldier would be "encouraged" to do so, even if he had spent his leave with a maiden aunt. During one pep talk I exhorted my black troops to cut down the VD rate, saying, "I've been telling you to keep yourselves clean till you're black and blue in the face." This was not my finest hour.

Reality surfaced when I was assigned to defend one of two black airmen who had killed a white guard while escaping from the stockade. Military "justice" in the 1940s was hardly worthy of the name. At that time, my only courtroom experience had been watching my father preside in Apache County Superior Court. To assign a second lieutenant with no law school training, let alone a law degree, to defend an accused murderer facing the death penalty was unthinkable. But that's what the Army did. The case still haunts me.

The trial took two days and it was a mismatch from the start. Opposing me was an accomplished attorney who presented his case with great flair. Despite my best efforts, my wretched defendant was sentenced to death by the six white officers who composed the court-martial board. I suspected that even Clarence Darrow would have lost in that biased court, but that didn't salve my conscience. When the sentence was carried out six months later, the nervous firing squad grotesquely bungled the execution, and an officer had to put the condemned man out of his misery with a coup de grace. A decade later, when I was Pima County attorney, I prosecuted a vicious, brutal homicide. I won the case, and the murderer was executed in the Arizona State Prison gas chamber. Few people, I'm happy to report, have had this close a look at both sides of capital punishment. For a brief period when I was a prosecutor, I believed that the death penalty was a deterrent and therefore justifiable; I no longer hold that view.

Tormented by the verdict, and tired of doing what General Patton called "shoveling shit in Louisiana," I badgered my commanders into allowing me to join a unit being trained as part of the invasion force scheduled to storm the islands of Japan. Germany had surrendered, and scuttlebutt had it that this was to be the last major battle of the war. But then *Enola Gay* intervened, dropping the first atomic bomb, and it was all over. I said to myself, "Well, Mo, I guess you have had your war. Now it's back to school and life as it's supposed to be lived." As usual, I was wrong. A few stateside warriors had to go over and clean up the remnants of a war while the men who had fought it came home.

The pain of going overseas was eased by the exquisite sense of irony. On a beautiful September morning we watched as the first shipload of exuberant combat veterans steamed into Seattle to be met by bands, dancing girls, balloons, and confetti. On the adjacent pier we watched wistfully, wondering what kind of reception we would get when we came home months, if not years, later.

I landed at Iwo Jima on D-day plus 155 with a piano and an assortment of softball gloves, bats, and balls—essential equipment for keeping the garrison troops from mutinying. There is nothing heroic about being on the scene of historic battles after the fighting's over. The GIs were sullen and homesick, the indigenous peoples shattered and distrustful. We tried to make the best of this cruel joke, but we were plagued with boredom and the sinking feeling that we were losing ground, especially jobs and girls, to veterans back home.

We broke the monotony by exploring caves and bunkers the Japanese had built, in search of rifles, pistols, and Samurai swords. The caves were off-limits because of the danger of booby traps and live shells; nonetheless, greed and ennui propelled us forward and we became first-rate souvenir hunters. We also bided our time playing poker; having learned the art from a few cowboys in St. Johns, I managed to build up a nice little nest egg from cocksure fighter jocks and other less serious students of the game.

The real antidote to boredom came when I started a basketball team that won the Mid-Pacific championship and, with it, a trip to Honolulu. There we frolicked in luxury: first-class quarters, scrumptious food, exotic drinks, even telephone calls home. When we flew back to Iwo, our homesickness had been much aggravated by this brush with civilization.

When it came time to close the Iwo base, one of my final military acts was to serve as master of ceremonies at a variety show—a poor excuse for entertainment featuring a ragtag assortment of musicians, comedians, and jugglers. As the show came to a close, I took the microphone and told the audience, "Gentlemen, I guarantee you this next act will bring down the house." On that cue, an engineer started up a bulldozer and roared up to the makeshift wooden stage, which I hastily vacated, and smashed the wooden structure to the ground.

It was time to go. We sailed back into San Francisco Bay in April 1946. There were no balloons. No brass bands. No dancing girls. No confetti. Nobody cared. We were met by inflation, unemployment, and uncertainty.

Returning to the University of Arizona boosted my spirits. I ran for student body president against a frat man by the name of Bill O'Brien. O'Brien's campaign was managed by a fellow Bostonian, Jim McNulty, who quickly became one of my best friends.

McNulty and I worked hard and played hard. We got into fairly serious trouble for organizing an assembly program that featured the mock shooting of ducks—in the university auditorium. As two hunters stalked the stage, they periodically aimed and fired their shotguns, loaded with blanks. At the gunshots, stagehands hidden in the rafters flung dead ducks into the audience. Thirty years later Jim won a seat in the U.S. Congress in the district adjoining mine. No man ever brought so much talent to the national legislature, but alas he was overwhelmed by the Reagan landslide and served only one term.

My college basketball career began on a fluke soon after the duck shoot. As the third-string center, I typically rode the bench, picking up more splinters than playing time. Then, in a key game against nationally ranked West Texas State, the coach yanked the starting center for dogging it. His substitute quickly got winded, and when the regular center, still pouting, took his sweet time doffing his warm-up jacket, the coach blew his stack. Looking down the bench, he yelled, "Mo, you get in there." My moment had come and I took advantage of it, hitting for ten points in the closing five minutes to pull out a close win.

My senior year, 1947/48, is a blur of happy memories: I was a full-time law student, cocaptain of a championship basketball team, and student body president. In the latter role, I earned a reputation as a dangerous maverick. First, I shocked the administration by demanding to oversee the expenditure of student funds; I then supported a takeover of the student bookstore; this was followed by the creation of a co-op grocery store to serve the many families of veterans studying under the GI bill. Predictably, I was roundly denounced by the Phoenix newspapers. They branded me a radical, and suggested that I be removed from office and thrown to the wolves. This was just the first of a lifetime of brushes with Phoenix newspapers—neither their depiction of my politics nor their proposed remedy has changed much o'er these many years.

On the basketball court the Arizona Wildcats were having a great season. We played at Madison Square Garden in New York City and Convention Hall in Philadelphia, receiving modest recognition from the pollsters. My last hurrah came against the University of New Mexico. On the day of the game, one of the Albuquerque papers featured a story about the Wildcat star with the plastic eye who was the student body president and leading scorer to boot.

That night I had one of those games you dream about. Everything I tossed up went in. With two minutes to play and twenty-four points to my credit, the coach took me out to a standing ovation. Our bench was right under the press table and an Albuquerque sportswriter leaned over and said, "Udall, you are a liar. No one shoots like that with a glass eye." I plucked the slippery orb out of its socket and handed it to him, saying, "Mister, I haven't been able to see much out of this one, you try it."

After graduating, I was approached by the newest team in the old National Basketball League, the Denver Nuggets. The Nuggets offered me the then-princely sum of $8,000 a year and said that I could attend law school in Denver while playing for them.

The 1948/49 Denver Nuggets rank among the worst professional basketball teams ever. Our performance on the court was abysmal, and we set a league record for consecutive losses. But we did travel in style, sort of. As our principal transport, our owner provided an ancient, dilapidated, rickety DC-3 in which we flew to such garden spots as Oshkosh, Sheboygan, Fort Wayne, Waterloo, Syracuse, Detroit, and Hammond, Indiana. As a rookie, I would carry the ball bag in one hand, a satchel of law books in the other. As a licensed pilot (I had obtained my flying license after being discharged from the Air Force), I frequently spelled the pilot at the controls—which did little to calm the frazzled nerves and queasy stomachs of my teammates as we lurched over the Great Plains in the turbulent winter air. (Later, flying would become a key part of my life, almost my very soul. As soon as I could afford one, I bought a small, single-engine Piper Cherokee. Over the next thirty years, flying enabled my children and me to savor from the air wilderness areas we would never have found time to hike. Being a pilot was also a boon in my legal and political careers: when I was first elected, my congressional district was among the largest in the country.)

Finally, mercifully, the season ended. The Nuggets went belly up, last in attendance, last in the league, and last in paying their players. I never did get my signing bonus; instead, the owner gave me a gilded, embossed certificate for $10,000 worth of Nuggets stock—as valueless today as it was then.

Worthless stock certificate in hand, I returned to Tucson, where I married and began a law practice with my brother Stewart. As a trial lawyer, I made my living by convincing a jury of twelve ordinary people that my client was right, the other attorney's wrong. It was sink or swim—if I won I could put food on the table and pay my bills. If I lost, my growing family scrimped. I loved the courtroom challenge and gradually became a fairly well-known trial lawyer.

In 1952, seeking a supplemental income and political experience, I ran for county attorney. I was only three years out of law school but thanks to some name recognition and old-fashioned door-to-door campaigning, I won—no mean feat for a Democrat in the face of Eisenhower's landslide.

One of the first cases I prosecuted involved a man accused of drunk driving. The defendant surprised me by hauling in five of his drinking buddies to attest to his sobriety on the night in question. In my summation, I told the jury that the defense's argument reminded me of the bartender who shoved the last five patrons out the door at closing time. When the group reached their car the leader turned to one of the men and said, "Simpson, you drive, you're too drunk to sing."

After I won the case and he had dismissed the jury, the judge told me a story about the two traveling salesmen who worked all day, rented a third-story hotel room, and then went out on the town. Plastered, the two returned to the hotel for a nightcap. Their besotted revelry was interrupted when one of them opened a window and fell out. His drunken partner consoled himself with another drink and then passed

102

out. The next morning he received a message that his friend was in the hospital in traction.

When his friend asked him what happened, the injured man said, "Don't you remember? I opened the window and said I was going to flap my arms and fly around the block and come back in the window."

His friend said, "Yes, I seem to remember that."

"Well, why didn't you stop me?"

"Stop you? I thought you could do it."

The judge went on to say that the beauty of my anecdote was that it had highlighted the absurdity of the defense's case so that the jury could not fail to discern it. This was an epiphany—an apt yarn, which took less than a minute to tell, could be more persuasive than an hour of logical argument.

From that moment on, I began to collect funny stories and use them regularly in opening and closing arguments. Whenever I heard a joke I thought I might be able to use, I scrawled it down. Later, as I got more deeply involved in politics, I discovered that many of my courtroom stories worked as well on the stump. When it became obvious to me that politics was my future, I began scribbling down political stories as well. As I made the transition from attorney to politician, the use of humor came naturally, and over the years it has served me when nothing else could.

Over three decades this scribbling has filled three looseleaf notebooks with stories, anecdotes, jokes, and one-liners that I periodically review and index. Once or twice a year, I'll spend a leisurely day at the beach or in the mountains browsing through the notebooks to refresh my memory. Gradually, I've come to embody the old saw: "That reminds me of a story . . ." Today I can almost always come up with an apropos story or relevant yarn for just about any occasion.

In 1954, Arizona's Second Congressional seat appeared

ripe for the taking, and I considered running for the House of Representatives, but for reasons of seniority and familial solidarity, I deferred to Stew (or Slu, as we still call him), who ran and won. In lieu of running for Congress, I mounted a campaign for a county judgeship. I lost that race, in part because my name was so well hidden on the voting machine that some of my friends told me they spent five minutes searching for it in vain.

In early 1960, my father was contemplating retiring from the Arizona Supreme Court. I decided to campaign for his seat. But fate had other plans: a few months later, in May 1960, Dad died. For the first time in twenty years, Arizona had a Republican governor. Searching for a worthy appointee who could win a six-year term in his own right the following November, the governor found just the right man: Superior Court Judge Jesse A. Udall, a staunchly conservative Republican and one of my favorite relatives. With Jesse's appointment I found myself doubly stymied: My brother had the congressional seat I wanted and I couldn't run for judge against my uncle. I paraphrased the Ancient Mariner and said, "Udalls, Udalls everywhere, and not an office to seek." Clearly, my destiny did not include Washington, D.C., or the state bench.

But less than a year later, I was in Congress, where I had longed to be for nearly ten years. Jack Kennedy had appointed Slu secretary of the interior, and I won a special election to fill his House seat. I decamped to Washington, taking my notebooks with me.

★ ★ ★ ★ ★ ★ ★ ★ ★ ★ ★ **8** ★ ★ ★ ★ ★ ★ ★ ★ ★ ★ ★

A "Caucasian in the Woodpile": The Seniority System and Adam Clayton Powell

★ ★

> Look, son, this seniority system is bad. It's indefensible, it stifles people, and it really can't be justified. But let me tell you one thing—the longer you're here, the better you'll like it.
>
> —*senior member of Congress*

Writing in *Harper's Magazine,* this is how Larry L. King described my arrival in Washington:

> He was then a month short of thirty-nine and looked something like a rodeo hand in short burr haircuts, bowties, and a wide leather belt studded with ersatz stones and a silver buckle; there was about him a disconcerting combination of painful country-boy shyness and a bawdy cowlot humor.

"Cowlot humor" to one side, Larry is one of my close friends, but this passage—which has stuck to me like a tick for fifteen years—reflects as much on his ignorance as it does on mine. I plead guilty to the burr haircuts, the bow ties, even the bawdy humor, but the "ersatz stones" were turquoise, the "silver buckle" a sterling example (no pun intended) of the Navaho jewelry that fifteen years later would be the rage in Washington. In short, I wasn't the rube Larry depicted—although I certainly did have a lot to learn.

As a freshman congressman I soon discovered that one oppressive reality—the seniority tradition—would greatly limit whatever I could hope to accomplish. In 1961, the seniority system controlled nearly every aspect of a congressman's life. It mandated matters varying from the substantive (your committee assignments) to the logistical (the location of your office and parking space in the House garage) to the inane (how punctually you were served in the Member's Dining Room).

After I had been in Washington a few weeks, I sat down and wrote a detailed letter to Speaker Sam Rayburn. I told the Speaker that, having had a good look around, I had some observations I wanted to share. First, I suggested that some mechanism ought to be implemented for ensuring that Congress balanced the budget each year. At that time, many congressmen customarily voted for all appropriation bills and against all tax bills—a politically safe but fiscally disastrous habit guaranteed to produce a tide of red ink. (If this sounds familiar, it's because they're still doing the same thing today. Actually, what I had in mind was something similar to Gramm-Rudman, the mandatory budget-balancing bill of 1985.) My second suggestion was that the Speaker appoint a special committee to review the seniority system, which was, in my considered opinion, long overdue for reform. I closed my letter by offering to meet at any time to discuss my ideas further. Rayburn was, in King's words, "a man congenitally offended by a single word when grunts or smoke signals might do," and he must have found this earnest entreaty both presumptuous and laughable. In any case, I never got a reply.

In their desire to hit the ground running, other brash freshmen have made the same egregious mistake of trying to do too much too soon. During his first year as a senator, John Kennedy was anxious to make a good impression on his elders. One afternoon, in a burst of creative energy, he rushed to the Senate floor, offered a flurry of amendments, proposed compromises, spoke on two or three bills, issued press statements, held a news conference, and then, exhausted, collapsed in a chair next to Carl Hayden, who had been in the Senate for more than forty years. Kennedy looked at the veteran and said, "Well, I guess you must have seen lots of changes in the time you've been here?"

"Yes," said Hayden curtly.

"What are some of the more important ones?" Kennedy asked.

"Well," said Hayden, "for one thing, in those days freshmen senators didn't talk."

Because my class of freshmen were sworn in in January 1961, and I did not arrive until May (having won the special election to fill Slu's seat), all the good committee slots were full. I was assigned to the lowest spot on one of the least prestigious committees, the Committee on Post Office and Civil Service. This is near the very bottom of the totem pole, the congressional equivalent of the Cleveland Indians, a study in futility where you can expect little recognition for either your sins or your accomplishments.

My colleagues told me not to grieve. "Hell, boy, you'll be able to put a new post office in every village and hamlet in your district!"

And I did. But the seniority system continued to frustrate and, increasingly, anger me. (To speak of seniority as a "system" is somewhat misleading. The seniority system is not a law or rule and, search as you may, you won't find its principles codified in a book anywhere. Like many of the customs that control the way Congress operates, the seniority system is a testimony to tradition—which makes it all the more binding.)

Paradoxically, when the seniority system that so chafed me first began to fix its grip on the institution in 1911, it was considered a reform—a way to curb the excesses of such tyrannical Speakers as Joseph Cannon and Nicholas Longworth, who appointed all committee chairmen and all committee members, and meted out other favors at their whim. (Congressmen joked that if you dared to cross Cannon he would banish you to the "Select Committee on Acoustics and Ventilation.") But like many enthusiastically embraced "reforms," the seniority system had unintended consequences. Over the next few decades, it ossified into a rigid, unresponsive practice that gave a few old men tremendous power and responsibility without any consideration of their ability. By the time I came to Washington in 1961, there had not been a serious challenge to the seniority system in more than two generations. Most congressmen, it appeared to me, seemed content to tolerate a process that rewarded longevity, not merit—and thus ensured mediocrity.

Here's how it works: Say, for example, I'm appointed to a committee on Monday. You are appointed on Tuesday. If we both stay in the House long enough (fifteen to twenty years is average), I will eventually become chairman and you will be number two. I might be a crook, an idiot, a drunk, a playboy, or even all four—but no matter how incompetent I am, or how brilliant and famous you are, I will forever be chairman and you will have little more real power than an incoming freshman.

There are, of course, arguments one can make in favor of some type of seniority system (for example, it does make sense to have experienced legislators in key positions), but in a rigid system, like that used by the House in the early

1960s, the disadvantages far outweigh the benefits. For one thing, a rigid seniority system reinforces the you-scratch-my-back-I'll-scratch-yours pork-barrel mentality common to all legislatures. In fact, the seniority system and the pork-barrel tradition go hand in hand. Politically influential movers and shakers understand that it behooves them to reelect their congressman, even if he is brain dead, so that his seniority, and with it, his ability to deliver the pork—post offices, military bases, dams, federal office buildings, etc.—continues to grow.

As I grew increasingly restive, I became active in the Democratic Study Group, an informal band of junior congressmen who favored reforming the seniority system. Although my sense of humor endeared me to a few of the older members, I eventually became known as a maverick—one of the "Young Turks" whom the elders regarded as an immense pain in the ass.

My reformist longings were given an outlet by an unlikely protagonist—Adam Clayton Powell. The seniority system had elevated Powell, B.A., M.A., DD, LLD, minister of the Abyssinian Baptist Church in Harlem, to one of the more powerful positions in the Congress, chairman of the House Committee on Education and Labor.

For three years Powell occupied an office—on his occasional visits to Washington—just two doors down from mine. He was one of the most unforgettable people I have ever met. A charming, humorous, charismatic black preacher, Powell was first elected to the House of Representatives in 1944; he would not face a close election until his defeat twenty-six years later. Throughout those years, this flamboyant character was never far from controversy.

Powell was a study in contrasts: brilliant but erratic; a self-styled "poor parish priest" who lived like a member of the jet set; a hip, magnetic black man who had little interest in fighting civil rights battles. But it was Powell's penchant for attractive women, his flashy manner of dress, his quick quips, and his frequent junkets to the most exotic locales, that had made him the most notorious member of the House of Representatives in half a century.

A colleague of mine, who served on Powell's committee, once told me of a visit he had made to the chairman's office. Arriving at the door, the congressman was greeted by a buxom receptionist, who escorted him past a number of stunning secretaries into the chairman's private office, which was carpeted with an exquisite Persian rug Powell had purchased on a junket to the Middle East. Embracing the junior member, Powell proffered an expensive Havana cigar he had just brought back from Cuba. He then sauntered to an antique sideboard groaning under a collection of exquisite French wines and Spanish sherries brought back from another "investigative" trip to Paris, and poured two glasses of port. Taking in the splendor, the younger man said, "Mr. Chairman, you really go first cabin." Powell grinned and said, "Yes, these are the fruits of serving Jesus."

On the floor of the House, Powell always put on a lively show. When another member proposed a vaguely worded amendment to one of his bills, Powell was dubious. "I'm not sure what this means," he said. "I suspect there may be a Caucasian in the woodpile." In another debate, Powell admonished, "Beware of Greeks bearing gifts, colored men looking for loans, and whites who understand the Negro."

Powell was beloved by his constituents. His simple and foolproof strategy for ensuring their fealty was to brand any criticism of his excesses as racist. From the pulpit he voiced his confidence in their staunch support: "I know you will vote for me until I die. And even after I'm dead I think some of you will write in my name." He was right. They still do.

However, as the civil rights movement began to flower in the early 1960s, other black leaders became increasingly dismayed by Powell's utter disinterest in joining the fight. For the first time in history, meaningful civil rights legislation was being introduced in the House and much of it was referred to Powell's own committee. But during the final debate over the 1964 Civil Rights Act, when many civil rights advocates went for days without sleep, Powell, incredibly, flew to the Bahamas. As the final vote was taken, Powell, the "champion of the Negro," was deep-sea fishing.

It wasn't that Powell was a hypocrite, it was just that when it came to the civil rights struggle, well, as he candidly put it, "I am probably the only living American, black or white, who just doesn't give a damn." Rather than join the legislative fray, Powell kept jetting off to the Caribbean to partake in highly publicized affairs and wild parties. He paid little heed to his critics: "I don't care what anybody says. I'll do exactly what I want to do. If it's illegal, immoral, or fattening, Adam Powell is going to do it. I intend to live my life."

Inadvertently, however, Powell was instrumental in helping me pass a bill reforming the franking privilege—which allowed congressmen to mail anything anywhere for free as long as it had some connection, no matter how tenuous, with official business. Powell was not, of course, the only member who abused the franking privilege, but when it was reported that he had sent a set of lawn furniture to his home in Bimini using "Official Business" tags, we were able to persuade the House to place some long-overdue limits on the practice.

By 1966, Powell's arrogant responses to questions about his life-style, his misuse of committee privileges, and his peripatetic junketing had chafed the House to the point of distraction. Fed up, the House instigated a full-scale inquiry into

111

Powell's conduct. Although the investigative committee's report was couched in diplomatic language, it described some "serious fiscal irregularities" in the way Powell ran his committee. For one thing, he had put his estranged wife—who lived in Puerto Rico—on the payroll at $20,000 per year, endorsed her paychecks, and kept the money. Perhaps this, the investigators sagely concluded, was one reason Powell's committee seemed to have an "unusually high cost of operation." Powell was plagued with other thorny problems, too. In Harlem, his failure to pay a $164,000 libel judgment had prompted a judge to issue a warrant for his arrest. Consequently, he was a fugitive in his own district—able to meet with his constituents only on Sundays, when legal papers could not be served.

When *Arizonans* began asking me about Chairman Powell's exploits during my 1966 reelection campaign, I decided that the time had come for someone to rein him in. I knew full well that this was bound to be a thankless task. If Powell was removed from his chairmanship, liberals and blacks were bound to cry that the House was "lynching" its only black chairman. For their part, conservative Democrats and Republicans wanted to banish Powell from the House entirely—a punishment I thought too severe, even unconstitutional.

By the time I returned to Washington in January 1967, I had decided that I would try to strip Powell of his chairmanship, in hopes of defusing the growing movement to deny him his House seat. The Capitol was abuzz with rumors that something big was in the offing. When old John McCormack, the Speaker of the House, heard about my plans, he was not amused. He barged into a meeting of the Democratic Study Group to chide me for having the effrontery to announce my intentions without consulting him. (Our relationship would never improve after this; it hit its nadir two years later when I mounted a symbolic challenge for the Speakership, and got clobbered for my pains.)

Despite being the focus of much scintillating gossip, Powell was still riding high. Even as newspapers headlined his latest junket, he issued still more provocative and defiant statements. He did not seem to harbor the slightest doubt that slavish deference to seniority, his symbolic standing with the black community, and the binding traditions of the House would protect him as they always had in the past.

When the House Democrats convened their closed-door caucus, the room was hushed as I moved to strip Powell of his chairmanship. Although he rarely attended these meetings, Powell had come to this one. Looking him in the eye, I said, "You are a gifted man; I envy the intellect, eloquence, and personality you have been given. Indeed, I have always believed that had your gifts been used in other ways you would have been one of the great men of our time."

Powell said little in his defense, perhaps knowing that the votes were there against him. My motion to install Kentucky's Carl Perkins as chairman of the Committee on Education and Labor passed overwhelmingly on a secret ballot.

Outside the Caucus, Powell described what had occurred as "a lynching, Northern style." Later, on national television, Powell said I was "Mormon racist"—although *The New York Times* noted that I was "a militant advocate of civil rights legislation."

The next day the full House convened. Republicans and conservative Democrats had announced their intention to deny Powell his seat. Since I had led the fight to take away his chairmanship, Speaker McCormack asked me to make the motion to *seat* Powell. This, we thought, would dramatize the distinction we were trying to make: the voters have an absolute right to send a representative—be he or she genius, idiot, nincompoop, or miscreant—to Congress, but they don't have the right to dictate who shall chair congressional committees.

When I reached the floor, Powell was already there. This was the first time I had ever seen him look worried. His normal jauntiness had evaporated, and he seemed to understand that, not only had he lost his chairmanship, there was a good chance that by sundown he would no longer be a member of the House of Representatives.

He came up to me and said, "Mo, I understand you'll make the motion to seat me."

I nodded.

"Do you control the debate time?"

Again I nodded. Then he asked if I thought it would help if he spoke in his own behalf. I replied that my whole argument would be based on due process and House precedent: he had not been given a hearing or trial, and the House had never rejected a congressman without such a hearing. I suggested that a subdued appeal for fair play and for his day in court would be helpful, but that any attempt to wave a red flag would be harmful to his case.

He nodded and in a few minutes came back with a speech written on a yellow legal pad. "My dear colleagues," it began. "I have been among you for twenty-four years. No one can say that I have not run my committee in a fair and responsive manner. Today, all I ask is a chance to be heard before unprecedented action is taken." Powell went on to suggest that perhaps other members' seats might be challenged if this precedent was established, and that "caution should be exercised before taking drastic action."

I was impressed by his sensitivity to the situation and his apparent understanding of the mood of his colleagues. I told him I would give him the coveted closing five minutes of debate.

As the hour-long debate began, the House galleries were

overflowing and the chamber was packed. The debate was a fierce one, and as various congressmen made a series of impassioned speeches, both for and against seating Powell, the tension grew ever more palpable. As the hour wound down, I yielded Powell the final five minutes.

From the manner in which he marched up to the lectern I knew that whatever humility he had felt was gone. During the Watergate hearings seven years later, Nixon staffer Charles Colson would say, "Contrition is bullshit," and Powell obviously felt the same way. He placed his yellow pad on the lectern and never glanced at it again. Instead, shouting in his best pulpit voice, he began haranguing the House.

"He who is without sin should cast the first stone," Powell began. *Oh, no,* I thought, dreading what was to come. "There is no one here who does not have a skeleton in his closet," Powell continued. "I know, and I know them by name. . . . Gentlemen, my conscience is clean. My case is in God's hands. All I hope is that you have a good sleep tonight."

Our strategy was completely undone. Powell's speech had taken the lid off the volcano. The vote (364 to 47) wasn't even close—Powell lost his seat.

What had happened between the time Powell had showed me his prepared remarks and when he had given his defiant speech? This: busloads of his Harlem supporters had arrived in front of the Capitol to protest his treatment. When forced to choose between swallowing his pride and just maybe preserving his seat, or protesting his innocence, he chose the latter. I think he desperately wanted to retain his seat, but when the time came, his nature compelled him, as in a Greek tragedy, to succumb to his fatal flaws. So Powell poured out his bitterness on the floor of the House, and then marched to the steps of the Capitol to be hailed as a martyr by his faithful followers.

As I had predicted, I got blasted from all sides for my efforts. I was damned by civil rights groups and deluged with letters from liberals. An example: "Of all the sanctimonious hypocrites, you are it. . . . Apparently it is right for the white man to cheat the taxpayer, but wrong for the black man." I was also hammered by racist whites. One wrote, "Louse. Louse. Powell's Louse . . ." Finally, I had strained my relations with the House Democratic leadership, who were largely opposed to depriving Powell of his chairmanship or his seat. Nevertheless, I still think that my attempt to have Powell sacked as chairman *and* my efforts to have him seated were consistent with standards of fair play and due process. At least privately, a number of other black leaders agreed. Andrew Young, now mayor of Atlanta, quipped, "Rosa Parks integrated buses, James Meredith integrated the University of Mississippi, Martin Luther King, Jr., integrated churches and lunch counters. But it was left to Adam Clayton Powell to integrate corruption."

Months later, Powell recaptured his seat in a special election ordered by the Supreme Court. After another battle, the House agreed to seat him, while garnisheeing one thousand dollars a month from his salary until he had repaid the money he had embezzled. Characteristically, Powell rarely showed up for work. He countered the inevitable criticism by saying, "part-time pay, part-time work."

In one sense, Powell was a living dinosaur—a relic of an age when public officials behaved with arrogance and impunity, confident that a compliant press would overlook their indiscretions. This was an era in which neither the House nor Senate had a code of ethics, much less a committee to enforce it. Congressmen did as they pleased and abuse of congressional privilege and nepotism were rife. But it was also an era where Washington journalists were more given to winks and nudges than to investigative journalism.

The Powell episode was a watershed for both the press and the Congress. Henceforth, the press would keep a much stricter accounting of the private behavior of public men and women. During the next decade, the media revealed a number of instances of misconduct in high office. Televised coverage of the bizarre exploits of Wilbur Mills and Wayne Hays, followed by the Watergate hearings, prompted an outraged public to demand reform. Today, although the comportment of congressmen is still not always what one would want, both the House and Senate have adopted codes of ethics and established committees to enforce them. Mandatory public disclosure of financial statements curbs the temptation to indulge in fiscal improprieties. Together, these reforms, in concert with a watchdog press, have done much to reduce wrongdoing. That is not to say that corruption has been banished. Isolated incidents of venality and hanky-panky still occur; men being men, perhaps they always will.

Powell's ouster had an equally dramatic impact on the seniority system. The immediate effect was to alert every chairman that the imperious behavior so often demonstrated in the past would no longer be tolerated. But Powell's lasting gift to the Congress was an impetus for reform. His outlandish behavior, his brazen flaunting of House privileges, his burlesque mockery of public opinion—all these unleashed a tidal wave of better-government reforms. The paradox, of course, is that had Powell's misconduct not been so flagrant, reform might have been much slower in coming.

Today the seniority system remains an important custom, but it is no longer as stifling as it once was. Although the House has a long way to go before it is a meritocracy, it has adopted, by caucus rule, an arrangement whereby senior-

117

ity counts for something but not everything. If, for example, there are eighteen Democratic seats on a committee, seniority automatically gets you up the first seventeen seats. Your ascension to the chairmanship, however, is not guaranteed; it must be ratified in a secret ballot by a majority of your colleagues. Once you've become chairman, your behavior is still subject to scrutiny, and your colleagues have an opportunity every two years to remove you for impropriety, unresponsiveness, or incompetence.

This was underscored in 1975, when four chairmen, who together had more than one hundred years of seniority, were toppled by the Democratic caucus, and again in 1985, when Les Aspin leaped over seven more-senior members to gain the chairmanship of the House Armed Services Committee. Two years later, however, Aspin almost lost the prize amid charges that he had misled fellow Democrats on his position on the MX missile and aid to the Nicaraguan contras. The message is clear: Congressmen serve at the behest of their constituents, chairmen at the pleasure of their colleagues; in either role they will be held accountable for both their legislative conduct and their private behavior.

★ ★ ★ ★ ★ ★ ★ ★ ★ ★ ★ ★ **9** ★ ★ ★ ★ ★ ★ ★ ★ ★ ★ ★ ★

The Straddle, the Weasel, the Waffle, the Fudge: The Art of Political Inconsistency

★ ★

> The candidate was reeling under charges that he was
> waffling on the issues. He summoned his staff and said,
> "What should we do about these charges? Should we
> deny them? Ignore them? Should we admit to part and
> deny the rest? Just what should we do?" At that, his
> staff shook their heads and walked out.
> —*Representative Brooks Hays*

In late October 1967, I returned to Tucson to give one of
the most difficult speeches of my career. I was scheduled to
address the Sunday Evening Forum, a monthly civic meeting
held in the main auditorium of the University of Arizona.
This was my home turf, the same building in which Jim
McNulty and I had staged our duck-hunting debacle twenty
years before. As I walked to the podium, however, my mood
was more somber than blithe. The title of my speech was
"The United States and Vietnam: What Lies Ahead?" and I
knew that my audience of 2,800 people was bound to include
large numbers of prominent citizens, many of whom would
not be pleased by the thrust of my remarks.

119

TOO FUNNY TO BE PRESIDENT

In 1967, the tide of public opinion had not yet turned on the Vietnam war. Protesters against the war were a distinct minority, and widely considered to be on the lunatic fringe. A few congressmen had come out against the war, but most Americans staunchly supported the president's policy. Now I was preparing to join the loonies and peaceniks with a speech that argued that the Vietnam policy embraced by my country, my president, and my party was tragically flawed. With my brother serving in President Johnson's cabinet, I knew the speech was bound to be a blockbuster both in my district and at the White House.

And so, I spoke:

Tonight I want to talk about war and peace, about presidents, dominoes, commitments, and mistakes. . . .

Two years ago, when this country had fewer than fifty thousand men in Vietnam, I wrote a newsletter defending the president's Vietnam policy and pleading patience and understanding for what he was trying to do. I have thought about that newsletter many times with increasing dismay and doubt as the limited involvement I supported has grown into a very large Asian land war with a half-million American troops scattered in jungles and hamlets, fighting an enemy who is everywhere and nowhere, seeking to save a country which apparently doesn't want to be saved, with casualties mounting and no end in sight. . . .

Many of the wise old heads in Congress say privately that the best politics in this situation is to remain silent, to fuzz your views . . . to await developments. . . .

But I have come here tonight to say as plainly and simply as I can that I was wrong two years ago, and I firmly believe President Johnson's advisers are wrong today.

I have listened to all the arguments of the administration,

read all the reports available to me, attended all the briefings, heard all the predictions of an eventual end to hostilities, and I still conclude that we're on a mistaken and dangerous road.

I went on to urge the withdrawal of United States forces from Vietnam and said I would work in Washington to achieve that end. The speech made headlines in papers ranging from the Nogales *Herald*, which didn't approve, to *The New York Times*, which did. Back in Washington, some of my colleagues complimented me for having the courage to speak out; others shunned me as a turncoat. Letters pro and con poured into my congressional office. One read:

Dear sir:
The following statement indorsed [*sic*] by sixty four relatives, friends, etc.—We hereby designate your reversed position regarding the Vietnam war as gutless. Also lacking the intelligence of a half-witted moron. At the next election we shall utilize every angle to cause your defeat. In our considered opinion you do not represent the indispensable man . . . p.s. The communists should present you, and others of the same category, a medal.

LBJ was outraged. As a congressman and senator, he had witnessed, and frequently employed, every possible variation of political fickleness, including the adroit sidestep, the straddle, the weasel, the waffle, the fudge, the flip-flop, and the "deep six," a technique perfected by Richard Nixon. Nevertheless, he would never forgive me for bucking him.

The ability to change one's views without losing one's seat is the mark of a great politician. If you're looking for world-class examples of fickleness, politicians are the ones to study. The late Senator Everett Dirksen, he of the wildly askew hair and sea elephant voice, once said: "I am a man of principle. And my first principle is flexibility." British prime minister Disraeli once justified his flexibility by saying, "I never deny; I never contradict; I sometimes forget" (sounds like Ronald Reagan).

It is easy to twit politicians for being inconsistent, for being "shifty," "tricky," for "shilly-shallying," but sometimes inconsistency is just a synonym for responsiveness. The fact is that in politics, as in any other part of life, nothing stays the same. Time passes, conditions change, values change—and politicians must adapt.

When I first went to Congress I made some commitments to myself: to make the tough and unpleasant decisions as they came; to speak out at times when remaining silent might be easier; to admit my own mistakes; and to advocate new policies when old ones, no matter how dearly held, had failed. These are noble sentiments, easier to espouse than to follow. The main difficulty is that in switching positions you run the risk of public ridicule, for nothing summons a baying pack of reporters faster than a politician saying, "I have changed. . . ." Once the hounds have treed you, you're in a real bind: A good reporter is never content simply to record your *new* position, he or she will also want a detailed explanation for the discrepancies between it and your *old* one.

The press, for reasons I've never been able to divine, has an obsession, bordering on the neurotic, with consistency. "If a politician murders his mother," journalist Meg Greenfield has written, "the first response of the press will likely be not that it was a terrible thing to do, but rather that in a statement made six years before he had gone on the record as being opposed to matricide." The press considers it *that* important for politicians to be consistent.

For some reason, voters, too, are unnerved by a politician who changes his mind. Knowing this, it's the rare politician who has the courage to say straightforwardly, "I was wrong. I have changed my mind." Think: When was the last time you heard a politician say anything remotely like that?

The ineluctable need periodically to change one's viewpoints, while appearing not to, explains why so many politicians become expert contortionists, even dissemblers. A clever pol can switch his colors better, and attract less attention while doing it, than a chameleon. Tom Connally, perhaps the last of the classic Texas senators, was once running for reelection and found himself perched in the back of a pickup truck in a little cotton-farming town in the eastern part of the state. At the end of his carefully imprecise stump speech a listener shouted out, "How do you stand on the cotton issue?"

Connally paused a second and then replied, "I'm okay on that one. Are there any other questions?"

Another congressman decided to canvass his district, seeking votes in the upcoming election. He soon discovered that his constituents were most upset about a proposed local ordinance to require goats to be kept in pens.

At the first house, the congressman identified himself and asked for the homeowner's vote.

"Well, Congressman, you're a good enough fellow, but where do you stand on this here goat-fencing law?"

The congressman hesitated, and then said that it seemed like a good idea to him.

"Well," said the homeowner, "I've ten goats myself and if'n I fence them in, I'll not be able to make a living. There's no way on God's green earth that I can support you!"

Chagrined, the congressman trudged to the next house, knocked on the door, and, when the owner appeared, meekly asked for the man's vote.

"First," challenged the owner, "where do you stand on this goat-fencing law?"

"That's an easy one," said the congressman, "I'm dead set against that income-robbing, no-good, discriminating law."

"Well," said the man, "I'm sure not for you, then. My neighbor keeps ten of the dirty, smelly beasts. They run all over my land, fouling my well and making an ugly mess of things. As far as I'm concerned, we need that law more than anything else."

Thoroughly deflated, the congressman approached the next house, knocked on the door, identified himself, and quickly said, "Now look here, about that goat-fencing law—I'm going to be all right on that one."

Politicians soon learn that you're often damned if you do, and damned if you don't. Over time, many develop the kind of double-jointed flexibility displayed by a young, destitute teacher who applied for a job in the hills of Kentucky. During his interview with the school board, the young man found himself in the middle of a spat about whether the earth was round or flat. "Young man, we like you," said the chairman, "and we might want to hire you. But first, we want to know when you teach about the world, do you teach it round or do you teach it flat?"

The teacher paused, wiped his brow, and said, "Well, sir, I can teach it either way."

First prize in the telling-them-what-they-want-to-hear category has to go to Governor "Uncle Earl" Long of Louisiana. Speaking in a parish where half the voters were Catholic, half Baptist, Long began by saying that the happiest times of his youth were on Sunday mornings, when he would hitch a pair of horses to a wagon and drive his grandmother and grandfather to the Catholic church. After the service was over, Earl continued, he would return home, hook up a fresh team, and drive his other grandmother and grandfather to the Baptist church. After the speech, Long's aide came up to him and said, "I didn't know you had a Catholic grandfather and grandmother. Uncle Earl replied, "Hell, we didn't even have a wagon!"

The heyday of waffling politicians occurred during Prohibition. Here, exhibiting great élan and nimble footwork, is a passage penned by Judge N. S. "Soggy" Sweat of Mississippi:

My friends,
I had not intended to discuss this controversial subject with you at this time. However, I want you to know that I do not shun controversy. On the contrary, I will take a stand on any issue at any time, regardless of how fraught with controversy it might be. You have asked me how I feel about whiskey. All right, here is how I feel about whiskey. . . .

If, when you say whiskey, you mean the devil's brew, the poison scourge, the bloody monster, that defiles innocence, dethrones reason, destroys the home, creates misery and poverty, yea, literally takes the bread from the mouths of little children; if you mean the evil drink that topples the Christian man and woman from the pinnacle of righteous, gracious living into the bottomless pit of degradation, and despair, and shame, and helplessness, and hopelessness, then certainly I am against it.

But—

if, when you say whiskey, you mean the oil of conversation, the philosophic wine, the ale that is consumed when good fellows get together, that puts a song in their hearts and laughter on their lips, and the warm glow of contentment in their eyes; if you mean Christmas cheer; if you mean the stimulating drink that puts the spring into the old gentleman's step on a frosty, crispy morning; if you mean the drink which enables a man to magnify his joy, and his happiness, and to forget, if only for a little while, life's great tragedies, and heartaches, and sorrows; if you mean that drink, the sale of which pours into our treasuries untold millions of dollars, which are used to provide tender care for our little crippled children, our blind, our deaf, our dumb, our pitiful aged and infirm; to build highways and hospitals and schools, then certainly I am for it.

This is my stand and I will not compromise.

Judge Sweat brings to mind Arizona's own Henry Fountain Ashurst, one of the state's first senators, who was known as the "Dean of Inconsistency." Ashurst was proud of the title; "the clammy hand of consistency has never rested for long upon my shoulder," he boasted. Another time, Ashurst proclaimed, "There has never been added to these vices of mine the withering, embalming vice of consistency."

Ashurst was a cowboy. Although he never went to school, he could recite every word that Shakespeare ever wrote. Barry Goldwater remembers as a boy meeting Ashurst when the senator used to stand on the street "with a black frock coat on and striped pants and a big red carnation, and every evening at five o'clock he'd recite Shakespeare to the secretaries coming out of the buildings. He was a good-looking guy and he would have women all around him."

Like many aspiring politicians, Ashurst thought a law degree would advance his career. According to Goldwater, "At that time the law firm that took care of my family's business was owned by the Ellenwood family, and old man Ellenwood said, 'Mr. Ashurst, if you'll go to the University of Michigan and get your law degree, we'll take you into the office.' In those days all you had to do to become a lawyer was to have another lawyer say you were competent. So Henry Fountain went to Michigan for two weeks and then returned to Phoenix. And old man Ellenwood said he was competent, so Henry Fountain became a lawyer. He couldn't even spell it."

Here now, more Ashurstisms.

On being defeated: "The welfare of the United States, and the happiness of our people, does not hang on the presence of Henry Fountain Ashurst in the Senate. When that realization first came to me, I was overwhelmed by the horror of it, but now it is a source of infinite comfort."

When beaten: "No man is fit to be a senator . . . unless he is willing to surrender his political life for great principle."

On growing old: "Always stand erect, and don't eat too much. . . ."

On communism: "The fanatical delusion of communism will evaporate."

On learning to speak: "I used to recite my speeches walking up a hill. It gives you wind power. I could throw fifty-six-pound words across the Grand Canyon."

The best example of Ashurst's "fifty-six-pound words" is this now-legendary opening statement, made before an unlettered, earthy justice of the peace in Winslow, Arizona, circa 1908:

Your Honor, as I approached the trial of this case today, my heart was burdened with crushing and gloomy forebodings and the immense responsibility of my client's welfare bowed me down with apprehensions. A cold fear gripped my heart as I dwelt upon the possibility that through some oversight or shortcoming of mine there might ensue dreadful consequences to my client, and I shrank within myself as the ordeal became more imminent.

Yet the nearer my uncertain steps brought me to this tribunal of justice, distinguished as it has been for years as the one court of the rugged West where fame attended the wisdom and justice of the decisions of Your Honor, a serene confidence came to my troubled emotions, and the raging waters of tumultuous floods that had surged hotly but a moment before were stilled. Your Honor, I was no longer appalled, nor longer feared the issue in this case. Aye, I reflected that throughout the long years of your administration as judge, there had grown up here a halo, as it were, of honor and glory illumining Your Honor's record, eloquent of a fame as deserved as that of the chastity of Caesar's wife, a fame that will augment with the flight of years and with increasing luster, light the pathway of humanity down the ages so long as the heaving billows of the stormy Mediterranean shall beat vainly upon the beetling cliffs of Gibraltar. . . .

Justice Waltron: Sit down, Mr. Ashurst. You can't blow any smoke up this Court's ass.

More Ashurst. On death: "There either is or there isn't a hereafter. If there is, I'll be there. But if there isn't, I'll never know it. If there is an eternity, don't think God will say, 'Henry Fountain . . . you've cavorted and raised hell and broken my commandments . . . so you'll have to stay out.' No, I don't think He'd want to run a heaven that would keep Henry Fountain Ashurst out."

In Ashurst's maiden speech to the Senate, he waxed eloquent about the potential of Arizona, which had just been admitted to the Union: "Mr. President, this great new baby state is magnificent, this great new baby is destined to join the pantheon of other splendid states in our fair union, this great new baby state is poised to become a veritable paradise. We only need two things: water and lots of good people."

Whereupon an old Senator from New England interrupted to say, "If the gentleman from Arizona will forgive me, that's all they need in Hell."

The following story was told by LBJ about an apocryphal state senator in Texas. It's adapted from a true story about Senator Ashurst, but here's the Texas version: "The senator was speaking down home," the president said, "and he started out talking about the beautiful piney woods of east Texas, and then he moved out onto the plains dappled with bluebonnets and then down through the hill country to the Gulf Coast. The crowd was becoming restless as he continued rhetorically to tour the state, going back to the piney woods and droning on about bluebonnets. When he finished his second circuit, he came up for air and then set off talking once again about the piney woods and the bluebonnets.

"At this, a good old boy rose up in the back of the room and yelled out, 'The next time you pass Lubbock, how about letting me off.' "

For all his Claghornian bombast, Ashurst was a man of integrity, and he let everyone know that there was an important distinction between flexibility and betraying a vote for, God forbid, financial remuneration. "When a public official accepts a gift," Ashurst said, "he dissolves the pearl of independence in the vinegar of obligation."

Ashurst was not, however, above casting a vote with a rheumy eye toward its political implications. He once said, "When I have to choose between voting for the people or the special interests, I always stick with the special interests. They remember. The people forget."

The events that made Ashurst a shoo-in to the Flip-Floppers Hall of Fame occurred during the early years of Franklin Roosevelt's presidency. As a staunch supporter of FDR and chairman of the Senate's powerful Judiciary Committee, Ashurst had a great deal of clout. When FDR grew tired of the troglodytes on the Supreme Court declaring his prized legislative initiatives unconstitutional, he asked Ashurst to remove the reactionary roadblock by packing the court with six more justices. Ashurst was happy to oblige; he drafted a bill and took it upon himself to shepherd it through his committee. But the bill quickly ignited a firestorm among civil libertarians and Ashurst found himself in an epic battle. Eventually, however, he prevailed: the bill was reported out of committee and sent to the full Senate.

Soon, though, his office was deluged with bundles of mail and telegrams condemning his bill. It did not take Ashurst long to see that his bill—and his career—were in trouble.

Ashurst, ever the Dean of Inconsistency, quickly chose pragmatism over loyalty. Not only did he abandon his own legislative progeny, he *led* the floor fight to defeat it—a flip-flop that even he marveled over in subsequent years. During the final stages of the debate, he received a telegram that said, "I thank God for your courageous stand on that Supreme Court bill."

Ashurst quickly sent a reply: "Which one?"

Representative Sidney Yates of Illinois tells a story about a politician who had made straddling the issues an art form. Asked for his views on the subject of inflation, the candidate said, "I'm totally against inflation." Well, said his questioner, "I guess you are for *de*flation." "No, I'm against that too." "Well," said the reporter, "what are you for?" The candidate hesitated and said, "I guess I'm foursquare for *flation*."

Yes, there's a lot to be said for inconsistency. As a politician you must be willing to change your mind as circumstances change or you may endanger your career. There is, however, a down side: No matter how many excuses you dredge up, your opponent will seize every opportunity to label you a "wishy-washy, flip-flopping wimp"—or worse. LBJ had a standard response to any opponent who impugned his integ-

rity with such slurs: he called him "a lying son of a bitch."
I usually try to preempt the critics by making light of my
switch. At the close of my Vietnam speech I said, "I don't
know how the ornithologists ever got involved in this war,
and I have little hope that this speech won't get me labeled
as some variety of dove, chicken hawk, pigeon, owl, or ostrich.
However, if it should happen that I dropped dead leaving
this meeting tonight, I would hope that my tombstone might
read: 'Here lies a realist.' "

If political flexibility is a type of yoga, Franklin Roosevelt
was the guru. Arthur M. Schlesinger, Jr., recalls how in 1936
FDR found himself in the embarrassing position of having
to make a speech advocating deficit spending—a speech that
would totally contradict a balanced-budget speech he had
given with great fanfare four years earlier. To make matters
worse, the new speech was to be delivered in Pittsburgh,
the same city in which he had given the earlier one.

"The earlier speech weighed on Roosevelt's conscience,"
Schlesinger wrote. "Moreover, Farley [the postmaster general
and party chairman] had lost no opportunity during the campaign to tell Roosevelt that 'the one criticism which is being
constantly hammered home and which seems to be having
the most effect is the charge that the President and his Administration are carrying on an orgy of spending and incurring
a tremendous public debt.' "

The president was worried. He instructed his speechwriter,
Sam Rosenman, to make sure that the new speech included
a "good and convincing explanation" for contravening the
earlier one. Rosenman made what Schlesinger called "a
prayerful reexamination" of the earlier speech. After his deliberations, he dutifully approached the president and
said that there was only one way to handle the problem.

"Fine," said FDR, "what do we do?"

"Mr. President," said Rosenman, "the only thing you can

say about the 1932 speech is to deny categorically that you ever made it."

As an administrator, Roosevelt was a duplicitous disaster by any standard. He refused to have lines of authority and he actively encouraged a kind of constructive tension between his cabinet members. One day, his wife, Eleanor, went to the Oval Office to watch him work. She had no sooner arrived when Interior Secretary Harold Ickes bounded into the room to tell the president of a great plan for public works to be administered by his department.

After Ickes outlined the proposal, Roosevelt replied, "Harold, you're absolutely right, absolutely right."

A few moments after Ickes left, Harry Hopkins, Ickes's main rival, arrived. He stated that he was concerned with the same problem and had designed a program to be handled by his agency that would achieve marvelous results.

Roosevelt said, "Hopkins, you're absolutely right, you're absolutely right."

As Hopkins left, Eleanor said, "Franklin, you shouldn't do this. These are two of your key administrators and each of them left here thinking that you'd approved his plan."

Roosevelt looked at his wife and said, "Eleanor, you're absolutely right, absolutely right."

★★★★★★★★★★★★ **10** ★★★★★★★★★★★★

The Wits and the Witless: Political Humor

★★★★★★★★★★★★★★★★★★★★★★★★★★★★★★

> Some people say we Democrats have to nominate a moderate in 1988, someone who doesn't say much, who says it with a slightly southern accent, who espouses strong conservatism with just a little dash of compassion thrown in. They've described a liberal Republican basically, sort of a George Bush with chest hair.
> —*Texas commissioner of agriculture Jim Hightower*

> Some critics complain that Gary Hart doesn't have any experience in foreign policy. But that's not true. Why just yesterday he had breakfast at the International House of Pancakes.
> —*George Bush at the 1987 Gridiron dinner*

Until about twenty years ago, most successful politicians were, of necessity, also entertainers. Before the advent of pollsters, media mavens, TV advertising, sound bites, PAC funds, and other related developments that have made a candidate's *image* more important than his *persona,* a politician rarely got anywhere unless he was capable of getting up on a wagon or stump and *entertaining* a crowd. Usually his audience would be gathered for a barbecue, a county fair, a high school graduation, a church picnic, a Fourth of July parade, or some other festive occasion. In such settings, pompous, long-winded speeches were never as popular as lighter, more humorous fare. Knowing that substantive ideas would go down better

133

if spiced with levity, a savvy politician tried to come off more like Johnny Carson than like George Will. Wit is equally valued—and valuable—in the clubby, hail-fellow-well-met atmosphere one finds on Capitol Hill. A good joke always finds a ready audience in the cloakroom or on the floor of the House. Here again, you'll find that good politics and good humor are often inextricably intertwined.

William Jennings Bryan was one of the surefire political attractions of his time. In those days before microphones, Bryan always tried to speak from a high platform so that his entire audience could hear him. One day a huge crowd came to hear Bryan, but only half the people could squeeze into the auditorium. Bryan's manager told him, "There are at least five hundred folks outside, pining for a word from you. You can't send them away disappointed."

"Find me something to stand on and I'll address them when I've finished inside," said Bryan.

All the manager could find, however, was a manure spreader. The farmers, of course, chuckled when Bryan climbed up on it, but he was equal to the occasion. "My friends," he thundered, "this is the first time I have ever spoken on a Republican platform."

Politicians of the deep South have always been justly famous for their unique blend of flowery oratory spiced with down-home humor. Louisiana governor "Uncle Earl" Long was a rabid populist and he used to delight his poor constituents with this story about a rich miser who died and was interrogated by St. Peter at the Pearly Gates. St. Peter told the man that, on cursory examination of the Book of Good Deeds, he did not seem to have done enough good in his life to warrant entry into Heaven. "Wait a minute," said the sinner, "In 1913 I gave a blind man selling pencils a nickel and let him keep the pencil." St. Peter flipped back through hundreds of pages until he finally found the entry. Anything else? he inquired. "Hold on, St. Peter," said the man. "In 1919 I gave a dime to a poor woman who was without cab fare in a blizzard." St. Peter, after much searching, located the reference. "Still not enough, though," said St. Peter. "Don't send me to Hades yet," pleaded the old scrooge. "In the early 1930s, I was going by an orphanage and I saw an urchin with no shoes on and I gave him a quarter." St. Peter checked and saw that this, too, was true. "I still don't think you qualify, but we'll appeal your case to a higher authority," St. Peter said, picking up the telephone. After an animated conversation, he hung up. "What did he say?" the anxious miser asked. "He says to give you back your forty cents and tell you to go to hell!"

Another of Uncle Earl's favorite stories was about a "thinking machine," what we would call a personal computer today. This thinking machine was a remarkable device, one that could answer any question its owner asked it. Questions like, Is that blonde over in the corner married? and, Who is going to win the fifth race at the track today? Although the owner took great advantage of the machine, deep down he resented it, for he was the kind of man who couldn't stand to have a machine outsmart him. One day he decided to trip it up by posing a question it would not be able to answer. He typed in, "Where is my dearly beloved father at this very moment?" The machine whirred and clicked and finally spat out, "Your dearly beloved father is in a pool hall in Pittsburgh, shooting a game of eight ball against a gentleman named Joe Sullivan. He is sitting down, and Mr. Sullivan is about to break." This made the owner furious, and he angrily typed, "I demand an apology. My dearly beloved father is not in Pittsburgh, he is in Philadelphia buried in peaceful repose on the side of a hill." The machine went *"clank, clank, burr, burr . . . repeat, reinvestigate"* and then spat out the following message: "Your dearly beloved father is still in Pittsburgh in the game against Mr. Sullivan . . . he is now three points down. Your mother's lawfully married husband is lying in peaceful repose on a hillside in Philadelphia, you bastard."

Political corruption has no place in good government, but everyone loves a scandal. Some states and communities, in fact, seem to thrive on them. Some years ago the people of Boston elected James Curley their mayor. He was in a jail cell at the time. In Chicago, an aide to Richard Daley used to tell a story about Hizzoner's first election: he collected 1,200 votes for junior class president from a class numbering 370.

The "Gret Stet of Loousianna" is another place where patronage, nepotism, and graft have been elevated to an art form. Governor Long used to jest that when he died he wanted to be buried in a church cemetery in a notoriously corrupt parish in southern Louisiana, "That way, I can still remain active in politics."

Ah, bayou politics. In 1940, Governor Richard Leche was jailed for accepting kickbacks in a road-building scandal. On his way to the pen, Leche waxed reflective, "For Louisiana politicians, bribery is an occupational hazard. When I took the oath of office I didn't take an oath of poverty."

Louisiana's recent governor, Edwin Edwards, is out of the same mold. When Edwards—who has been, by his own count, the subject of *eleven* grand jury investigations—was running in 1983 against then-governor David Treen, he told reporters, "If we don't get Treen out of office soon, there won't be any money left to steal." As the election neared with Edwards in the lead, Edwards said, "The only way I can lose is if I'm caught in bed with a dead girl or a live boy." After Edwards won, Treen commented, "It's difficult for me to explain

Edwards's popularity. But how do you explain why nine hundred people drank spiked Kool-Aid with Jim Jones?"

Congressman James R. Jones (no relation to Jim Jones) equates the practice of politics with teaching and preaching. "I put them all in the same category," he explains. "They are the noblest of professions because they touch lives and set social and moral values in a way that no other profession can." Most of the politicians I know agree with Jones; certainly, I do. But, pound for pound (and I'm not talking about Tip O'Neill), politicians are the butt of more jokes than any other discrete population.

Congressman William Hungate, now a federal judge, was one of those rarest of birds: the elected official who leaves office in his prime, under his own power, of his own accord. A pianist and raconteur, Hungate was criticized during the Watergate impeachment proceedings for singing in public a song he had composed about the coverup. In 1976, Hungate retired. His moving farewell address to his colleagues ended: "May the future bring all the best to you, your family and friends, and may your mother never find out where you work."

It's true: as an institution Congress has fallen flat on its face. Congressmen are not amused when pollsters discover that they rate slightly below used-car salesmen in the public's esteem. This is not new. Sixty years ago Speaker Nicholas Longworth said:

I have been a member of the House of Representatives for twenty years. During the whole of that time we have been attacked, denounced, hunted, harried, blamed, looked down upon, excoriated, and flayed.

I refuse to take it personally. We did not start being unpopular when I became a congressman. We were unpopular before that time. . . . From the beginning of the

137

Republic it has been the duty of every freeborn voter to look down upon us, and the duty of every freeborn humorist to make jokes of us.

Always there is something wrong with us. We simply cannot be right. Let me illustrate. Suppose we pass a lot of laws. Do we get praised? Certainly not. We get denounced by everybody for being a "meddlesome Congress," a "busybody Congress."

But suppose we take warning from that experience. Suppose that in our succeeding session we pass only a few laws. Are we any better off? Certainly not. Then everybody denounces us for being an "incompetent Congress," a "do-nothing Congress."

We have no chance—just absolutely no chance. The only way for a congressman to be happy is to realize that he has no chance.

Will Rogers made a career of ragging Congress. Here are some of his best zingers:

★ They have an unwritten law in the Senate that a new member is not allowed to say anything when he first gets in, and another unwritten law that whatever he says afterward is not to amount to anything.

★ Congress has promised the country that it will adjourn next Tuesday. Let's hope we can depend on it. If they do, it will be the first promise they have kept this session.

★ Congress meets tomorrow morning. Let us all pray to the Lord to give us strength to bear that which is about to be inflicted upon us.

★ Come pretty near having two holidays of equal importance in the same week—Halloween and election. And of the two, election provides us the most fun. On Halloween they put pumpkins on their heads and on election they don't have to.

★ Once a man holds a public office he is absolutely no good for honest work.

★ You know, congressmen are the nicest fellows in the world to meet. I sometimes really wonder if they realize the harm they do.

For those who agree with Rogers that politicians are a plague on mankind, I offer the "Politician's Psalm":

The politician is my shepherd . . . I am in want.
He maketh me to lie down on park benches.
He leadeth me beside the still factories.
He disturbeth my soul.
Yea, though I walk through the valley of the shadow of the Depression and recession,
I anticipate no recovery, for he is with me.
He anointeth my small income with great taxes.
My expenses runneth over.
Surely unemployment and poverty shall follow me all the days of my life,
And I shall dwell in a mortgaged house forever.

Emmanuel Celler, who served in the House for more than forty years, summed up what it takes to be the ideal congressman: "the wisdom of a Solomon, the perspicacity of a bill collector, the curiosity of a cat, cunning of a fox, thick skin of an elephant, eagerness of a beaver, amiability of a lap dog, kindness of a loving wife, diplomacy of a wayward husband, and the good humor of an idiot."

The Congress never looks more ineffectual, or reaps more abuse, than when we are trying to adjourn. Every two years, all the bills we've dillydallied over pile up in a gigantic logjam. Sometimes the government even runs out of money and federal employees are temporarily dismissed and sent home in a dither, simply because Congress hasn't been able to pass a stopgap funding bill. This situation does, however, spawn some good jokes.

A few years ago, as Congress frantically tried to finish its work, Senator Russell Long was presiding over a conference committee that had labored through a lonely Saturday afternoon and evening. About 3:00 A.M. on Sunday, Long threw up his hands in exasperation. "It's time for us to make some decisions here," he boomed at the gaggle of lobbyists, staffers, and congressmen present. "What we have to do is act like the world is coming to an end in fifteen minutes, and we need to make the most of it."

My assistant, Bob Neuman, once told Eleanor Randolph, a reporter for the *Washington Post,* that Congress's last-minute frenzy was not unlike lovemaking: "Think of the House and Senate as a couple. They have almost two years of foreplay, and it's not until the last two weeks that they get down to the real thing."

During one closing session, Dick Tuck, the infamous prankster who has driven generations of Republicans bonkers, was invited by Senator James Abourezk to sit on the Senate floor. This was highly unusual, and Senator Pat Moynihan objected. "This is outrageous," Moynihan railed, in full oratorical frenzy—but with a twinkle in his eye. "Why, this is the worst affront to the democratic process since Caligula rode his horse onto the floor of the Roman senate."

Former congressman Philip Burton was well known for his energy, relentlessness, and, if need be, creative parliamentary shortcuts when it came to getting his bills passed. One of Burton's pet projects was to enlarge the National Battlefield Park at Manassas, Virginia, the site of the Civil War battles of Bull Run, as the South named the bloody encounters.

In the House, Phil was able to pass a bill augmenting the park, but he was stymied in the Senate by Virginia Senator Harry F. Byrd. In the waning days of a session, Phil snuck a provision to enlarge the battlefield into a Senate bill where, he hoped, it would go unnoticed by the weary Byrd. But Byrd, to the dismay of the chagrined Burton, discovered the plot and mustered his friends to defeat the bill.

"Byrd just about died," Abourezk recalled at the time. "The Burton ploy has so terrified him that he won't leave the chamber even for a short nap, because he's afraid Burton will sneak another bill past him." (Burton eventually got the battleground enlarged—but only after Byrd retired.)

One senator surveyed the chaos of a closing session and grandly referred to the entire proceedings as the "acne of ridiculosity." One of his colleagues explained that he probably meant "acme." Semantics aside, who was right?

Sometimes during these late hours one or two members will seek solace in drink. One night Senator Ted Stevens of Alaska fulminated that the Republicans were being run roughshod by the Democrats. "There's just enough Scotch in me to demand that I get my fair rights," he roared to the bemusement of the newsmen wearily keeping the deathwatch.

Later that evening, after his colleagues expressed their astonishment that he would publicly confess to being drunk, Stevens hastily sought recognition to insist that he had been referring to his Scottish heritage, *not* the amber liquid of the same name.

Congressional adjournment reminds me of the town council meeting interrupted by an earthquake. As the council members dashed outside, the clerk hesitated long enough to record: "On motion of the city hall, the council adjourned."

Another target of public scorn—and a longtime peeve of

mine—is the much-abused seniority system, which used to invest a select few congressmen with almost dictatorial powers. Although reforms have diminished the power legislative barons now wield, congressional leadership, or the glaring lack thereof, remains an easy target for the critics.

In the late 1800s, during a period when the Republicans had an overwhelming majority, Speaker of the House Thomas Reed had unfettered power over the House's agenda—a power that he frequently used to steamroll Democrats. In a Rules Committee meeting, Reed once slapped a bill on the table and said to the Democrats present, "Gentlemen, we have decided to perpetrate the following outrage."

"But what of the rights of the minority?" a Democrat meekly protested. "The right of the minority," Speaker Reed mocked, "is to draw its salaries and its function is to make a quorum."

During my career I was often on the losing end of such dictatorial decisions. Parliamentary procedures killed my strip-mining bill time and time again despite its overwhelming public support. The final blow came when Gerry Ford, Nixon's successor in the White House, buckled under election-year pressure from coal industry lobbyists and twice vetoed a reasonable compromise bill.

During one of the many debates on the bill, I told this story to illustrate my conviction that the bill would ultimately prevail: After Stalin died, Khrushchev wanted to get rid of his body. He called President Kennedy and asked if Stalin could be buried in the United States. "No," said JFK, "I'll get too much criticism if I allow that. Why don't you call British prime minister Harold Macmillan?" Khrushchev did and got a similar turndown; Macmillan recommended he try President Ben-Gurion of Israel. So, Khrushchev called Ben-Gurion, who said, "Yes, if you come in the middle of the night, you can bury Stalin's body in a remote spot. However," he continued, "I must remind you that this country has the world's highest rate of resurrection."

As I predicted, the resurrection of the strip-mining bill did occur, and Jimmy Carter, who had replaced Ford, signed it into law. (Carter, in my opinion, was one of the nation's finest presidents when it came to the environment; in particular, he deserves kudos for throwing the weight of his administration behind the Alaska Lands bill. I think his now-tarnished reputation will improve with time and better understanding of the unpredictable and intractable events that plagued his ill-starred presidency. True, his patient course did not free hostages in Iran. Yet his control of the executive branch looks positively inspired—and aboveboard—when compared with the criminal chaos that resulted when President Reagan turned the "cowboys" on his National Security staff loose in the Iran-contra affair.)

No discussion of congressional foibles and wit is complete without mentioning former congressman Brooks Hays of Arkansas. One of the House's beloved figures, Hays, an ordained Methodist minister, was renowned for injecting yarns and parables into his colorful and persuasive speeches. A progressive man during a reactionary era, his support for the integration efforts of President Eisenhower during the Little Rock schools crisis put him at odds with his governor, Orval Faubus, and his constituency. His defeat was a defeat for the House and a signal that civil rights advocacy could be fatal to an honest southerner's career.

Hays once said, "Next to fried foods, the South has suffered most from oratory."

On another occasion, Hays told a story about a Southerner's funeral. After the deceased had been buried, the deacons retired to the church house, where, as was the custom, a lively wake got under way. A few hours later, one of the well-oiled deacons fell down and broke a leg. "Another dea-

143

con," Brooks continued, "observed that the accident had cast a pall of gloom over the entire proceedings."

House Speaker Thomas Reed considered himself a great statesman. In 1896 he was asked by a reporter whether he would receive the Republican presidential nomination. "Well," he replied, "they might go further and do worse and they probably will."

They did.

A congressman named Springer once told the House that he would rather be right than president. Speaker Reed promptly retorted, "The gentleman from Illinois will never be either."

Another amusing Speaker, "Uncle Joe" Cannon, once said, "Sometimes in politics one must duel with skunks, but no one should be fool enough to allow the skunks to choose the weapons."

One recently deceased congressman—let's call him William—was a cantankerous man with few friends among his colleagues. When I heard that William had passed away, I was reminded of the Quaker who was asked to say a few words at the funeral of a little-loved man: "Well, I can say one good thing about William. He wasn't as mean sometimes as he was usually."

An elaborate protocol, heavy on the rhetorical courtesies, governs public relationships between senators and representatives. This excerpt from the 1966 *Congressional Record* documents a most unusual exchange between Senator Young of Ohio and Senator Gruening, who was presiding over the Senate for a few hours one afternoon:

Sen. Young: I propound a parliamentary inquiry: Would it be a violation of the rules of the Senate were I to assert in this Chamber at this time that Representative Hays of Ohio and one-term Representative Sweeney of Ohio, are guilty of falsely, viciously and maliciously making stupid, lying statements assailing the loyalty and patriotism of Senators, including the Junior Senator from Ohio, and that they are liars in alleging that we "have aided our enemies"?

Sen. Gruening: . . . It has been held out of order for Senators to refer to a Member of the House in opprobrious terms, or to impute to him unworthy motives.

Sen. Young: I, of course, abide by the ruling of the Chair, and I respect it. If, however, on some future occasion a similar contemptible attack is made on me with the insect-like buzzing of lying allegations by either or both of these publicity seekers, I shall surely embalm and embed them in the liquid ambers of my remarks. [*Loud laughter*]

In 1964, Senator Gruening and Senator Wayne Morse were the only two senators to vote against the Gulf of Tonkin Resolution, which greased the skids for our ill-considered escalation of the Vietnam war. In that same year, Gruening asked me to become the House sponsor for his controversial bill on population control. I told him that since I had six children, it might be hypocritical of me to sponsor such a bill, but that I would nonetheless. After I introduced the bill, I sent him a note saying that I was following him off the cliff, and that I expected him to find me another job when the voters ran me out of office. He sent back a terse note that simply said, "Leaders often find themselves temporarily alone."

A mention of tough Wayne Morse reminds me of the popular congressman who died and went to Heaven, but to his horror was denied entry and sent to a location with a hotter climate. Weeks later, another congressman traveled the same route.

When he approached Satan, he asked for the first congressman, a man named Smedley. "Is Smedley here?" he asked.

145

"Yes," replied the Devil, "but he is damned disliked here."

"Well, I can't understand that. He was one of the most respected men in Washington. What happened?"

"Oh, not too much. He just made a very bad impression when he arrived."

"What do you mean?"

"Well, when Smedley arrived, he said he owned this place, that his constituents had been giving it to him for twenty years."

Now that I've started, allow me a few more examples of time-honored congressional humor: During a budget debate, Senator Everett Dirksen grew tired of Majority Leader Lyndon Johnson's use of misleading statistics. "Statements made by the majority leader are all right so far as they go," said Dirksen. "But it is like the man who fell off the twentieth floor of a building. As he passed the sixth floor, a friend shouted to him, "Mike, so far you're all right."

From today's Speaker, Jim Wright, on the impossibility of pleasing one's constituents: "When I spent a long vacation in my district, there were loud complaints that I was spending too much time there and should be in Washington. But then when I didn't make it home for several months, others said, 'Who does that guy think he is? We only see him during elections.'

"When I came home shortly after being sworn in, driving my old car, they were upset because it looked like something farmers used to haul trash. But, by gosh, when I bought a new one they were sure the lobbyists had gotten to me. If I came home wearing an old suit people said, 'Look at him. Just an old bum.' Yet when I wore a new one, I heard, 'He's gone high-hat with that Ivy League suit of his.' One Sunday I missed church and some people said that 'being down in Washington had made an atheist of me.' Several

146

weeks later, when I did get to church, they said, 'Why, that pious fraud! He's just trying to dig up votes!' "

And the next one really happened, so I was told: A constituent came into a congressional office and said, "Congressman, I've been a supporter of yours for years. I voted for you three times for sheriff, twice for county commissioner, once for state senate, and four times for Congress. I've never asked for a favor, but there's one thing I now want you to do." "Yes, of course," said the congressman, "anything at all." "Well, I want you to help me get my citizenship papers."

An Alabama congressman once said of a Texas colleague: "He's so incompetent he could screw up a two-car funeral."

Someone once said that politics is the art of taking money from the rich and votes from the poor while promising to protect each from the other. Georgia senator Eugene Talmadge knows how to sing that song. After telling a home-state crowd of their woes and the dangers ahead, he said, "I swear, sometimes I think the po' folks of this state have only three friends left in this world: Gawd Almighty, Sears and Roebuck, and Eugene Talmadge."

An Oklahoma candidate for Congress was setting a new handshaking record while campaigning. Said a farmer, "If that guy was milking cows, he would have drained every cow in this county."

A man by the name of Lex Johnson campaigned for office before the Civil War and said, "Elect me. We can lick those yellow-livered, soft Yankees with cornstalks." After the war he ran again, saying, "Folks, elect me and we'll get this state back on its feet." A heckler interrupted and said, "Just a minute, Lex. Before the war you said we should elect you and we'd lick those Yankees with cornstalks." To which Lex replied, "Yes, that's right, man, but those Yankees wouldn't fight with cornstalks."

A reporter interviewed an old senator recently: "Well, sir, I guess you've seen a lot of changes in your time here?"

"Yes, and I have been against every blamed one of them."

He was one of those politicians who finally left office because of illness . . . the voters got sick of him.

If the use of rapierlike wit was an Olympic sport, Senator Bob Dole would be the gold medal winner. When Dole was once shown a photograph of former presidents Ford, Carter, and Nixon, he said, "There they are—See No Evil, Hear No Evil, and Evil."

In 1986 there were a lot of complaints from all around the country about negative campaigning in Senate races. It used to be that a candidate had a choice between taking the low road and the high road. These days, though, it seems like it's a choice between the low road and the gutter. In my own campaigns I try to heed the wise old Navaho adage, "He who slings mud loses ground."

While canvassing house-to-house late one evening, a congressman came to where a large party was in progress. When the host discovered his caller's identity, he cordially invited the congressman in. But the campaigner first wanted to know what kind of party was taking place. The host said, "All the men strip naked, wrap a towel around their heads, and run through a room where all the women are watching. The game is to see how many of the men the women can identify."

Aghast, the congressman said, "Oh, my God! Surely you don't think I can afford to participate in such a party." "Oh, don't worry," the host assured him. "Your name has already been called four or five times."

A Pope and senator were killed in the same air crash. When they arrived at the Pearly Gates and identified themselves, St. Peter told the Pope to wait while he attended to the senator. As the Pope looked on, Peter took the senator to a luxurious twenty-room mansion and said, "Senator, this is your home. Enjoy it and if you need anything, please call us at once."

Peter then escorted the Pope to another building and showed him his new quarters, a studio apartment. Puzzled, the Pope said, "St. Peter, I don't understand. You gave that politician a fine mansion and settled me in this little apartment. Since I spent my whole life doing the Lord's work on earth, I am unable to see the reason for the disparity."

St. Peter said, "I'd be glad to explain. You are Pope Number 186 we have received in Heaven. But this is the first senator we have laid eyes on."

"You're on Your Own, Big Shot": Dinner Speaking and Other Nightmares

★★★★★★★★★★★★★★★★★★★★★★★★★★★★

An eager young man took a speech course to better his chances for advancement. Practicing extemporaneous delivery at class, he picked a topic out of a hat. It was "sex." Later he told his wife of the effort, but said he had spoken on sailing. An acquaintance called her to tell how well her husband had spoken in class. "I don't understand how he could talk about that," she said. "The first time he did it he got sick to his stomach . . . and the second time his hat blew off."

March 1987. Staggered by daily revelations of new developments in the Iran-contra scandal, President Reagan's popularity plunges to a new low. After canning chief of staff Don Regan, Reagan brings aboard Howard Baker to effect his political resurrection. Baker advises the president to stop hiding from the press. You should hold a press conference, Baker suggests, and you should definitely attend the press corps's Gridiron dinner. It's time to beard the lion in his den.

Following Baker's advice, the president attends the dinner—an annual event where politicians and the press take turns lampooning one another—and wows 'em. Although he's the butt of dozens of jokes, Reagan is the hit of the evening, giving as good as he gets. His affability captivates the crowd.

"With the Iran thing occupying everyone's attention, I was thinking," the president confessed. "Do you remember when I said 'we begin bombing in five minutes?' Remember when I fell asleep during my audience with the Pope? Remember Bitburg? . . . Boy, those were the good old days!" Referring to Nancy Reagan's months-long attempt to dump Regan, the president joked, "Nancy and Don at one point tried to patch things up. They met privately over lunch. Just the two of them and their food tasters.

"Not only is the Iran-contra scandal being investigated by an independent counsel, a special review board, and two congressional committees," the president continued, "there was also my trip to Bethesda [Naval Hospital, where he underwent prostate surgery]. I tell you, one more probe and I've had it."

Not to be outdone, the press serenaded Reagan with this song, sung to the tune of "Try to Remember":

Try to remember
The time in September
When you said yes,
Or was it "golly."
Did you dissemble
The truth last December
With Ollie, Ollie, Ollie?

In another skit, an actor playing Colonel North sang that "Just for freedom's sake, fellas, I would love to do it all again." The reply, to the tune of "Hello, Dolly!":

Oh, no, Ollie,
Oh, no, no, Ollie.
That's not exactly what we had in mind.

TOO FUNNY TO BE PRESIDENT

So take the stand, Ollie.
Tell the story of your glory,
Cov'ring your behind.

On leaving the dinner, Supreme Court Justice Antonin Scalia was asked for his comments by a *Washington Post* reporter. "I can't imagine this happening in any other country," Scalia said. "One of the virtues of the American republic is that we don't take ourselves too seriously." British ambassador Sir Antony Acland concurred: "It was great fun, very unique, I am not sure we could have anything like this in Britain."

The origins of the political dinner are murky, but the Gridiron Club of Washington, D.C., an association of prominent political journalists, hosts the oldest, most prestigious, and—occasionally—the funniest of the lot. For more than a century, the Gridiron's dinner has been one of Washington's most popular fetes, attended by hundreds of journalists, politicians, and their guests.

The Gridiron provides a rare opportunity for governors, mayors, senators, congressmen, and sometimes even presidents to break bread with the press. The usual adversary roles are checked alongside the coats as the politicians say, "Well, boys and girls, here I am. Have at me. I can take a joke. I am neither god nor king. I am a citizen along with you. Help yourself—have some fun at my expense." Where else but in America would the most powerful politicians shamelessly covet invitations to a dinner, knowing full well that before the evening is over they will have been slandered, dismembered, and roasted?

The well-lubricated evening is punctuated with skits, songs, and wickedly witty speeches (within limits: the dinner is conducted in a spirit of fellowship and good will—the rule is that a "joke may singe, but should never burn"). The Gridiron provides journalists with a chance to exhibit their creaky voices and piddling theatrical talent. It's also a testing ground for politicians: Can they take the Club's barbed humor in stride? Or will they stalk off in a pout?

Eighty years ago, William Howard Taft, the three-hundred-pound president, provided a hippopotamic target for Gridiron gag writers. He later wrote in a memoir:

The Gridiron dinners, at which of late years I was a regular attendant, are worthy of mention. They furnished a great deal of fun, some of it bright and excruciating, and all of it of a popular flavor, because it was at the expense of those of the guests who were in the public eye. After some training, both as Secretary of War and as President, I was able to smile broadly at a caustic joke at my expense and seem to enjoy it, with the consolatory thought that every other guest of any prominence had to suffer the same penalty for an evening's pleasure. The surprise and embarrassment of foreign ambassadors at their first Gridiron dinner, and their subsequent wholehearted appreciation of the spirit of these occasions, showed how unique a feature they were of Washington political life.

Before the evening is over, the politicians have their turn, too. If, in their attempts to slay the press, the politicians come across as gracious or, better yet, funny, they will enhance their reputations among the Washington press corps. But woe to the politician who sulks, or is perceived as a stick-in-the-mud, or tells tasteless jokes, as former New York mayor John Lindsay once did, that just don't carry the crowd. In the same vein, Senator Malcolm Wallop set his career back when he gave a five-minute monologue on portable johns, which had been an issue in his campaign.

President Benjamin Harrison was the first president to attend a Gridiron dinner, and the ordinarily aloof and colorless politician stunned and delighted the assembled newsmen with a humorous speech lampooning the press. The speech was doubly remarkable because of Harrison's low standing for decisiveness in the White House.

Afterward an admirer came up to Harrison's assistant and said, "Your man Harrison is a wonder. I didn't think it was in him."

"Oh, he's all right on his feet," the aide replied, "It's only when he sits down that he falls down."

President Grover Cleveland was the only early Gridiron era president not to attend a dinner. His absence did not deter the newsmen from mocking him, and Cleveland let it be known that he was not amused. The chronicler of the Gridiron's history, Arthur Wallace Dunn, wrote, "Although the Gridiron Club had come to stay long before the end of Mr. Cleveland's first term, the relations between the newspaper men and the President continued to be strained. In a measure this hostility contributed in no small degree to the failure of Mr. Cleveland to be reelected in 1888, and if it had been left to a vote of the correspondents in 1892, Mr. Cleveland would not have been nominated nor elected."

Cleveland, years after his retirement, rued his poor press relations and said if he were to do it again, he would have attended the Gridiron to soothe hard feelings. (Jimmy Carter later had a similar experience—he attended only one Gridiron during his administration.)

Teddy Roosevelt had the kind of grace under fire that newsmen admire. Responding to a jest directed at him, Roosevelt said, "After this spontaneous effusion, I am reminded of Mr. Campbell's attack on me in the New York legislature, when I introduced a certain bill which, he charged, occupied a 'quasi' position. Whereupon Colonel Michael C. Murphy

154

said: 'How dare ye quote Latin on the floor of this house, when ye don't know the Alpha and Omega of the language.' It was all Greek to brother Murphy."

After John F. Kennedy won his first Senate race in 1952, he was widely criticized for buying the victory with his father's money. To twit Kennedy about this, Gridiron members introduced him with a song, "For the Bill Goes to Daddy." Responding, Kennedy brought down the house by reading a telegram supposedly from his father: "Dear Jack: Don't buy a single vote more than necessary. I'll be damned if I'll pay for a landslide."

In 1983 President Reagan broke precedent when he actually performed in a skit. Dancing out onstage at the end of a conga line, clad in a huge sombrero and flashy serape, Reagan sang his own version of "Mañana." A year earlier, Nancy Reagan stopped a critical press dead in their tracks—and softened their harsh portrayals of her—with a song-and-dance routine spoofing her expensive clothing. In 1984, Washington Redskins fullback John Riggins was seated next to Supreme Court Justice Sandra Day O'Connor at a White House Correspondents dinner. Later Riggins was found asleep on the floor. "This," one observer suggested, "gave new meaning to the old term 'working the floor.'"

The Gridiron's blend of fellowship, humor, entertainment, and fine food has proved so successful that it has spawned a number of clones, including the "roast," first popular for taking the stuffing out of stuffed shirts. Gradually, over a period of decades, the political dinner has become something of a national tradition: many hundreds are held in all parts of the country every year. The underlying agenda for many such dinners, of course, is fund raising. But no sane taxpayer is going to don black tie and wade into a crowd of sweating politicians and lobbyists in order to get a watery drink and two pieces of inedible chicken for $50, $100, even $1,000 a plate unless the evening offers something in the way of entertainment—a chance to laugh at and with those who govern.

There are, of course, those cynics who say that political dinners are inherently self-congratulatory influence-peddling feasts—and that the whole charade ought to be abolished. They're probably right. But you can make a case that by providing an opportunity for citizens and taxpayers to dine and laugh with their elected officials the political dinner does have some redeeming social value.

I plead guilty to having attended more than two hundred political dinners during the past fifteen years. Some would say this is cruel and unusual punishment. And it is true: political dinners *can* be stultifyingly boring, torture of the most heinous sort. But being asked to speak at one of these affairs can sometimes be an even greater nightmare.

While waiting to give his address, the poor speaker must try to gag down a few bites of ghastly vegetables and gelatinous meat, while carrying on a thoughtful conversation with the two total strangers flanking him, whose sole purpose in life appears to be to prevent him from reviewing his scribbled notes.

And then come the introductions.

Ah, introductions. If I ever were to become king, my first act would be to issue an edict outlawing the bombastic introductions so common to political dinners. Brooks Hays once said to the giver of an overly laudatory introduction about him, "If you do not go to heaven for charity, you will certainly go somewhere else for exaggeration or downright prevarication." Of another grandiloquent introduction, Hays has said, "I hope that the Lord will forgive this man even as He does heathens, atheists, used-car salesmen, and fishermen."

When I labor under the burden of being introduced at stupefying length, I'll say something to the effect: "Thank you very much. Of all the introductions I have received in a long career, that is absolutely the most recent."

Occasionally, though, a master of ceremonies will liven up the evening by making a gaffe while introducing a guest. One emcee ruined his evening (but made that of the other guests) by saying, ". . . and our distinguished guest tonight, Congressman Smith, is a public servant who is equal to few and superior to none."

Another emcee brought down the house when he announced, "Now, ladies and gentlemen, I will ask Senator Crosby to come to the rectum."

Sometimes I've had fun with an honored guest during an introduction by saying, "I've been reading our guest's new biography, entitled "The Life and Times of _____, or, Demagoguery's Finest Hour."

To his eternal shame and our delight, another toastmaster once introduced the governor of the Virgin Islands as "the virgin of Governor's Island."

Some years ago, an emcee got a laugh when he opened the evening by saying that he felt like Elizabeth Taylor's sixth husband on his wedding night: he thought he knew what he was supposed to do, but he didn't know if he could, uh, make it *interesting*. Later, after this joke started making the rounds, another emcee told it—not knowing that John Warner, who *was* Taylor's sixth husband, was in the audience. Warner was not amused, and he gave the chagrined emcee a tongue-lashing he would not soon forget.

Over the years I have developed an introductory style that could best be described as lean and mean. If, for example, I have to introduce a gaggle of people at the head table, I'll follow tradition and say, "Please hold your applause until all the honorees have been introduced . . . but on second thought, some of these people don't deserve much applause, so if you feel compelled to applaud some of them individually,

157

go right ahead." One of my favorite introductions is to reverse the E. F. Hutton line: "When our guest speaks—no one listens." Or paraphrase the Smith Barney ad: "He made money the old-fashioned way—he stole it."

In 1953 I had the honor of introducing Adlai Stevenson, a man I greatly admired, at a fund raiser in Tucson. Most of the guests were longtime Stevenson supporters who knew him better than I did. The program was running late, and as I rose to give the introduction, Stevenson eyed me with the look of a man being led to the gallows. Obviously, he had suffered hundreds of boring, seemingly endless introductions, and he probably didn't expect mine to be much different.

I said, "Ladies and gentlemen. Our guest tonight is, as in that time-honored cliché, a man who needs no introduction . . . and I'll be damned if I'm going to give him one. Here he is, Adlai Stevenson, the next president of the United States." Stevenson was momentarily stunned, but as I sat down he shot me a perplexed glance that said, Thank you, thank you.

Contrast this with the emcee who, after rambling on and on about the featured guest and throwing in a few thousand well-chosen words about himself, finished his introduction with: "Well, so far this evening we have had our attention directed to a turkey stuffed with sage. We will now focus on a sage stuffed with turkey."

I remember hearing one colleague introduced in the following way: "The next speaker is a man of whom it can honestly be said, 'He has no enemies.' I must report, however, that he is thoroughly detested by every friend he's got."

Over the years I have tried to develop an appropriately self-deprecating manner when required to respond to introductions. I try to be gracious in the face of outrageous provocation, humorous in handling all insults, patient while enduring the unendurable, and humble when gushing praise makes me want to seek shelter under the table.

A sample opener: "I thank you for that kind introduction. I wanted to come here tonight in the worst way—so I tried Ozark Airlines. We took the economy flight—the one that does a little crop-dusting en route."

At one formal fund raiser, I arrived late wearing a suit instead of black tie. I told my audience that my plane was late and I had lost my luggage. But those travails, I continued, had given me a brainstorm: "I now know where to hide the MX missile," I said. "I will put it in a suitcase and check it on Piedmont Airline's midnight flight to Louisville. You will never see it again, nor will the Soviets have any idea where it is."

Once Hubert Humphrey waited through preliminary announcements, additional short remarks by head-table guests, speeches by local politicians, and, finally, a fustian introduction by the emcee. When Hubert finally got to the microphone he said, "I'm just tickled to be here, though I hadn't planned to stay the weekend."

I once had the difficult job of telling Hubert that because of the crowded schedule, I would have to limit his remarks to three minutes. "Three minutes!" Hubert cried. "Mo, I can't clear my throat in three minutes."

Another famous figure was beseeched by a friend to attend and speak at a political dinner. As the evening wore on and on, the guest's patience evaporated. After expansive opening remarks by his friend, who was serving as master of ceremonies, there was a musical interlude, then the first course, then more introductions, the second course, a report from the treasurer, the third course, a couple of skits, dessert, and finally, well past midnight, the emcee, awash in Scotch, lurched up to pontificate about his friend's qualifications. He finished by saying, "And now ladies and gentlemen, our distinguished speaker will give us his address."

Whereupon the irate guest got up and said, "Ladies and gentlemen, my address is 625 Park Avenue, and I bid you *Good night!*"

(My editor just interrupted me: "Come on, Mo, it's a pretty funny line, but it wasn't delivered by a 'famous figure.' You made it up," he continued, "or stole it—again without attribution—from one of your pals, right?" Maybe so. Like Oliver North, I don't seem to remember.)

The ideal political dinner speech, in my opinion, should be more in the vein of Hunter Thompson or Garry Trudeau or Mark Russell than John Stuart Mill. I always try to hook my audience immediately by beginning with a story. Here's a favorite: There was once a politician who was as stultifyingly boring as he was handsome. He looked like a distinguished statesman, but as a speaker he was an unmitigated disaster. In an attempt to salvage his career, the politician hired a gifted young speech writer. The young man wrote witty speeches sprinkled with quotations from Thucydides, Aristotle, Jesse Helms, even Bob Dole—all the classic thinkers. The politician's career took off; he became governor, senator, and soon was being touted for the presidency.

After several years, the young man came to him and said, "Sir, I've been working for you for years now, and I think I have had something to do with your success. I deserve a raise."

The senator thought for a minute, then replied, "You've worked hard, and I appreciate your help, but I think I'd have gone about as far on my own. We're paying you eight hundred dollars a month, and I just can't do any better than that."

Crushed, the young man returned to his small cubicle. That evening, as was his custom, he met the senator at a dinner and handed him the text of his speech, which he had not read. When it came time for the senator to begin his address, he strode confidently to the podium amidst thunderous applause, and began, "My dear friends, I come to you tonight with a message of hope, to tell you that this nation can solve its problems."

He turned the page and read on: "I come tonight to tell you that we can double our expenditures for education and health. I come tonight to tell you that we can clean up the environment, make our highways safe, strengthen our defense, roll back the Iron Curtain, banish communism from the hemisphere, and even bring peace to the Middle East. And, while doubling our expenditures to do all this, we can cut taxes and, in a short time, pay off the national debt."

As he turned the page, the senator hesitated, thinking that this was surely going to be one of his finest speeches. Then, in a stentorian rush, he read on: "My dear friends, I deal not in glib generalities, I deal in specifics, and tonight I shall reveal a new ten-point program that will, if followed, lead to the peace and prosperity of which I speak. I do not propose to beat around the bush, I propose to unveil this program here, and to unveil it now. . . ." An expectant hush settled over the audience. "The first point in my ten-point program is . . ." The rest of the page was blank so he quickly turned to the next page, where he found: *All right, big shot, you're on your own.*

A speech's summation is as important as its beginning. If you just dribble to a close, your audience will think you a dribbler, and with good reason. But if you close with a rousing line or relevant joke, your audience will conclude that you made some sense—even if you didn't. As with sales spiels, the closing words are of first importance.

I have had some success using variations on this story, into which I simply insert the appropriate name of the city or state where I am speaking: A traveling minister came to Springfield, Illinois. He asked Abe Lincoln to rent him a hall in which he could have a meeting. Curious, Abe asked him what the meeting was going to be about. The minister told him it was to discuss the second coming of the Lord. Lincoln objected, "It's no use, Reverend. If He's been to Springfield once, he'll never come again."

Sometimes I'll end with a story about a drill sergeant who was watching his platoon march back and forth on a military reservation and then was struck speechless as the platoon marched toward a cliff. The drill instructor had forgotten the command for "halt." A horrified onlooker shouted at the sergeant, "Say something, for God's sake, even if it's only good-bye!" And so to you, my friends, I say, "Good-bye."

Here are some remarks I made at the Gridiron back in 1982 that illustrate how topical humor can enliven a political speech (remember, appropriateness and timing, plus delivery and surprise, are all important).

Mr. President, former friends of David Stockman, Liberals, Americans, friends of the Navaho Indians, George Will's vocabulary teacher, and anybody who may have stumbled in here by mistake.

I hear all this talk tonight about the Great Communicator. Well the G.O.P. has always had a variety of talented orators, even some superstars.

Surely Nelson Rockefeller is entitled to the Communicators' Hall of Fame for the great sign of the one finger he gave that day in May to student protesters at Syracuse University. That clearly had to be a great moment in the annals of reverse heckling by politicians.

I've studied that event closely, and I'm here to report

that Nelson was not trying to be obscene. He was simply demonstrating how his brother turns you down for a loan at Chase Manhattan.

Barry Goldwater was another great communicator. You remember him saying that in the event of nuclear war we'd just "circle the wagons." Barry's often wrong, but he's never in doubt. Barry can get to the nub of a problem quickly. I thought one of his finest hours was following the nomination of Judge Sandra Day O'Connor, who's with us here tonight. She was attacked by Jerry Falwell, who said that every good Christian should be concerned about this appointment. Barry was asked what he thought, and he said every good Christian should kick Reverend Falwell right in the ass. Barry meant well, but I knew it wouldn't work. As a practicing Christian, Falwell would always turn the other cheek.

Judge O'Connor put on the robes and is hard at work on the Burger court. I heard a Republican tell a joke the other day: "Do you know the difference between the Ku Klux Klan and the Supreme Court? The Supreme Court puts on black robes and scares hell out of white folks, and the Klan puts on white robes. . . ."

At the court and elsewhere it's not been a good year for atheists. But the atheists finally did get one of those dial-a-prayer telephone lines. When you dial it, no one answers. . . .

I'm told that General Haig has had a bad month with staff leaks and so on. He then called the suicide prevention hot line and they put him on hold.

Ah, the Grand Old Party. I've been monitoring their programs carefully. LBJ gave us guns and butter, but the Reagan administration gives you guns, cheese, and teenage chastity—New Federalism and a war on puberty.

For those of you who don't understand Reaganomics, it's based on the principle that the rich and the poor will get the same amount of ice. In Reaganomics, however, the poor get all of theirs in winter.

Now something about this administration, which was also true of past Republican staffs. President Calvin Coolidge invited Will Rogers to the White House and the president said to the comedian, "Tell me the latest jokes." And Rogers said, "I don't have to. You have appointed them."

Speaking of appointments, the great state of Colorado gave us Jim Watt and Anne Gorsuch, who have done for the environment what Bonnie and Clyde did for banks.

Incidentally, while I'm speaking of Jim Watt, you understand that he's been under a charge of contempt of Congress and is facing a possible fine of one thousand dollars. Well, Secretary Watt has asked me to advise you that one thousand dollars does not even begin to express his contempt for this Congress.

I wish Secretary Weinberger were here tonight. I would like to introduce him to Al Haig. Someone said in Haig's presence the other day that Caspar Weinberger is his own worst enemy. And Haig replied, "The hell he is—not while I'm alive." Haig believes that war is wrong. He's against it because it tends to increase tensions between the participants.

Now let me end by saying something of a more serious nature. Members of the Gridiron, we've been through a lot of campaigns together. With bad nights, bad food, and early morning baggage calls. We've also had our share of mutual misunderstandings and irritations. But I'd like to think that when we disagreed, we disagreed agreeably.

"You're on Your Own, Big Shot"

The United States is the world's oldest democracy, and we should all treasure the fact that we live in a country where public figures and a free press can laugh together. So may the Gridiron last a long time and may it, as the saying goes, "singe, but never burn."

Tongue Twisted: Malaprops and Metaphorical Bloopers

★ ★

> If Lincoln were alive today he'd be turning over in his grave.
>
> —*Gerald R. Ford*

Dinner speaking (and legislating) is rife with perils and pitfalls, foremost of which is the dreaded *malaprop*. (William Safire, word maven for *The New York Times,* claims there ain't such—that the word I want is *malapropism,* but I don't think there will be a schism if I drop the *-ism*.) Since everyone has, at one time or another, succumbed to this tongue-twisting affliction, all of us can sympathize with the pitiable speaker who utters the fateful blooper.

There have been masters of the malaprop and mixed metaphor in many professions—consider Hollywood producer Sam Goldwyn: "An oral contract isn't worth the paper it's written on"; "Include me out"; and baseball's Yogi Berra: "That place is so crowded that nobody goes there anymore"; "If I hadn't woke up, I'd still be asleep"—but politicians seem particularly susceptible to this malady. A classic bon mot: "Senator, if we don't stop shearing the wool off the goose that lays the golden egg, we are going to pump the well dry."

Tongue Twisted: Malaprops and Metaphorical Bloopers

State senator John Parker of Massachusetts has a fine collection of verbal bloopers. An example: During a debate over the merits of pasteurized milk, a New Hampshire pol said, "What the people of this state deserve is clean, fresh, wholesome pasteurized milk. And I'm going to the state house and take the bull by the horns until we get it."

On the campaign trail, the deadly malaprop follows the politician like a poor relative, popping up when he least expects it. Said one aggrieved candidate: "Throughout this entire campaign I have been slandered by innuendo—both direct and indirect."

A southern politician who had suffered a narrow loss in a hard-fought campaign said, "My opponent deserves to be kicked to death by a jackass . . . and frankly, I'd like to be the one to do it!"

The malaprop also stalks the halls of Congress, claiming unwary victims of both parties. Former chairman of the House Committee on Armed Services, F. Edward Hebert, once observed, "The only way we'll ever get a volunteer army is to draft 'em."

During a debate over how best to win the loyalty of foreign nations, a young, idealistic congressman was plaintively pleading for programs designed "to win the hearts and minds of the downtrodden" when Representative Mendel Rivers, a crusty southerner, interrupted. "Bullshit," Rivers roared. "I say get 'em by the balls and their hearts and minds will follow."

Commenting on a colleague's abilities, a senator said, "He's got a lot of depth on the surface, but deep down he's shallow as hell." In the same vein, someone (perhaps it was I) once said of Sam Steiger, a former congressman from Arizona, "He always makes a good first impression; to detest him, you really have to know him."

167

Richard M. Daley, Jr., the son of the late Chicago mayor, once served in the Illinois legislature. While his career already includes a number of notable achievements, perhaps most memorable was his suggestion that the state honor the late senator Everett M. Dirksen with a statue. To facilitate the process, Daley proposed to create a "Commission on Erections and Mounting."

One of the masters of the malaprop was Representative Elford A. Cederberg of Michigan, who once referred to a young attorney as "still green behind the ears."

Representative Silvio Conte of Massachusetts, one of my favorite Republicans and a man who is renowned for over-heating during debates, once declaimed, "This is no time to pull the rug out in the middle of the stream."

UPI columnist Dick West also collects choice misstatements. One of his favorites was coined by New York Congressman Alfred Santangelo, who rose in indignation about a proposal to have a national lottery. Such a thing, Santangelo declared, "was morally repugnant to millions of people, not only in the United States, but also in the Twenty-fourth Congressional District."

While explaining that a group of people faced a dilemma, Congressman John Dent said, "They were torn between two fires."

Senator Roman Hruska struck a blow for the average man during a debate over the seating of President Nixon's first nominee for the Supreme Court, Judge Harold Carswell. To a critic who complained that Carswell was a mediocre judge, Hruska shot back, "There are a lot of mediocre Americans. Don't *they* deserve some representation on the court?"

According to Dick West, the all-time champion congressional tongue twister was the late senator Kenneth Wherry of Nebraska. The many cherished Wherryisms include his introduction of Senator Spessard Holland of Florida as the "distinguished senator from Holland." Wherry habitually referred to Chiang Kai-shek as "Shanghai Jack," and supported him in his battles against the Chinese Communists and "Mousey Tongue," the leader of "Indigo China."

Another artful malapropist was Senator Homer E. Capehart of Indiana. He once addressed a colleague as "the senior senator from Junior." In another debate Capehart got so carried away with the rhetorical courtesies that he referred to himself as "the distinguished senator from Indiana."

Senator Joe McCarthy was known for tongue tripping— particularly after a high-proof lunch. Of a witness's testimony he once said, "That's the most unheard-of thing I ever heard of."

Bureaucrats, too, beget malaprops. Archivist West awards an honorable mention to an Agriculture Department official who testified before a senate committee during the Billie Sol Estes inquiry. Defending the department's failure to anticipate a problem, the official said, "Unfortunately, we are not equipped with hindsight in advance." West puts this type of statement under the heading, "Hitting the nail on the head in a nutshell."

During the campus demonstrations of the 1960s, a congressman proposed an amendment to cut off financial aid to any student found guilty of participating in unsanctioned demonstrations. "This amendment," he roared, "will put some starch in the backbones of weak-kneed college administrators."

It was Senator S. I. Hayakawa of California, I think, who said, "The best cure for insomnia is to get a lot of sleep."

The higher a politician aims his rhetoric, the more likely it is that he will launch an unguided missile. Speaking at a patriotic event honoring Abraham Lincoln, a politician said, "It is indeed fitting that we gather here today to pay tribute to Abraham Lincoln, who was born in a log cabin that he built with his own hands." Another senator, frustrated by the continuing strife in the Middle East, recently wondered, "Why can't the Jews and the Arabs just sit down together and settle this like good Christians."

Nervousness also produces memorable slips. A young man being honored at a banquet was summoned to the head table. The mayor handed him a trophy and asked him to say a few words. The boy did: "From the heart of my bottom, I thank you." After being given a coveted award, another flustered honoree replied, "I sure don't appreciate it, but I really do deserve it."

The late senator Joe Montoya of New Mexico will live forever in the Malaprops Hall of Fame. Montoya once arrived ninety minutes late for a dinner meeting in Albuquerque. He rushed into the ballroom and was handed a speech and a press release covering its high points. Montoya strode to the podium. "Ladies and gentlemen, it is a great pleasure to be with you today." He hesitated, looked down at his script, and read, "For Immediate Release. . . ."

One longtime Rocky Mountain governor was prone to bouts of fumbleitis. Trying to protect him from himself, his staff made sure his speeches were typed in large letters with short, simple, declarative sentences. But once, as he was ponderously droning through a speech on highways and taxes, the governor read, "This, gentlemen, is our program for highways. . . . Pause and smile. . . . Now, with regard to taxes . . ."

Senator Strom Thurmond once chaired an investigative hearing. Before he left his office, Thurmond's staff provided him with an opening statement and a list of questions for each witness. Arriving in the hearing room, Strom read the opening statement—and then kept right on going: "If the first witness answers 'Yes,' then ask him so and so. . . . If the witness answers 'No' or 'I'm not sure,' then ask him such and such." As the crowd started to titter, an aide rushed over and grabbed the paper from Thurmond's hand.

The late governor of Arizona, Wesley Bolin, is renowned for this example of sparkling logic: "We'd like to avoid problems, because when we have problems, we can have troubles."

During their 1986 Texas gubernatorial race, Mark White, Jr., and Mark Clements spent the whole campaign playing demolition derby on the low road. The voters had a choice, said one disgruntled commentator, "between the evil of two lessers."

Philadelphia's former mayor, Frank Rizzo, was defensive about his administration. To a question that implied that the City of Brotherly Love was not so brotherly after dark, the former cop replied, "The streets are safe in Philadelphia, it's only the people who make them unsafe."

Barry Goldwater, of course, has made shooting from the hip an art form. For example: "The only summit meeting that can succeed is one that does not take place." Also: "Thank heaven for the military-industrial complex. Its ultimate aim is peace in our time." Barry was also the only politician I've ever met who could get God, motherhood, the flag, and the Fourth of July into one sentence of his speech. He'd say, "You know, I'll always remember how as a little kid my mother would take us down to the courthouse after church on the Fourth of July to see them raise the flag." They probably stopped for apple pie on the way home.

State legislatures can spawn malaprops and sundry bloopers at a staggering pace. The *Wall Street Journal* cited these gems from a recent session of the Michigan legislature:

★ "Now we've got them right where they want us."

★ "Before I give you the benefit of my remarks, I'd like to know what we're talking about."

★ "There comes a time to put principle aside and do what's right."

★ "I don't see anything wrong with saving human life. . . . That would be good politics, even for us."

★ "This bill goes to the very heart of the moral fiber of human anatomy."

★ "It's a step in the right direction, it's the answer, and it's constitutional, which is even better."

★ "Some of our friends wanted it in the bill, some of our friends wanted it out, and Jerry and I are going to stick with our friends."

★ "I'm not only for capital punishment, I'm also for the preservation of life."

★ "From now on, I'm watching everything you do with a fine-toothed comb."

★ "The chair would wish the members would refrain from talking about the intellectual levels of other members. That always leads to problems."

★ "Mr. Chairman, fellow members and guests. That's a goddamn lie!"

★ "I don't think people appreciate how difficult it is to be a pawn of labor."

★ "This state's atypical. We've got some real weird ducks and I think that's reflected in this senate, with all due respect."

★ "Let's violate the law one more year."

★ "Mr. Speaker, what bill did we just pass?"

An intentional use of a malaprop can be an easy way for a speaker to get a laugh. For example, I've frequently referred to Henry Kissinger as "a legend in his own mind." Kissinger himself has a great sense of humor, a thick German accent, and a wonderful sense of timing, all essential elements in

172

his self-deprecating, yet occasionally pompous style. After one diplomatic meeting he announced, "Golda Meir and I agree on everything . . . including the fact that we don't see eye to eye." Kissinger's sense of humor enabled him not only to survive Watergate but to emerge with his prestige relatively intact. Making light of the scandal, Kissinger would often say, "The illegal we do immediately. The unconstitutional takes a little longer." Another Kissingerism: "The history of things that didn't happen has never been written." Kissinger also had the last word on fame's perquisites: "Now when I bore people at a cocktail party they think it's their fault."

Euphemisms and malaprops are kissing cousins, and one of the Nixon administration's greatest claims to fame was that it set new records in the Euphemisms Sired by Republican Administration category—although, at last count, the Reagan crowd was fast overtaking them. One Nixon spokesman described the White House's stance on an important piece of legislation as "unyielding but flexible rigidity." Here's two beauts from Al Haig, who earned all-star status while serving Nixon as Secretary of Snarled Syntax and Gobbledygook: "You'd better caveat that statement" and "At the moment we are subsumed in the vortex of criticality."

One year the National Council of Teachers of English awarded its Doublespeak Award to the United States Department of State for its effort to redefine "killing" as "unlawful or arbitrary deprivation of life." The Federal Aviation Administration went them one better when, in a report about an accident that had claimed 180 lives, it referred to the "premature impact of the aircraft with the terrain below." If I'm not mistaken, that's what we used to call a "crash." During the Three Mile Island disaster, utility officials fretted that a hydrogen buildup in the reactor could lead to "a rapid energetic disassembly"—an explosion.

173

A Nixon appointee asked Gerald Cullinan, the Oxford-trained official of the AFL-CIO's Letter Carriers Union, for some personal advice. After Cullinan had pontificated at great length, the official said, "On balance, I think it is safe to say that I couldn't conceivably disagree with you less."

To paraphrase John O'Donnel's favorite line: "He may waddle like a duck, quack like a duck, and associate with ducks, but he retains a clear, uncontested constitutional right to insist that he is a prothonotary warbler."

Former governor Richard Hughes of New Jersey told of campaigning in a particularly tough section of the Jersey waterfront. He asked a longshoreman if he had any problems he wanted to discuss.

"You politicians have got to do something about those bleeping taxes," the longshoreman replied. "If you don't, they are going to throw my bleep out of my house and I'll end up in the bleeping street."

A female reporter traveling with Hughes asked him to repeat the longshoreman's message. "The gentleman," replied Hughes, "says that unless we revise our fiscal policies, he might lose his residence."

A few years ago, George Smathers was running against Claude Pepper in a Senate race. In a speech in rural Florida, Smathers did a euphemistic hatchet job on Pepper. It's now recognized as a classic of the genre: "Are you aware that Claude Pepper is known all over Washington as a shameless extrovert? Not only that," Smathers went on, "but this man is reliably reported to practice nepotism with his sister-in-law, and he has a sister who was once a thespian in New York. Worst of all," Smathers said mournfully, "it is an established fact that Mr. Pepper, before his marriage, practiced celibacy."

Smathers won.

It takes courage to eschew euphemism—courage that many

politicians, bureaucrats, and generals lack. During World War II General Stilwell was hounded out of Burma by the Japanese. A few years later General MacArthur was overwhelmed by Chinese forces at the Yalu River in Korea. When asked by a diplomatic reporter whether his movement had been a "tactical retreat," Stilwell rejected the euphemism and said, "I claim that we took a hell of a beating."

Contrast that with MacArthur, who, when facing a similar situation, called a press conference to announce, "Should the Red Hordes continue to pour across the Yalu, it might not only render impossible the resumption of our offensive, but conceivably could eventuate in a movement in retrograde."

Beyond euphemism we enter the tortured realm of obfuscation in which no politician—with the possible exception of Al Haig—was ever more comfortable than Governor Nelson Rockefeller. Asked at a press conference for his views on the war in Vietnam, Rocky energetically declared, "My position on Vietnam is very simple. And I feel this way. I haven't spoken on it because I haven't felt there was any major contribution that I had to make at the time. I think that our concepts as a nation and that our actions have not kept pace with the changing conditions. And therefore our actions are not completely relevant today to the realities of the magnitude and the complexity of the problems that we face in this conflict."

"What does that mean, governor?" a reporter asked.

"Just what I said," Rocky replied.

★ ★ ★ ★ ★ ★ ★ ★ ★ ★ ★ ★ **13** ★ ★ ★ ★ ★ ★ ★ ★ ★ ★ ★ ★

"Get Cancer, You Parasite": Letters from Home

★ ★

> Of all the rats and snakes elected to represent the people
> and carry out their wishes, you rank head and shoulders
> beneath the lowest.
> —*a friendly letter from home*

I cannot understand why more people don't write their congressmen. Even though the two most precious rights in a democracy are voting for an office holder and then communicating your dissatisfaction with him or her, a large number of Americans do neither. It doesn't matter whether you think congressmen are overpaid cretins—these are the people whose votes will determine whether we have balanced budgets or outrageous deficits; war or peace; tax raises or cuts; clean or fouled air. And yet I once took a survey and found that less than 5 percent of Americans had ever exercised their God-given right to raise unshirted hell with the people they put into office.

This is a shame. Too many Americans have yet to discover the simple joy of venting their spleen; they must not know what fun it is to put their feelings about Senator X's farm policy or Congressman Y's latest brush with the law down on paper. If you think your congressman's stance on abortion or aid to the Nicaraguan contras or Star Wars leaves something to be desired, unholster your pen and let him have it. Alternatively, if your less-than-honorable Honorable has been

176

caught with his hand in the till or in bed with a page, and you think such comportment is not in keeping with his image as a family man and deacon of the local church, why, *tell him so!* God knows there must be *something* you're outraged about—the budget deficit is running $160 billion per year; the public debt, less than $1 trillion when Reagan took office, has skyrocketed past $2 trillion; the trade deficit is climbing like a gut-shot panther; the average rain in the Eastern United States is as acidic as tomato juice; infant mortality among babies born to blacks is twice that of whites; and a million Afghans have died since the Russians invaded their country. Meanwhile, unable to fiddle, Reagan chops wood.

Time is growing late. Don't sit there mutely while the republic founders! Take pen in hand, write a letter, give your congressman the benefit of your wisdom. He needs it.

Sometimes citizens are reluctant to write because they share the cynical but understandable notion that congressmen have neither the time nor the inclination to read their mail, that a letter probably won't be answered, that one letter won't make any difference. But all three notions are wrong.

Although it is impossible for me to read every letter that comes into my office, I do read a representative sample every day. The letters I don't have time for are read and answered by a staff member. Rest assured, you will receive a reply from me—unless you've suggested I do something anatomically impossible. Some members of Congress insist they read every piece of correspondence that comes into the office. If they do, they have precious little time to do anything else.

As to whether a letter *can* influence a congressman, on several occasions a single, thoughtful, factually persuasive letter did change my mind. For example, heartfelt letters I received during the mid-1960s were instrumental in changing my positions about dams in the Grand Canyon, and the Vietnam war.

TOO FUNNY TO BE PRESIDENT

Ironically, in this high-tech telecommunications era, mail plays a more crucial role in the legislative process than ever. The reason? In the days of Clay and Calhoun, Webster and Lincoln, congressmen lived among their constituents for nine months each year, and thus became intimately familiar with their beliefs, problems, ire, and hopes. Today we rarely get to spend even sixty days a year in our home states. And so the mailbag has become the "hot line" to the people.

The art of writing a letter to a congressman is fading but not lost. To be sure that your letter gets read and noticed:

★ Make sure the letter is legible. If your spouse can't decipher your handwriting, I can't either.

★ Be brief. Every day I get hundreds of letters. Don't send me a tome when an epistle will do. "Has any foreign person not a Communist or a cannibal approved our foreign policy?"

★ If you're writing about legislation (as opposed to, say, help in cutting red tape, jump-starting a balky bureaucrat, or locating a missing Social Security check), state your arguments as concisely as the subject matter will permit. Less is often more: In the midst of a heated debate about a new wilderness area in Arizona, I received a neatly typed letter that simply said, "Happy retirement, Mo."

Ten years ago I wrote a handbook for newly elected members of Congress entitled, *The Job of the Congressman*. The book gave rookie legislators some tips for answering the mail soon to deluge them. But how can you prepare someone for a letter like this:

Udall you are a worthless bum and our biggest problem. Is there any way possible to ship you to the South Pole, permanently, so we would not hear from you again?

Also, would you take all the lice in Washington with you? The only thing you are good at is spending other people's money. You do absolutely nothing else. Also, Udall, stay off TV as you turn my stomach and I have lost some meals, and, at the price of food, you cost me a lot of money.

So, ashhole [*sic*] Udall, as from the above, you know my education is not as good as yours, but I know an ashole [*sic*] without smelling it.

It's clear that he knows one without spelling it as well.

Was I offended? No, not really. If heaping abuse on me makes that gentleman's day, well, that's just another service we public servants can provide. Congressmen expect to be lightning rods for the wrathful, and as I do with all such letters, I saved that one for posterity in my "Friendly Letters" file. Whenever I need a fresh dose of humility, I'll pull it out and reread some of my favorites. If, however, a letter *does* offend me, I'll sometimes take the time to compose an "up yours" reply.

The acknowledged champion of the stinging retort was the late senator Stephen Young of Ohio, a man who made short-temperedness an art form; the caustic comment, high literature. To a woman who had been pestering him mercilessly, Senator Young wrote, "Dear Madam: You should know that some idiot in your town is sending me a series of crazed letters—and signing your name." If Young was in a rush, he would cross out the offending text with a red Magic Marker and then scrawl in letters large enough to ensure notice his simple, yet eloquent reply: "KISS MY ASS!"

Some of the most vitriolic mail comes from people who turn into pussycats when confronted in person. The first bill

I sponsored that became law was introduced at the behest of the Civil Service Commission and was intended to settle the question of whether illegitimate children of civil servants were eligible for benefits. The courts had ruled in different ways, and the commission wanted the matter settled one way or the other, they didn't care which: "Just get us a yes or no so we can send checks." Thus I became the sponsor of a bill making illegitimate children "children" for the purposes of civil service retirement. Inevitably, the bill soon became known as the "poor bastards bill."

In spite of that irreverent appellation, or perhaps because of it, the poor bastards bill breezed through the House and Senate and was signed into law by President Kennedy. The next weekend I was in Arizona and I met a disputatious merchant who was a member of the John Birch Society and a regular contributor to the Friendly Letters file. He said, "Congressman, you guys are throwing our money away in Africa, Europe, and everywhere else. What I want to know is, When are you going to do something for the poor bastards in this country?"

It was a softball question tossed from heaven. "Sir," I said, "I'm glad you asked that question. Why, just last week . . ."

Not all obscene mail comes from right-wing zealots and the loose-wired issue freaks of conservative extremist groups. Environmentalists—those "tree-hugging, posy-picking, Snail Darter lovers" so disdained by the right wing—are quite capable of nasty letters. During a bitter legislative battle over a proposed seaport near Seattle, I was outraged by an egregious attempt by other congressmen to circumvent my committee's jurisdiction. In a fit of pique, I told a reporter that I was angry enough to consider voting against the resolution halting the port project.

This aroused Seattle-area environmentalists to a state of high fury. Wrote one:

Dear Congressman Udall:
I used to defend you among my co-workers in the Carter campaign as the ideal vice-president if Jimmy could get over being mad at you. I've probably had more kind words to say about you over the years than any other politician, and I even sent you a contribution to your campaign. After what you said about the oil port question I'd like to say just one more thing to you: "Go fuck yourself!"

I sent a copy of this letter to the congressman who opposed me on the seaport issue with a note, "I think he may be against me on this one."

Nothing ever arouses more fury among the voters than attempts by members of Congress to vote ourselves a pay raise. From the tone of most letters, you would think our intent was to repeal the Bill of Rights, ban baseball, and authorize an IRS audit of Mother Teresa.

"Morris K. Udall," said one, "Just how hoggish can you get. . . . How many families are you supporting? Get your hand out of our pockets." I didn't have the gall to write back and tell him that, being a divorced father, I did have two families to support.

A colleague from California, Jerome Waldie, once told me that he was getting merciless mail on the issue. He reached into his jacket and took out a letter:

Dear Mr. Waldie,
As a retired telephone operator living on a fixed income with medical costs and food prices going up every day, I am absolutely outraged and shocked by your support

for a big pay raise. I hope that you choose to change your mind on this or suffer the consequences.

> Indignantly,
> Your
> Mother

Here is a succinct example of the postcard genre:

If you scum in Congress vote yourselves fat raises again like in 1968, I and my friends will not file or pay any 1972 tax! Get Cancer, you Parasite!

A similar epistle, perhaps from the same correspondent:

Dear $2100 and wage freezer Morris Bastard Udall!
If you and your bastards in Congress vote yourselves another fat pay raise plus benefits, I hope you get Cancer! I and my wage frozen friends will not pay or file any income taxes . . . so help me God! You scumbags let food prices skyrocket while you silly pricks live off the fat of the land! If you were paid hourly you would starve to death!

Friendly letters don't stop at Christmas. I typically send hundreds of Christmas cards to supporters and friends, but one year my Christmas card list got mixed up with another one. A few weeks later one of my cards was returned with my greeting—"Peace on Earth, Goodwill to Men"—crossed out. In its place someone had written: "You must be out of your stupid mind—if you have any."

Watergate spawned a few nasty letters. During his last troubled year in office, Richard Nixon's die-hard supporters wouldn't stand any criticism of their hero. To a letter I sent to those urging me to change my views about wanting Nixon to resign, I received the following telegram: "You are a no good son of a bitch. Suggest you resign. Strong letter follows."

Lots of folks write in asking for help. Nothing fancy, just help. Not long after I stopped practicing law to become a congressman I received the following letter:

Thank you sir for your very kind letter of December 4th. I do, however, have a further question. The big one. So far all of Congress has evaded it. How do I obtain a divorce? If I don't receive some satisfaction by February, I fully intend to contact a reporter and be on my way to Washington D.C. Sir, I have had more than enough. I don't intend to go on in this manner longer than February 1963. Thank you. . . .

Kids write, too. I once received a letter, painstakingly scrawled by a young boy, imploring, "Dear Congressman, my mother won't let me go out after 5:30 at night. She told me if I didn't like it to rite my congressman. Sincerely, Randy."

Occasionally, a congressman's morality is the topic of a letter. In 1968, after years of effort, the Arizona congressional delegation succeeded in passing the Colorado River Basin Project Act. That evening we celebrated. The next morning the Arizona *Republic* ran a photo showing Representative John Rhodes, Senator Carl Hayden, my brother Stewart (then Secretary of the Interior), and I raising glasses of champagne in tribute to our hard-fought victory.

Attached to a jagged clipping of the photo came the following letter:

Dear Mr. Udall:
I am compelled by my conscience to pen this letter of protest. I cannot remain silent about the photograph

which appeared on the front pages of Arizona newspapers on Friday last.

My blood ran cold when I perceived the telltale signs of alcoholic indulgence: the crooked grins, the eyes unnaturally bright, the frozen grips on the rum cups, and the utter lack of dignity and decorum.

My worst suspicions were confirmed when I read that my elected representatives in Congress were swilling the poison that robs men of their reason (and young women of their virtue). Snort! Smack! Slurp!

There, for all to see, are four of Arizona's most prominent men—otherwise respected and responsible officials of our national government. I can only pray that other readers were able to discern, as I was, the insidious influence of strong drink. It is visible in the gleeful clinking of the wine glasses, in the giddy conspiratorial atmosphere, in the slavering of wine-wetted lips, in the salacious leer that unmasks alcohol-inflamed minds, and in the shameless savoring of seductive sin.

For shame!

It is all there, for the whole world to see and be instructed thereby. Surely the good, God-fearing people of Arizona will not forever tolerate this brazen flaunting [sic] of morality.

Arizona stands at the crossroads. Downward the smooth broad path leads to debauchery, degradation, and the early dissolution of our sovereign state.

Upward?

Upward the rocky slope leads to sobriety and salvation.

> Your faithful Servant,
> Rev. Bill Bowler

Reverend Bill didn't mince words. That tongue-lashing was enough to make me want a beer.

In December 1976, I was cleaning the gutters on my garage of detritus accumulated during two years of presidential campaigning. My ladder slipped and pitched me down eight feet onto the cruel pavement. I broke both elbows and a wrist.

My notoriety was still high enough that the next day photographers arrived to document my anguish with a pathetic bedside photo. They talked my wife Ella into holding a telephone to my ear while I acted as if I was taking a call from a well-wisher.

The wire-service photo ran in hundreds of newspapers around the country and I received a number of nice cards and supportive letters. Lest I wallow in the warmth of good wishes too long, my wife started her own collection of letters from folks who didn't think Mo Udall was the greatest thing since disposable diapers. Her basket of insults and slurs included a missive from a taxpayer in Indiana who enclosed the photo with this empathetic inscription: "You cross-eyed bastard should have broke your neck!"

On some issues the hate mail is really hateful and reveals the depth of anger, fear, racism, and paranoia to be found in this country. During the furious gun-control debate following the assassinations of Robert Kennedy and Martin Luther King, Jr., I knew that no matter what stand I took I would be hammered from both sides. So I went on the offensive with a preemptive strike designed to defuse emotions. On television I called for understanding and said I would try to listen to all sides and do what was right for my country and my conscience. But when it comes to gun control, politics is thicker than blood. For my pains I received the following:

Dear Mo,
In spite of your statement on TV that you knew that you would receive a rash of letters from "crackpots" or whatever you called us, I am writing you advising

you of my feelings on the gun legislation which will no doubt get out of committee this week.

I am going to watch your voting on the subject, and if you vote for this "pro-communist" (and I may be quoted) legislation, I will pledge my full support to defeat you in the coming election, *in spite of the fact that you are my cousin.*

Yours truly,
Robert

Robert's letter was only one of hundreds that flooded my office. One particularly vicious letter was dated June 6, 1968, the day Bobby Kennedy was shot.

My dear Mo,
The other day, I heard some of our good Morman [*sic*] boys talking about boiling the Udall boys in oil. They seemed very hostile towards you boys for something that your brother came out in the paper about letting the black minority into the priesthood of the Mormon Church. An awful disrespectful and crazy thing to do. Mo, you being raised a good Morman must know that the great Mormon Church will never bow and let the filthy gangster-ridden hands of MAD! MAD! Lyndon to even touch it.

And Mo, this for you to always remember, stop shedding your crocidile [*sic*] tears for the black Minority— at the expense of the White Majority. What they want is not "equality," but "top quality!" And anyway, you are just playing into the Communist hands with such capers, what you have to face, coming this fall is the Angry White majority.

To the Mormon boys, I suggested that they just get

you to vote "yes" on Lyndon's gun law, and that would settle your pockmarked RADICAL HIDE for all time.

Mo, you are not a "liberal," you are just a "radical."

You have been running about in evil company. Now, you may vote for this gun law—but 99% of the people of Arizona are against it. And if it wins, you will lose your freedom as well as your country. It is just for a Communist Takeover! And Mo, you may come out and work for it and vote for it. But you will become a HAS BEEN Congressman. It will ruin your whole political career. Get wise, Mo—all our communications media, radio, television, motion pictures, and the press are all owned by our enemies. And they are full of lies.

Yours for God and Country,
D. Moore, Yuma, Arizona

"For God and Country"? Sometimes those letters were too much to grin and bear.

During the Reagan years one anonymous correspondent wrote,

Udall,
You're enough to make a fellow puke. You just can't bear it that we at last have a truly decent man in the W. House. You Dems have never put anything there but SCUMBAGS!

It just kills you trash that we have a President who wants to protect us from the vipers of Central America.

You are a bastard of the first water. To hell with you libs, especially you smelly Demos.

Have a painful day,

Reagan, of course, is not universally beloved. From another citizen I received this:

Congressman Mo Udall,
Saw you on NBC-TV tonite about the strip-mining bill violations.

It was written all over your face, so why didn't you come out and say it?

THAT RONALD REAGAN OUGHT TO BE LOCKED UP!

The worst Pres. in the history of our nation. Trouble is, the bottom line is, how did we ever get him? Our system is screwed up.

Jim Carrigan

P.S. A crying shame. I weep for our country.

On a lighter note, sometimes letters propose solutions to problems that have vexed the experts. One obviously over-taxed citizen offered a novel way to raise more revenue:

Dear Congressman Udall:
I read where Congress is staying up late at night trying to find something else to regulate or tax.

Have they thought about sex?

It is a luxury; would not produce undue hardship; could be spread over a large segment of the population; would let the teenagers contribute; would give the old-sters a tax break; and is not discriminatory to race, religion, or national origin.

The Punch Line:
Getting Laughs Almost Anywhere

★ ★

Today's generation of politicians is less seasoned, more serious, richer, and less humorous. I'd say of the 435 members in the House of Representatives, only twenty-five or thirty possess oratory stimulating enough to inspire other members to interrupt a gossip session. The ability to deliver a riveting speech, rich in substance, enlivened with humor and anecdote, is a dying art in Washington today.

To be sure, there are still some politicians who excel in the use of political wit. Senator Bob Dole has a rich repertoire and the delivery of a stage-trained comic; on a good night he can keep any audience enthralled for as long as he wishes. If properly armed, Senator Ted Kennedy can delight a crowd with his sense of humor; although not a sharp extemporaneous speaker, he garners one-liners from an extensive network of gag writers and comedians. A list of other renowned orators would include perhaps two dozen politicians, among them: Republican Senator Alan Simpson of Wyoming; the Democratic Speaker of the House, Jim Wright of Texas; Representative Henry Hyde, Republican from Illinois; Democratic Representative Tom Foley of Washington; and—forever, it seems—Representative Claude Pepper, Democrat, of Florida. But for every politician who spices his message with wit, there are dozens more who drone through their ghostwritten speeches without a trace of humor or the ability to draw a flicker of a smile from the most sympathetic audience.

Politicians who use humor effectively are a declining breed. Television's infatuation with fluff and the pithy ten-second sound bite, the frenetic pace of high-tech (and passive) modern life, and the near-total dependence of most politicians on speech writers seem to be the prime culprits for this decline.

I sometimes worry that the vaunted American tradition of political humor has lost its vitality; a venerable heritage that unites George Washington, Abe Lincoln, Will Rogers, even Ronald Reagan, is in danger of withering away. And I'm mystified by this, especially so because experience suggests that humor is possibly the most potent tool a politician can wield. Since any speech benefits from the addition of a few amusing stories or relevant anecdotes, it seems to me that any politician who fails to use humor is simply missing the boat.

"Humor is essential to prevent audiences from adopting the MEGO [My Eyes Glaze Over] look," reminds Representative Pat Schroeder of Colorado, one of a handful of congresswomen who use it effectively. "Why, sometimes even my worst enemies will laugh when I tell a good joke."

If humor *is* such a valuable tool, why are so many politicians and others reluctant to employ it? The three most common reservations I've heard expressed are:

★ "Telling jokes detracts from the 'serious' business of my work."

★ "I just can't tell a joke."

★ "I don't know any funny stories and I couldn't write one if my life depended on it."

To the first objection I say, Nonsense! A speaker can be both humorous *and* substantive; in fact, you can make a strong case that if you're the former, you're more likely to be the latter. Look at Abe Lincoln, John Kennedy, Jim Wright, Bob Dole, Adlai Stevenson, Gene McCarthy—the list could go on.

As for not being able to tell a joke, you (and here I'm speaking of anyone who speaks in public) don't have to be a professional comedian to use humor effectively. With a little practice almost anyone can learn to tell a decent joke, deliver a punchy speech.

The third reservation—not knowing any jokes—can be rectified simply by keeping your eyes and ears open. Life is full of humorous moments—too many, some say—if we have the will to notice. (As for actually *writing* jokes, I've only thought up a small percentage of the thousands I've told and often wonder, Where *do* my jokes come from? After the recent "Baby M" custody case, the Pope announced that surrogate motherhood ran counter to the precepts of the Church. "But what about Mary, mother of Jesus?" a wag soon asked. "Wasn't she a surrogate?" It's next to impossible to trace the origin of this (or any other) joke; somebody spawned it but only God knows whom. Another case of immaculate conception.

DON'T BE AFRAID TO STEAL GOOD JOKES

Jokes are public, not private property, and you can't be prosecuted for borrowing them. Like most political humorists, Mark Shields admits to having done his share of pilferage. "Jokes have a copyright of about twelve hours," he says. Columnist Art Buchwald propounds "Buchwald's Rule": the first two times you use a joke, give your source credit. From then on, to hell with it! Be shameless—claim it as your own. After all, your source undoubtedly stole it from somebody else. (This is why at a luncheon or dinner you should always volunteer to speak first—particularly in Washington, where jokes circulate at the speed of light. That way you don't run the risk of someone else stealing your thunder.)

The truth is, there is very little new political humor. A good story is timeless, and most political jokes are recycled tales. You could take Abe Lincoln's joke book, substitute autos or airplanes for horses and carriages, change time and place, and end up with a witty, timely joke.

PRACTICE YOUR PHRASING, DELIVERY, AND TIMING

Anyone who has ever had the task of "being funny" at a cocktail party or benefit luncheon knows the perils, the pains, the hard work that humor, stand-up or otherwise, entails. Worse is the fear of the microphone. Just remember that there are few "natural" comedians; being funny isn't some mysterious, arcane black art like, say, defrosting a turkey in a microwave. Being humorous is a *skill,* which you can learn and develop through practice.

Delivery—by which I mean phrasing, body language, timing, and inflection—is about three-fourths of the art. Politician A can tell a story and roll them in the aisles; pol B can tell the same story and bomb out. The late senator Henry "Scoop" Jackson appreciated a joke, even when he was the target, but was absolutely hapless when it came to telling one. Jackson once attended a luncheon where the emcee told a story about President Nixon returning to the White House after his resignation. Entering the Oval Office, he stumbled and bumped into President Gerry Ford. "Oh, *pardon* me, Gerry," Nixon said. "I already did, Dick," Ford replied.

The next night Jackson ventured to tell the same anecdote. Unfortunately, when he delivered the punch line he had Nixon saying, "*Excuse* me, Gerry," and Ford replying, "I already did, Dick." Nobody got the joke, and, of course, nobody laughed.

192

But let's not pick on Scoop—the fact is, most people are inept when it comes to cracking a joke. It took a whole galaxy of gag writers to prepare a funny speech John Glenn gave one year at the Washington press corps's Gridiron dinner. By the end of the evening the writers were joking that "it took more people to get John Glenn up onstage than it did to get him to the moon."

A gag writer might spend an hour getting a joke's phrasing just right. But when it comes to *telling* the joke, timing becomes critical. Telling a joke is like dancing a waltz—you must have a feel for the tempo. Inexperienced humorists sometimes make the mistake of rushing to the punch line. Unfortunately, this approach prevents the audience's anticipation from ripening; the joke may get a laugh, but it will be an abbreviated one. Conversely, some speakers telegraph the punch line with exaggerated body language, as if to say, "Here it comes, folks. Get ready to laugh." This, too, detracts from an anecdote's punch. Another egregious mistake is to begin chortling *before* the punch line is delivered. From the audience's point of view, premature chuckling is anything but laughable.

Jack Benny may have been the unequaled master of timing. Remember his classic story about the mugger who corners him in the alley, puts a gun to his head, and says, "Your money or your life"? Benny, a legendary penny-pincher, is silent for thirty seconds, until the robber gets irritated and repeats, "Your money or your life!" After another brief pause, Benny says, "I'm thinking." What makes this joke work isn't dialogue—it's *timing*.

KNOW YOUR AUDIENCE

Every audience is different, and what will carry the crowd at one setting, won't at another. A speaker always has to

193

tailor his anecdotes to suit his listeners: a joke that is appropriate at a rodeo in Arizona might not be at a black-tie dinner in Washington. For example, portable toilets were an issue during Wyoming Senator Malcolm Wallop's first campaign; and "john" jokes drew laughs in his home state. But the same jokes were considered tasteless when Wallop told them to a mixed audience in Washington. Be careful not to commit gaffes in pursuit of laughs.

Another thing to bear in mind: Occasionally, you will encounter individuals and crowds who won't laugh at *anything*. How these dour people survive the vicissitudes of daily life is beyond me, but I do my utmost to avoid them. (I still shudder when I recall the time I spoke to an audience of Party officials in Siberia. The crowd—which seemed to view laughter as a subversive act—sat stonefaced as I bombarded them with a number of my best jibes, including one from Khrushchev: "Politicians are all alike. They'll promise to build a bridge even where there's no river.") When I *do* draw a sullen crowd, I try to keep in mind the old Texas adage: "If you don't strike oil in the first few minutes, stop boring."

Avoid Smug Jokes—Tell Self-deprecating Ones

Nobody likes a smug politician. Jimmy Carter sometimes made the mistake of aiming his best zingers at the press— "I'm not going to say anything terribly important tonight, so you can all put away your crayons"—rather than at himself. Carter failed to understand the first rule of political humor. By contrast, Ronald Reagan is a master of the self-deprecating joke. With volumes of anecdotes about his age and selective memory, he can get a laugh out of any crowd. My experience has been that putting myself down—humility is attractive—

is the best kind of humor: it creates empathy, humanizes any message, and puts people at ease. Self-deprecating jokes have the added benefit of inoculating one against egomania. Whenever my ego threatens to get overblown, I puncture it with a story from the early stages of my 1976 presidential campaign such as this one: I was in New Hampshire, thousands of miles from home, with my car stuck in the snow. My advance woman urged me to shake a few hands in a nearby barbershop. I stuck my head in the door and blurted, "Mo Udall, I'm running for president!"

The barber replied, "Yeah, I know. We were laughing about it just this morning."

In the same vein, if the press or your opponents are telling a joke *on* you, the best thing to do is to *appropriate* it and tell it on yourself. A couple of years ago, George Bush attended a spate of funerals for foreign dignitaries. People soon began describing his motto as "You die, we fly." Instead of getting huffy, Bush appropriated the joke, told it wherever he went, and invariably got an appreciative laugh.

Self-effacing humor can also be the best way for a politician to deal with any delicate subject. One respected member of the House is gay, and occasionally he'll be asked, "Congressman, are you *still* a practicing homosexual?" His stock response is, "*Practicing?* No, I don't need to practice—I've been doing it long enough."

AVOID RACIST AND ETHNIC JOKES

Sacred cows may make great hamburgers, but it's only common sense for a public servant to avoid jokes with ethnic or racist overtones. Nonetheless, I'm continually amazed at the number of politicians who land in hot water for telling a joke based on tired ethnic stereotypes. (Remember Earl Butz? The secretary of agriculture who lost his job for telling a racist joke about blacks and watermelons?) Haven't these people gotten the message? Don't they understand that humor can wound as well as enhance any career?

"With all of today's caucuses and groups, you're not permitted to be nearly as ethnic in your humor," says Mark Shields. "There are no Pedro, Pat, or Manny stories being told. You *can* make fun of your own group, but you can't make fun of anybody else's. The one group anyone can make fun of is WASPs. They're fair game. You can try, 'Quiche is their idea of soul food' anytime. Remember, there is no Episcopalian Antidefamation League. I've checked."

Unless you're very sure of your audience, your standing in their eyes, and your material, it's best to avoid all ethnic jokes. If you do attempt an ethnic joke make sure it is empathetic, not based on a painful stereotype. For example, I occasionally tell the story that my World War II roommate and 1976 campaign treasurer, Stanley Kurz, once offered to make me "an honorary Jew." Flattered, I asked what were the perks, the benefits, to which he replied, "Two thousand years of persecution—retroactive."

SEXIST JOKES ARE TABOO, TOO

Women voters provided the margin of victory in half a dozen Senate races in 1986; they are the reason the Democrats control the Senate today. Obviously, no politician can afford to offend his female constituents with blatantly sexist jokes. Being of an older, less enlightened generation, it's sometimes hard for me to tell whether a joke is sexist or not. But many jokes men tell clearly are. Here's an example of the kind of joke that is now taboo: At the unveiling of a statue honoring Jake Potofsky of the Amalgamated Clothing Workers, an attractive, well-endowed woman rushed up to Potofsky and said, "Oh, Mr. Potofsky, I've come a hundred miles to see your bust unveiled."

"Madam," replied Jake, a male chauvinist if there ever was one, "Believe me, I'd gladly do the same for you."

Recently, Senator Pete Domenici got into trouble for joking, "I'm blessed with the talent of . . . whipping the electorate to a frenzy. Just like with the singer Tom Jones, women often throw their panties at me when I speak. It happened again just yesterday. I just don't know what got into Senator [Barbara] Mikulski." This brought down the house, but it also brought down the wrath of Mikulski. Ironically, Domenici had reservations about this joke when he first heard it, but went ahead when reassured that "Mikulski has a great sense of humor." The moral is: when in doubt, don't.

Of course, not all sexual jokes are *sexist;* there are some you can tell that won't get you branded as an M.C.P. Secretary of the Treasury Jim Baker stole the show at the Gridiron one year with this entry:

"I had a terrible dream last night: I dreamed that the three most powerful Americans—the president, the Speaker of the House, and the chairman of the Federal Reserve—suddenly passed away. All three appeared in St. Peter's waiting room.

"A voice came over the intercom telling the president to go to Room One. He went inside and found himself with a huge gorilla. The voice then said, 'Ronald Reagan, you have sinned, and you must spend eternity with this gorilla.'

"The voice over the intercom then sent Tip O'Neill to Room Two, where the speaker found a mad dog. 'Mr. Speaker,' the voice on the intercom said, 'you have sinned and must spend eternity with this mad dog.'

"Then the voice sent Paul Volcker to Room Three. He went in, and to his surprise he found himself with Bo Derek.

Then the voice came over the intercom and said, 'Bo Derek, you have sinned. . . .' "

WHENEVER POSSIBLE, USE TOPICAL JOKES

Jokes are like seafood: the fresher, the better. "A joke *cannot* be too topical," says Mark Shields. "If you make a reference to something that happened between the salad and the soup, it works. There is no one dining out today on great Jim Watt stories. Donald Regan stories are long gone, too." Good one-liners are current and topical, and if they are really good, they wear out fast.

LAST BUT NOT LEAST, BE GENTLE

Effective humor is never cruel, ridiculing, or belittling. Ideally, it should be gentle, nudging at a weakness rather than exploiting a glaring personal shortcoming. The best jokes are those that make all of us laugh *together* at the vagaries of life or the human condition—not at some ethnic group or someone's religious beliefs.

In early 1987, at the height of the Iran-contra affair, Ronald Reagan's popularity sank to a new low. At the Gridiron dinner, Speaker of the House Jim Wright joked, "For six years, we went around saying Ronald Reagan didn't know what was going on. And now, when he says the same thing about himself, we say he's lying." This joke is funny, but I like it because it's *generous*—its main target is Reagan's fickle critics, rather than the embattled president himself. Or is it?

Told well, the right joke can make everyone in the audience feel a little better about mankind, and a little closer to one another, and closer to the speaker. That's why humor is still one of the healthiest exercises of a democracy—also why I've done what I can to remind you of the rich heritage of American political humor. I've even included a selection of jokes and short tales in this chapter. These are drawn from several large black notebooks I've been toting around for thirty-five years.

A reminder: The first task for all of us, whether delivering a commencement address or a toast at your daughter's wedding, is to practice—and then to speak without notes, if possible. The appropriate opening joke will go a long way in overcoming your fear and winning your audience. Feel free to incorporate the jokes I've listed on the following pages. These can be dusted off and made appropriate for almost any occasion by changing the names and places and by altering the opening lines. Keep it short and make it funny.

Aging and Death

An old man was interviewed by a newspaper reporter on his one hundredth birthday. "To what do you attribute your longevity?" asked the reporter.

The centenarian thought for a moment and began ticking off items on his fingers: "I never smoked, I never drank liquor, I never overate, and I always rise at six in the morning."

"I have an uncle who did all those same things, yet he only lived to be sixty," the reporter said. "How do you account for that?"

"Well," said the old man, "he just didn't keep it up long enough."

Following a long and eloquent sermon on the importance of fellowship and getting along with one's neighbors, the preacher asked the congregation, "Is there anyone present who has led such a life that he does not now have any enemies?"

An old man stood up and said, "Right here, parson."

"Congratulations," said the preacher. "Please tell the congregation how you did it."

The old man looked around the room, winked, and said, "I outlived the bastards!"

Every losing politician should heed the words of an old hillbilly often quoted by former vice president Alben Barkley. Uncle Zeke was renowned for his wisdom. When asked why he was so wise, he said, "Waal, I've got good judgment. Good judgment comes from experience; and experience . . . waal, that comes from bad judgment."

Senator Theodore Green, who served in the Senate until his nineties, always carried a little black date book. At one Washington party a lady saw the senator put on his spectacles and begin to study the little black book.

"Senator, can I help you find something?" she asked.

"No, this is only my engagement book," the senator said.

"Oh, I imagine you are trying to see which party you are attending tomorrow?"

"No," the senator replied, "I am trying to find out where I am tonight."

Here's a useful piece of graffiti that was found recently in southern California: "Death's the greatest kick of all; that's why they save it till last."

During a hotly contested Democratic caucus in New Jersey, several candidates were vying for the party's nomination for a congressional seat. All of the eager aspirants were of tender years, save one old bull. During his moving plea for the nomination, the elderly candidate boasted of his youthful vigor and proclaimed that he would be as energetic a campaigner as any of his younger foes.

After he had finished and hobbled back to his seat, one of the delegates turned to his neighbor and said, "He may still have his youth, but we've got to find someone who hasn't had it quite so long."

There is an engaging legend throughout the land that advancing years mellow one and somehow bring out the kindliest impulses of one's nature; that the countryside swarms with repentant scrooges.

My own observation has been that when a bastard grows old . . . he simply becomes an old bastard.

A reporter was interviewing an old senator: "Well, sir, I guess you've seen a lot of changes in your time in Washington."

"Yes, son, I have. And I have been against every damned one of them."

"The trouble with our time," said one old senator to another, "is that the future is not what it used to be."

The recent debate over whether the Democratic party needs to change its stripes reminds me of this story: In Minnesota, a family of Scandinavian heritage was mourning their recently deceased patriarch. To their chagrin, they discovered that they had no recent photograph to remember him by, so they asked a local artist to paint a posthumous portrait. The family members described the deceased in great detail—his habits, his physical makeup, his height, the color of his hair and eyes.

A month later the portrait was finished, and the family

201

gathered for the unveiling. The cover was removed and one of the man's sons walked up to the painting and looked at it closely, finally kneeling to get a different perspective. The nervous artist finally said, "Ole, what do you think? Isn't that a good likeness of your father?"

Ole replied, "Yah, suure. I guess that's the old man all right, but my, how he has changed."

Death, it has been said, is nature's way of telling us to slow down.

Most of us know Gertrude Stein's final line spoken to her friend Alice B. Toklas, but Lord Palmerston's, as he lay dying, is even better: "Die, my dear Doctor? That's the last thing I shall do."

At an Arizona–Arizona State football game there wasn't a ticket available for weeks. On the forty-five-yard line a fan sat with an empty seat next to him. A spectator asked the man if he knew who owned the seat. "Yes, I do," the fan replied sadly.

"Then why isn't it being used on the day of the biggest game of the year?" the spectator asked.

Mournfully, the man said, "Well, my wife and I have season tickets and we always come together. But last Friday she died."

"Oh, I'm sorry to hear that," the spectator said. "But why didn't you give her ticket to one of your children?"

"Oh, I couldn't do that. They're all at the funeral."

A candidate for governor of Arizona was campaigning in the Gila Valley. Early in the morning he climbed through a fence to talk to a baling crew. Of one young man he asked, "What's your name?"

"Hoopes, sir," the young man replied.

"Are you by chance related to my very good friend, Gerald Hoopes?"

"Yes, sir, he's my father."

"Well," said the candidate, "how is he?"

"He's been dead for five years."

Taken aback, the politician said, "Well, I'm sorry to hear that. But please give my best regards to your mother." The young man promised to do so.

About ten hours later, the politician wearily headed back down the valley. He stopped for gas and, lo and behold, there was the same baling crew—only the politician didn't recognize them. He glad-handed his way over to the same young man.

"Hello, I'm running for governor. What's your name?"

"Hoopes, sir."

"Are you related to my old friend Gerald Hoopes?"

"Yes," said the young man, his eyes rolling. "He's my father."

"Well, he's a great man, a good friend of mine. How is he?"

"Still dead."

As Lincoln prepared to leave the White House to travel to Gettysburg to deliver what turned out to be a historic speech, he paused to look over a fresh report from one of his generals. One of his assistants rushed in and hurried him out the door, insisting that there was no time to lose. Lincoln said he felt like the man in Illinois who was going to be hanged and as he passed down the road on the way to the gallows, the crowd kept surging into his way and blocking his passage. The condemned man at last called out, "Boys, you needn't be in such a hurry . . . there won't be any fun until I get there."

203

An old man lay on his deathbed as his minister gave him the last rites. "Will you accept Jesus as your savior and renounce the devil?" said the minister. There was a long pause, then the man said, "Reverend, I'm in no position to offend anyone."

When Thad Stevens was gravely ill, a friend visited him and said, "Thad, you look well—your appearance is good." Stevens smiled weakly, "Ah, John," he replied, "it's not my appearance that concerns me now, but rather my disappearance."

When Sir Winston Churchill was asked on his seventy-fifth birthday if he had any fear of death, he replied, "I am ready to meet my Maker. . . . Whether my Maker is prepared for the great ordeal of meeting me is another matter."

Churchill was not above insulting his foes abroad. He once managed to assail both Lenin and Stalin in the same breath, saying, "The Russian people's worst misfortune was Lenin's birth, their next worst, his death."

Mark Twain read the obituary pages and found that an old adversary had passed on. A few days later he was asked if he had attended the funeral. "No," he said, "but I did send a message of approval."

A woman whose husband had deserted her and gone to Brazil learned that he had died and left her a considerable sum in insurance. Soon afterward, a cable arrived asking what to do with the remains. She sent back a cable saying: "Embalm, cremate, and bury in steel box . . . take no chances."

A former governor of Louisiana tells a story of a man who made a great deal of money in New York and resided there for many years. During that time he bought a burial plot in a New York cemetery. Later, he retired and moved to Florida, and after several years, he bought a burial plot there. A few months later he became gravely ill. His relatives gathered at his bedside to offer their farewells. In a very delicate manner one of them asked, "Sir, we think that you will be with us for a while, but, just in case, do you want to be buried in the cemetery in New York or in the burial plot you own here in Florida?"

The sick man raised his head and said, "Surprise me."

An Arkansas coroner's jury was unable to reach a verdict as to the cause of death of a recently deceased farmer. They finally compromised and returned a verdict that read: "We find the deceased came to his death on the night of March 2 by reason of an Act of God—under very suspicious circumstances."

W. C. Fields was in a hospital. He was visited by his Uncle Claude, who was surprised to find W. C. reading the Bible. He inquired if the actor had turned over a new leaf and was looking for comfort and instruction from the good book.

Replied Fields, "Look, Uncle Claude, with my age, my illness, and my conduct, I'm just looking for loopholes."

FDR told the story of a Wall Street tycoon, an outspoken enemy of Roosevelt's, who would buy the newspaper each morning, look at the front page, curse, and throw the unread newspaper in the trash can. One day, the newsstand proprietor asked the tycoon why he bought a paper, glanced at it, and then threw it away. "I'm looking for an obituary," he replied.

"But sir, you don't find obituaries on the front page, they are toward the back."

"Son," said the millionaire, "believe me, the obituary I'm looking for will be on the front page."

At a time of grave crisis during the Civil War, Abe Lincoln was awakened late one night by an opportunist who reported that the head of customs had just died.

"Mr. President, would it be all right if I took his place?"

"Well," said Lincoln, "if it's all right with the undertaker, it's all right with me."

Animals and Others

Whenever I hear someone say that American businesses need to be "more competitive," I think of this story: Attempting to increase productivity in the henhouse, the rooster escorted his hens to an ostrich egg and said, "I do not criticize; I do not disparage; I merely bring to your attention what has been done by others."

During my career, my opponents have often asked me to participate in a "political compromise." I tell them, "The lion and the lamb can lie down together . . . but the lamb won't get much sleep."

The balky process of congressional reform brings to mind the time a minister sold a mule to a neighboring farmer. Before handing over the reins, the minister told the farmer that the mule had a gentle soul and should be treated with kindness.

Some days later the minister was passing the farmer's field and saw the farmer standing in front of the immobile mule. The farmer told the minister that the mule wouldn't work.

"Let me show you how to get him going," said the minister. He seized a nearby two-by-four and smote the mule between the eyes, whereupon he raised up and began to pull the plow.

"I thought you said to treat him kindly," said the farmer.

"Yes," said the minister. "But first you have to get his attention."

Senator Dale Bumpers once complained that the U.S. Senate wasted an exorbitant amount of time during its prolonged debates. He recalled the politician who stopped at a farmhouse and asked the farmer to identify the scrawny animals out front.

"Those are razorback hogs," the farmer replied.

"How long does it take to get them up to size?" the politician asked.

"About three years," said the farmer.

"That's an awful long time, isn't it?"

The farmer thought about it a minute, and said, "What's time to a hog?"

An old politician may forgive, but he never forgets. It's like the story of the fellow who was bitten by a rabid dog. The victim rushed to the hospital and called for his doctor. As the doctor entered the emergency room he saw his patient feverishly writing on a legal pad. The doctor examined him and said he didn't think the injury would prove fatal, and that there was no need for a will.

"Oh, this isn't a will, Doc, I'm just making out a list of people I want to bite."

A politician often finds himself in a political dilemma, torn between two choices. On one such occasion I said I felt like a dog in heat: You can't really win—if you run fast, they come up and bite you in the ass; and if you slow down, you get screwed.

The Reagan budget deficits have brought us into an era of "diminished expectations." A wealthy man was going away for a month and asked a neighboring farmer how much he would charge to board his horse. The farmer said it would cost fifty dollars a month and he would keep the manure. The rich man thought that was a bit steep, so he went to the next farm. There he was told that the fee would be forty dollars a month and "we keep the manure." Noting a downward trend, the rich man drove another mile to an old ramshackle house. There he was told that the monthly fee would be five dollars. After agreeing to the terms, the wealthy man said that all the other farmers were demanding to keep the manure. "Why didn't you insist on such a stipulation?" he asked.

"Well, mister, at five dollars a month, there ain't going to be much manure."

Choices

Given the vilification that comes with it, you'd think congressional service would be one of the least sought-after professions; nonetheless, there is never a shortage of candidates ready and willing to spend their own money in pursuit of a congressional seat. A Capitol Hill veteran explained this phenomenon by recounting Mark Twain's story about the young cowboy who on each monthly payday rode into town and lost his wages playing poker.

After months of watching him lose, a sympathetic bartender took the young cowboy aside and told him that the game was as crooked as a dog's hind leg—the cards were marked and the dealer had aces up his sleeve. Shortly thereafter, the bartender saw the cowboy back in the game. He sent one of his barmaids over to ask the cowboy why he didn't believe him.

"I do believe him."

"Then why are you back playing poker?"

"It's the only game in town."

And there is always the choice of not attending a dramatic performance that you've already experienced. Emerging from the weight of Wagner's *Parsifal* one night, Noel Coward was heard to remark, "Who says opera isn't what it used to be? That's the trouble, it is what it used to be."

Soon after the airplane took off the stewardess came down the aisle with a tray of complimentary drinks. A businessman asked for a scotch and water. His seatmate twice declined the stewardess's offer and when, after she served the businessman his drink, she persisted in asking him if he would like a cocktail, he refused again, saying, "I'm a minister of the gospel and I would rather commit adultery than have a drink."

The businessman handed his glass back to the flight attendant and said, "Oh, I didn't know we had a choice."

At a social engagement, Churchill's bitter foe, the American-born Lady Astor, reacted to a Churchillian aside by saying, "If you were my husband, I would put poison in your coffee." He replied, "Madam, if I were your husband, I'd drink it."

A senator up for reelection was asked by a reporter how he felt about the military-industrial complex. "I think I'm undecided—but I'm not sure," the senator replied.

His inquisitor said, "Senator, I want to congratulate you on the straightforward manner in which you dodged my question."

It was Dante who said, "The hottest places in hell are reserved for those who, in a time of great moral crisis, maintain their neutrality."

A minister put out the following message on the sign in front of his church: "If you are tired of sin—come in!" Someone wrote underneath: "If not, call 987–6543."

The minister was giving his annual hellfire-and-brimstone, damnation and Judgment Day sermon. He said, "Brothers

and Sisters, on this terrible Judgment Day there will be lightning and thunder and terrible storms. On this Judgment Day,
there will be weeping and wailing and you are all going to
gnash your teeth."

The lady in the front row said, "But, Reverend, I ain't
got no teeth."

He replied, "Madam, on the great Judgment Day, teeth
will be provided."

Senator Zebulon B. Vance was once asked where he stood
on prohibition. "I will reply to the gentleman's request by
saying that my head is roughly inclined to the great policy
of prohibition, but my stomach yearns the other way. I may
say, therefore, I truthfully declare myself divided on the issue."

In answering a questionnaire asking, "What is the greatest
public problem—ignorance or apathy?" one respondent
wrote: "I don't know and I don't care."

The Irish, Westerners, and Other Ethnics

> God created the Irish, the perfect manifestation of the
> human species, and then he created whiskey.
> —*Tip O'Neill*

Although I've cautioned readers on the dangers of using sexual
innuendo or ethnicity—and that means race, color, creed—
as a basis for jokes and stories, you'll see that I'm ignoring
my own advice in this section. Many speakers cannot resist
the temptation. Here are a few harmless examples that should
infuriate just about everyone.

As for westerners: Well, I guess most of us are considered
somewhat exotic by easterners.

Lord Chesterfield once described Ireland as a place where
God had done so much—and man so little. But it would be

hard to underestimate the contribution the Irish have made to the American heritage of political humor. Jokes about Irish politicians are one of the richest veins a political humorist can mine; after two hundred years, the stereotype of the Irish as a hard-drinking, song-singing, somewhat irresponsible lot eminently qualified for public office has taken on near-mythical proportions. If my experience is any guide, this stereotype, much more than most, is pretty close to the mark.

On his deathbed another old Irish pol confessed, "Half the lies told about me are not true."

After my close friend Representative James McNulty of Bisbee, Arizona, lost his reelection bid, he held a wake. At the wake McNulty told the story of an eighty-year-old Irishman who during his lifetime had witnessed a long and sad list of invasions, famines, and revolts plague his country. "Ah, yes, we Irish have lost all the wars," the old man lamented, "but we have all the good songs."

Irish priests and Notre Dame football provide a font of grand stories. One of my favorites concerns a parish priest who had a habit of preaching hellfire-and-brimstone sermons to his congregation whenever Notre Dame suffered a particularly galling defeat the previous Saturday. On this particular Sunday the good father pounded the pulpit and grew red in the face as he warned his quivering congregation that the day of retribution was near and that their preparations were glaringly deficient.

"All of you who want to go to heaven," he thundered at the wide-eyed parishioners, "stand up!"

Everybody in the church stood. Except for Murphy.

"Everyone who wants to go to hell," he shouted, glaring at Murphy, "Stand up!"

Only Murphy rose. "And so it is to hell that you want to go, is it, Mr. Murphy?" "No, father," said Murphy. "I just didn't want to see you standing up there all by yerself."

During that era when Tammany Hall had its greatest influence in New York City politics, there was a ward boss by the name of "Big Tim" Sullivan. Big Tim was built like a prize-fighter; his booming voice made men quake and women swoon. One election night Big Tim won reelection by a vote of 8,571 to 2. His supporters were joyful at Big Tim's over-whelming victory, and expected him to share their glee. Instead, when they arrived at his house they found him staring in a sullen rage at the tally sheets. Asked why he was so glum, Big Tim explained, "It was last week that Joe Doyle come to me to say that the fellow running on the Republican ticket was a relative of his wife's and that the women in the family were at him hot and heavy to vote for the missus's kinfolk.

"In the interest of peace and harmony in the home, I told Joe to go ahead and vote Republican. But what I want to know now is," Big Tim shouted, slamming his fist on the table, "Who was the *other* son of a bitch who voted Republican without my permission!"

During his 1904 presidential campaign, Teddy Roosevelt made a whistle-stop train trip. During the course of one impassioned speech, the president was interrupted when a man emerged from a nearby saloon and cried out, "I'm a Dimmycrat! I'm a Dimmycrat!"

Exasperated, Roosevelt addressed the heckler. "Why, sir, are you a Democrat?" "Because me grandfather was a Dimmycrat, and me father was a Dimmycrat, and I'm a Dimmycrat," the heckler retorted.

Sarcastically, Teddy rejoined, "My friend, suppose your

grandfather was a jackass, and your father had been a jackass?
What would you be?"

Instantly the Irishman replied, "A Republican."

The famed mayor of New York City, Jimmy Walker, who
was known for being quick-witted, was once asked by then-
governor of New York Franklin Delano Roosevelt, "Why
is it that the Irish always answer a question with a question?"

"Do we now?" responded Hizzoner.

Another legendary Irish-American mayor, James Michael
Curley of Boston, had a controversial career. After a particularly vicious attack on him, the great pol replied, "Ah, it's
all a part of the great game of politics, where the epithets
are not to be taken too seriously."

A noble view did not prevent Curley from giving as good
as he got, especially if his opponent was a fellow Irishman
and member of the Roman Catholic Church. In one election,
Curley noted that his opponent, Murphy, had recently moved
to a house adjacent to a Protestant church. Though Murphy
was known to be a devout Catholic, Curley charged that
the real motivation for the move was so that he wouldn't
have to walk so far to worship. While poor Murphy was
forced to spend valuable time denying the charge, Curley
was not idle. As Murphy attempted to set the record straight,
the mayor reported that he had been told by a counterman
at Thompson's Saloon, a notoriously honest fellow, that Murphy had been seen ordering a rare roast beef sandwich on
Friday last.

"Whilst I," said the outraged Curley, "was at St. Mary's
walking the Stations of the Cross."

Many years ago Arizona had a noteworthy Irish politician
named William "Buckey" O'Neill. O'Neill decided to make

candor the focus of his first campaign, and his declaration of candidacy should be enshrined in the political hall of fame, under the category of "frankness above and beyond the call of duty."

"I announce for this office entirely on my own responsibility," O'Neill stated. "There has been no 'anxious public' urging me to do so; there has been no solicitation of friends; nor have the 'wishes of many prominent citizens' made the slightest effort to bluff me into doing it.

"To be frank, it is not a case where the office is wearing itself out hunting the man. Here it is the man wearing himself out for the office, and for the simple reason that it is a soft berth with a salary of two thousand dollars per annum attached.

"As for my 'special qualifications,' the truth is, I don't have any. Although I have no particular advantage over 75 percent of my fellow citizens in the county, I do believe that I am fully competent to discharge all the duties incident to the office—if I am elected.

"If you coincide in this opinion support me if you see fit. If you do not, you will by no means jeopardize the safety of the universe by defeating me."

He was dead right: After Buckey was trounced, the universe went on its way unimpeded.

A candidate was visiting the Indian reservation, seeking votes, and was given permission to speak before the tribe.

"If elected," he cried, "I'll get schools and hospitals for the Indians."

"Goomwah!" shouted the crowd.

"You'll get gas heat in every teepee."

Again the crowd shouted, "Goomwah!"

After the speech, the chief said to him, "You're a good friend of the Indians. Please come into the corral so we can present you with a fine pony. But be careful and don't step in the goomwah."

When I first became chairman of the Interior Committee, an Irish colleague came up to me in the cloakroom and said, "There is an old Irish legend that when an infant is placed in his cradle immediately after birth, an angel of the Lord hovers over him and kisses him. If the angel kisses him on the forehead, the child will grow up to be a great thinker or philosopher; if the kiss is on the throat, a great singer or orator; if on the heart, a great humanitarian.

"The angel has kissed you in several places," my friend concluded, "including one which will make you a great chairman."

The recent controversy over the 1987 immigration bill brings to mind the time a wise old Indian chief came to Washington, D.C., to visit President Truman. After a polite conversation the Indian gave some parting advice to the president: "Watch your immigration laws very carefully—we got careless with ours, and look what happened."

Indians often have to put up with the cultural intolerance of their neighbors. Arizona senator Carl Hayden, whose political career began when he won a race for sheriff, told of the time that a group of righteous churchwomen came to him to complain about an old chief who lived outside town with three wives. The women demanded Hayden do something about it. Hayden saddled a horse and rode out to see the chief. When he arrived, and had greeted the chief, he explained, "Under the white man's law, you can only have one wife. Decide which wife you want, and tell the other two they will have to go."

The chief sat silent for a moment, then grunted, "You tell 'em."

Hayden, knowing he was whipped, climbed back on his horse and rode home.

Anxious to know the future, PLO leader Yasir Arafat goes to visit a fortune-teller. She looks at the lines in his hand and says, "I see many things in your future."

"Tell me one," Arafat prompts.

"I see that you will die on a Jewish holiday," the fortune-teller replies.

"That's very interesting," Arafat replies. "But there are many Jewish holidays. On which *one* will I die?"

"It does not matter," the lady says. "Any day you die will be a Jewish holiday."

Barry Goldwater's father was Jewish, but he married a gentile, and Barry himself was raised as an Episcopalian. During the early stages of the 1964 presidential campaign, when it looked as if Barry might defeat Lyndon Johnson, the journalist Harry Golden quipped, "Somehow I always knew that our first Jewish president would be an Episcopalian."

Barry Goldwater tells about his brother, Bob, an excellent golfer who went back to Westchester County, New York, to play in a tournament at one of the stuffy country clubs. There was a sign that read GENTILES ONLY.

When Bob Goldwater took to the practice area the day of the tournament, the manager came running out very embarrassed and, pointing to the sign, said, "Mr. Goldwater, I'm afraid you won't be able to play here on account of our rules."

"That's all right; I'll only play nine holes; my mother was Episcopalian."

I've always been fond of a sign posted above an old saloon's bar in Tombstone, Arizona: "I ain't what I oughta be; I ain't what I'm gonna be; but I ain't what I was."

There are a few of my favorite grave markers in Boot Hill Cemetery in Tombstone, Arizona, which I represented for several years. Among them, that of a well-known hypochondriac: "I told you I was sick." One that Harry Truman used: "Johnson—he done his damndest." One that read: "Hung by mistake." And,

> Here Lies Les Moore
> Four slugs from a .44
> No Les no more . . .

Westerners have a proud tradition of loyalty to friends. There is an ancient story about the old cowpuncher who was asked by an easterner visiting the dude ranch if there were any rattlesnakes around.

"Lots of them," the cowpoke said.

"Well," persisted the easterner, "What do you do if one bites you on the arm?"

The cattleman replied that you apply a tourniquet, cut the area of the bite open with a knife, and suck out the poison.

"And what do you do if a snake bites you in the leg?"

The cattleman again replied that you apply a tourniquet, cut the area of the bite open with a knife, and suck out the poison.

"What if the snake were to bite you where you sit down?"

Said the cowboy, "Well, that's when you find out who your friends are."

217

When Margaret Heckler was unceremoniously dumped out of the Reagan cabinet so that she could be "promoted" to the ambassadorship of Ireland, I told this joke:

A prospector came down out of the mountains pulling a burro behind him. Reaching town, he tied his burro up in front of the local saloon. A drunk cowboy came stumbling out of the door, sized up the prospector, and, pulling out a six-gun, said, "Mr. Miner, I want to see you dance." Bang, bang, bang! the cowboy fired off three rounds near the miner's feet. The cowboy enjoyed the spectacle so much he fired off three more shots, then stopped to reload. The next thing he knew the miner was holding a shotgun an inch from his nose.

"Hey, Mr. Cowboy," said the miner, "have you ever kissed a burro's ass?"

The cowboy looked at the miner, then at the burro, and said, "No, sir, but I've always wanted to."

Lawyers

Many—some say, too many—politicians are lawyers. It's not surprising, therefore, that jokes about lawyers, justice, and the legal process are often heard in politics. Here's a sample:

During his first campaign for the House, Bill Hungate was told that to carry a certain county he needed to be endorsed by an influential elderly editor. Hungate went to see the editor and spent about an hour with him, doing his best to charm the old gent.

At the close of their meeting, the editor said, "Son, I like you and I think we're going to endorse you, but one thing first—I hope you're not one of those god-damned lawyers."

Hungate hesitated for a moment and then said, "Well, sir, yes, I am. But if it helps, I'm not much of one."

The judge addressed the court: "Gentlemen, before the trial begins, I want to make a statement. Yesterday, the plaintiff's attorney came to my office and left me $5,000. This morning, the attorney for the defendant came to my chambers and offered me $10,000. I want the record to show that I'm giving back $5,000 to the defendant and will try this case strictly on its merits."

In Arizona the old-time lawmen have a saying, "You can get much further with a kind word and a gun than you can with a kind word alone."

The story is told of an explorer coming upon a tribe of cannibals who were about to sit down to a hearty meal of human flesh. Chatting with the cannibals' chief, the American was astonished to find that he had been educated in the United States and had a law degree from a prominent university.

"Do you mean to say," demanded the explorer, "that you attended law school only to return here to eat humans?"

"Oh, yes," replied the chief. "But, of course, now I use a knife and fork."

Lyndon Johnson said that a town that can't support one lawyer can always support two.

Seeking a handsome settlement for injuries he had sustained when his wagon was run off the road by a big-city driver, a farmer took his case to court. An attorney for the defense grilled him. "Did you say to the defendant immediately after the accident that you were hurt?

"Well," said the farmer, "sort of."

"Please answer my question," repeated the attorney. "Did you say you were hurt and, if not, why not?"

"Let me explain," said the farmer. "You see, when that

big Caddy hit my wagon, it knocked me off the road and into a ditch. My horse was knocked across the road and broke his leg. And my dog was pinned under the wagon. Your client took one look at the yelping dog and the writhing horse, and went back to his car and got a big pistol. Next, he walked over and shot my horse. Then he went over and shot my dog. Finally, with his pistol still smoking, he came to where I lay bleeding in the ditch and asked, "How about you? Are you hurt?"

There is a story told about Federal Judge Leon Yankwich of Los Angeles, who was almost totally blind and had thick glasses that looked like telescopes. A Phoenix lawyer was making a long and technical argument before him, reading from a prepared text. For several minutes he didn't glance up from his notes, and when he did, the judge was not on the bench.

The Phoenix attorney whispered to his partner, "Where did that little S.O.B. go?"

Yankwich, who had climbed down off the bench to read over the lawyer's shoulder, said, "Here I am."

A law firm sent a junior associate to plead a case in another town. Soon he sent the office a telegram: "Justice has triumphed." They wired back: "Appeal at once."

There was another young lawyer who showed up at a revival meeting and was asked to offer the opening prayer. Unprepared, he gave a prayer straight from his heart. "Oh, Lord, stir up strife amongst these, thy people, in order that this, thy servant, may not perish."

A wealthy Oklahoma oil baron died after a protracted illness, and his attorney gathered the entire family for the reading of the will. Relatives came from near and far to see if they were included in the bequests.

The lawyer ceremoniously opened the will and began to read:

"To my cousin Nancy, I leave my ranch.

"To my brother George, I leave my bank.

"To my neighbor and good friend, Oscar, I leave my oil stocks.

"To my uncle Stanley, I leave an office building in Tulsa.

"And finally, to my cousin Willie, who always wanted to be remembered in my will, 'Hi, Willie.' "

The juror was asked if he was prejudiced against the defendant.

"Oh, no, judge. I think we ought to give him a fair trial . . . and then I think we ought to take the son of a bitch out and string him up!"

A lawyer, a priest, and an accountant hired a boat and went fishing off the Florida coast. As luck would have it, the boat smashed into a reef and the fishermen were left perched on a small rock. The three had a discussion about who was best suited to swim the mile to shore through a school of sharks. Concluding that they all would die if they stayed on the rock, the lawyer eventually decided to give it a try.

He dove in the water and the sharks swarmed around him, but then, instead of attacking, they formed lines on either side and escorted him to the beach.

"Thank God!" said the priest. "It's a miracle."

"Miracle, hell," said the accountant. "It's professional courtesy."

I once had a client whose favorite expression was "most un-Christian, most un-Christian." After I went to Wash-

221

ington, my law partner sent me a clipping describing a recent incident where a drunk came home one night, took a foot-long crucifix off the mantel, and beat his wife over the head.

Underneath the clipping my partner wrote, "I think this most un-Christian."

I said, "The only way it would be more so would be to have done it on Mother's Day."

During a trial in Tucson, one of the attorneys repeatedly requested the testimony of a witness from the Arizona Corporations Commission. Unbeknownst to the attorney, however, the sought-after witness was long dead.

Attorney Tom Chandler could stand it no longer. "Your honor, if they are going to call that particular witness, they'll need a recess and a shovel."

In a community in Texas, a not very upright character was sentenced to thirty days for stealing a ham. Two weeks after he had started his sentence, his wife visited the judge and begged for his release.

"Is he a good husband?" the judge asked.

"No, sir, he's a no-account."

"Does he treat the children well?"

"No, sir, he's right mean to them."

"Well, does he stay at home when he's not in jail?"

"No, sir, he runs around a lot."

"Then," said the judge, "why in the world do you want him out of jail?"

"I'll tell you, judge," the woman said, "we're about to run out of ham."

In Utah, Death Row convicts get to choose the method of their execution: firing squad or hanging. I heard of the man

222

who chose the firing squad and, when asked if he had a final request, said to the executioner: "Yes. A bullet-proof vest."

Representative Brooks Hays told of a slow-talking lawyer who so delayed the courtroom proceedings that the judge was prompted to say, "Lawyer Chambers reminds me of the girl in Arkansas who talked very, very slowly. She sat in the moonlight with her boyfriend and he asked her if she was a virgin. By the time she could tell him she was . . . she wasn't."

And Andrew Young picked up this piece of advice from a government lawyer charged with regulating business: "Nothing is illegal if one hundred well-placed businessmen decide to do it."

Loyalty, Consistency, and Courage

Senator Henry Fountain Ashurst once said, "I have no trouble with my enemies, but my friends, yes, they are the ones that keep me walking the floor nights."

A man died and went to heaven. Through a miracle he was permitted to visit hell. Then, in an even larger miracle, he was allowed to return to earth. Upon his return he was surrounded by incredulous friends who inquired whether he was more impressed with heaven or hell.

"If you go for alabaster cities, pearly gates, streets paved with gold, angels flitting around making beautiful music, then there is simply no place like heaven.

"But, if you like the warmth of old companions, and the joy of renewing old associations long past, you really can't beat hell."

Sometime after the Civil War, when U.S. Grant was president, his old comrade in arms, General Sherman, declined to correct a policy of Grant's. When asked why, he replied, "Grant stood by me when I was crazy, and I stood by him when he was drunk . . . and now we stand by each other."

It is said that if you find a starving dog, feed him, and make him prosperous, he will not bite you. This is the principal difference between a dog and a man.

Jim Wright once lamented his unfair treatment at the hands of his hometown constituents: "When I returned to my district office there were long and loud complaints that I was spending too much time there and should be in Washington. Then, when I didn't make it for several weeks, others said, 'Who does that guy think he is? We only see him during elections.'

A colleague once told me, "This job has done wonders for my paranoia: now I have real enemies."

Lincoln commented after an election loss suffered at the same time his longtime rival Stephen Douglas had lost, "His defeat gives me more pleasure than my own gives me pain."

Tales of losers remind me of the story of the angry lawyer who had just lost an important case and reacted to the decision with an air of offended majesty that was not lost upon the judge. "Is your conduct meant to express contempt for this court?" the lawyer was asked by the judge. "Express my contempt for this court?" said the lawyer. "No, your honor, I'm trying to conceal it, but I find it damned hard to do."

The public rivalry between Sir Winston Churchill and George Bernard Shaw has given rise to one of the most famous of the rhetorical ripostes, though Leon Harris, in his book, *The*

Fine Art of Political Wit, says it is possibly apocryphal. Shaw is said to have sent Churchill two tickets to his new play which was opening in London, ". . . and bring a friend, if you have one." Churchill replied that he was busy that evening, but asked Shaw to send him a pair of tickets to the second performance, ". . . if there is one."

Whenever I read of illegalities committed "in the interest of national security" by the CIA—an agency created to counter Soviet intelligence agencies—I am reminded of the old philosopher who said, "Choose your enemy wisely, for in time you will become like him."

Politicians would do well to remember H. G. Wells's dictum: "To be honest, one must be inconsistent."

I once told a Washington audience that the Nixon administration's greatest claim to fame was that it kept the world safe for euphemisms after an administration spokesman described the White House's stance on an important piece of legislation, "unyielding, but flexible rigidity."

It has always seemed to me that the Republican party has more than its share of know-nothings. Whenever I get trapped in a verbal exchange with one of these obtuse people, I think of the story about that friend of William Jennings Bryan who stopped him on his way to a debate. The friend asked the Great Orator the subject of the debate. Bryan said that the subject was an obscure issue, one he knew nothing about.

"How, then, are you going to debate?"

"Sir, I shall take the negative. . . . You don't have to know anything to oppose a proposition."

225

Then there was the politician who proudly proclaimed himself "a liberal conservative . . . or was that a conservative liberal?"

I have often called attention to the use of fancy words to cover up reality by government or military officials. I contrast General Douglas MacArthur, who had his troops *repulsed* at the Yalu River during the Korean War, and General Vinigar Joe Stilwell, who was driven back from Burma by the Japanese in World War II. When Stilwell was told his action had been a "tactical retreat," he retorted, "I claim that we took a hell of a beating."

When asked if he was a Democrat or a Republican, Mark Russell answered, "I am a four-square, undecided independent . . . I think."

When I see congressmen rant and rave about budget deficits, while at the same time voting for their own pet pork-barrel projects, I'm reminded of the man who went into a restaurant, hung his expensive new topcoat on a coat rack, and sat down to eat. He looked up to see a thief grab his coat, put it on, and begin to run away.

The owner, enlisting a nearby policeman's help, gave chase. When they caught up, the police officer ordered the thief to halt. But the thief kept running, and the cop drew his pistol to fire.

Seeing this, the coat owner shouted, "Shoot him in the pants!"

During the tumultous riots in Paris during the French Revolution of 1848, the leftist leader Ledru-Rollin was quoted as saying, "Where is the mob? I have got to follow them, I am their leader."

When I came to the Congress I was confronted with the oldest and most basic questions of a representative democracy: For whom does a legislator vote? Should a congressman vote his or her strongly held convictions? Or those of a majority of the constituents?

In this now-classic statement, Edmund Burke rejected the "weather vane" view of the legislator's role. "Your interests must come ahead of mine, your opinion and wishes ought to have great weight and high respect," Burke told his constituents. "But your representative owes you not his industry, but his judgment, and he betrays instead of services you if he sacrifices it to your opinion."

Few politicians have the courage to champion a losing cause, even if they know it's right. A high school football team from the relatively big town of Safford, Arizona, was playing a team from the hamlet of Solomonville. The lads from Solomonville were badly outmatched in size, depth, and talent. Their only asset was one very big kid, Rudolfo.

Solomonville's coach decided to exploit his only weapon. When his team gained possession, the coach shouted, "Give the ball to Rudolfo! Give the ball to Rudolfo!"

When the quarterback did not follow his instructions, the coach again shouted for Rudolfo to get the pigskin. Finally, the harried quarterback stood up and shouted back, "Rudolfo don't want the ball!"

Adlai Stevenson was not above voicing his disappointment when he lost. After the 1952 election, he recalled a Lincoln story told after one of Abe's own setbacks. "I feel a little like the boy who stubbed his toe in the dark while running to meet his sweetheart. The boy said he was too big to cry and far too badly hurt to laugh."

227

President Ford's bullheaded attitude on oil prices in 1976 was like that of the bull who stood in front of the onrushing train. A farmer said to the bull, "I certainly admire your courage, but I must unconditionally damn your judgment."

At one dinner party at which Churchill had put down his customary amount of claret and brandy, a socialist member of Parliament, Mrs. Bessie Braddock of Liverpool, confronted Churchill saying, "Mr. Churchill, you're drunk!" He replied, "And you, Bessie, are ugly. But tomorrow morning, I'll be sober, but you'll still be ugly."

Politicians

Senator Sam Ervin of North Carolina became famous for his rich store of country humor during those critical months he chaired the Senate Watergate hearings. Yet my favorite Ervin story originated in 1954 when he was a freshman senator. During the bitter debate over whether to censure Senator Joseph McCarthy, two senators nearly came to blows. Ervin rose and the Senate quieted. He said the scene reminded him of the time his Uncle Ephraim, who had been tortured for years by arthritis, went to church. The mountain preacher asked various members of the congregation what the Lord had done for them. All replied at length about the wonders of the Lord's blessings.

Then the preacher pointed to crippled Uncle Ephraim, bent double in one of the pews, and demanded to know what the Almighty had done for him.

Croaked Uncle Eph: "Brother, he has mighty near ruint me."

"And that is what Senator McCarthy has done to the Senate," Ervin concluded.

Every good Democrat knows that Republicans aren't the most compassionate people on earth. Once, at the end of a floor debate in which conservative Republicans were trying to cut funds going to illegitimate children, Representative Bob Eckhardt, Democrat of Texas, went to the microphone and said quietly: "I'm not so much concerned with the natural bastards as I am with the self-made ones."

Here's a warning to every incumbent:

After serving in Congress for fourteen years, Representative Tom Downing started his 1972 campaign. He asked the first man he met if he would vote for him for Congress. The man said, "Sure I will. Anything would be better than what we have up there now."

After the 1984 Democratic primary season came to a close, Senator Fritz Hollings looked back on the experience with some wistfulness. "You know, Thomas Wolfe lied, you can come home again. In fact, in my case, the people of New Hampshire insisted on it."

A guest seated in the visitors' gallery of the Senate watched intently as the chaplain opened the day's proceedings with an invocation. "Does the chaplain pray for the senators?" the man asked. "No," replied his companion. "He looks at the senators and then prays for the country."

During his lengthy tenure as chairman of the House Judiciary Committee, Emmanuel Celler was once asked how he stood on a given bill. With disarming candor Celler replied, "I don't stand on it. I am sitting on it. It rests four-square under my fanny and will never see the light of day."

In 1934, during a debate over one of the key New Deal bills, one government official ventured the opinion that the legislation might be unconstitutional. Giving voice to the mood of the times, another official interjected, "Hell, what's the Constitution between friends."

Asked at a press conference about the chances of a certain bill passing the Senate, Republican Minority Leader Everett Dirksen said, "Ha, ha, ha. And, I might add, ho, ho, ho."

When asked for a comment about a particularly offensive statement by my fellow Arizonan, the very conservative Representative Sam Stieger, I paraphrased Voltaire: "I disagree with almost everything he says; and I am prepared to incur only minor injuries to defend his right to say them."

One of my favorite Texans is Bob Strauss, the former Democratic National Committee chairman and one of the gifted politicians of my era. Strauss could follow you through a revolving door and come out first. Some said that for forty years Strauss took money from the rich and votes from the poor, convincing each group that he was protecting them from the other.

Some politicians believe that when they have coined a slogan they have solved a problem.

Adlai Stevenson used humor to make a point on serious subjects. While discussing education, he quoted the prisoner who said to his cellmate, "I'm going to study and improve myself. While you'll still be a common thief, I'll be an embezzler."

Speaking of taxes, Stevenson said, "There was a time when a fool and his money were soon parted; now it happens to everybody."

The Nixon administration's agricultural policies were ruinous for farmers, and his agriculture secretary, Earl Butz, was held in "minimal high regard" throughout the Midwest. When I was campaigning in Iowa in 1975, I used to joke that things were getting so bad that it might be necessary to bring back the old "Earl Butz" tractor. This was a tractor that had no seat and no steering wheel—a tractor designed for a farmer who's lost his ass and doesn't know which way to turn.

I'd follow that joke by asking the crowd if they knew the difference between a pigeon and an Iowa farmer. The pigeon, I said, can still make a deposit on a new tractor.

The politician's prayer: "O Lord, give us the wisdom to utter words which are gentle and tender . . . for tomorrow we may have to eat them."

Sometimes politicians are criticized for treating major issues with levity. Representative Bill Hungate of Missouri took such abuse after the protracted impeachment hearings of Richard Nixon. Said Hungate: "I would apologize to some if they have found my attempts at humor offensive. But I have never thought a sense of humor needed to destroy your sense of responsibility, and, in my case, I felt it was better to have a sense of humor than no sense at all."

California Congressman Phil Burton, famous for his legislative arm-twisting, was once disappointed by a secret caucus vote. As he reviewed the vote, Burton recalled the crusty newspaper editor who asked that the following be put on his headstone: "Life is a god-damned treacherous, stinking game . . . and 999 men out of every 1,000 are bastards."

During the heady period following John Kennedy's inauguration, someone commented to Speaker Sam Rayburn about the tremendous brilliance and intellect of the new Kennedy team—in the mind of the commentator, the best set of brains ever brought to Washington. "That may be true," said Rayburn, "but I'd feel a lot better if just one or two of them had ever run for sheriff."

During the early days of the Republic, Henry Clay encountered his ancient foe, John Randolph, on a narrow sidewalk bordering a muddy street, a quagmire of hay, horse manure, and chicken droppings. Randolph, who was wearing a gun and was accompanied by two bodyguards, said, "I never step aside for scoundrels." Clay considered the odds for a moment, and then, stepping aside, said, "I always do."

When former Iowa congressman and later Senator John Culver was first elected, he set out for Washington. The night before their journey east, Culver and his wife overheard their three children saying their bedtime prayers. The youngest one said,

Now I lay me down to sleep,
I pray the Lord my soul to keep.

God bless Mommy, Daddy, Grandma, and sister. . . .
And now, good-bye God . . . we're going to Washington.

Presidents

Of the twelve presidents during my lifetime, Jack Kennedy was, in my opinion, the wittiest, with Ronald Reagan and perhaps FDR running second and third. Among the others,

Coolidge had the driest wit; if Harding, Hoover, Nixon, and Carter were humorous it wasn't in public; Harry Truman's earthy humor and quick shots at more pompous opponents were very popular; Gerry Ford and Dwight Eisenhower were a bit awkward in delivering a one-liner, but not at all reticent about laughing at their own mishaps; and LBJ was a master of Texas-style humor—barbecued with braggadocio.

Ronald Reagan is undoubtedly the liveliest wit in the White House since Kennedy, though looking over the presidents who have served in between, that's not saying a hell of a lot. Reagan is quick with a quip, has a one-liner to fit every occasion, and understands the importance of timing in telling jokes. He has even managed to pull off the unthinkable— to tell an off-color joke before a large audience: "When you go to bed with the federal government," the president once said, "you get more than a good night's sleep."

Over the past few decades the presidency has increasingly come to be viewed as a twenty-four-hour-a-day job, and Reagan has been much criticized for decamping to his California ranch whenever the mood strikes. But Reagan is just reviving a long-dormant tradition in which presidents routinely packed off for months at a time, as this 1816 notice from the *Niles' Weekly Register* attests: "Washington, June 6—The President and his family left this city yesterday for Montpelier, where it is expected he will spend the summer months; there being no public business, at this time, particularly requiring his attendance at the seat of government."

Herewith a sampling of other presidential anecdotes:

No president has used political humor to better effect than Abe Lincoln—although he was often criticized by the press and public of his day for treating tragic events lightly. Lincoln had a perfect answer for his critics.

Lincoln told of the long-legged boy who was "sparking" a farmer's daughter. When her father caught them kissing, he grabbed a shotgun. The boy jumped through a window, and started running across the cabbage patch, scaring up a rabbit. In about two leaps the boy caught up with the rabbit, kicked it high in the air, and grunted, "Git out of the road and let somebody run that knows how."

Lincoln also told of the Kentucky horse sale where a small boy, the son of a horse trader, mounted a horse to show off its fine points. A man whispered, "Look here, boy, hain't that horse got the splints?" The boy replied, "Mister, I don't know what the splints is, but if it's good for him, he has got it; if it ain't good for him, he ain't got it."

When he was speaking to an audience of lawyers, Lincoln often told of the strict judge who "would hang a man for blowing his nose in the street, but . . . would quash the indictment if it failed to specify which hand he blew it with."

When Lincoln presented the proposed Emancipation Proclamation to his cabinet, they unanimously opposed it. He said, "On this issue the nays have seven, the ayes have one—the ayes have it."

When a woman chided Lincoln, saying he should *destroy* the rebels, not speak kindly of them, he answered, "What, madam, do I not destroy my enemies when I make them my friends?"

Throughout his career, Republican Senator Albert Fall was a political opponent of Woodrow Wilson, and he helped torpedo Wilson's great dream: the entry of the United States into the League of Nations. But when he heard that President Wilson had suffered a stroke, Fall went to visit him.

He said, "Mr. President, all the Senate is praying for you." "Which way, senator, which way?" Wilson bitterly retorted.

Calvin Coolidge didn't mind the press criticizing him for his lack of humor: "I think the American public wants a solemn ass as president . . . and I think I'll go along with them."

Coolidge also possessed a surefire strategy for avoiding blunders—he wouldn't talk. At one point during the monumentally boring 1924 presidential campaign, Coolidge agreed to take questions from a group of reporters.
"Have you any statement to make on the state of the campaign?" the first reporter asked.
"No," replied Coolidge.
"Can you tell us anything about the world situation?" a second queried.
"No."
"Any information on Prohibition?" a third prompted.
"No."
As the disappointed reporters left, Silent Cal called out, "Now remember, boys, don't quote me."

Coolidge was once asked how many people worked in the White House. With his usual loquacity, he replied: "About half of them, I guess."

Teddy Roosevelt once said his vice president and successor, William Howard Taft, was a man "who means well feebly."

Thomas Marshall wrote: "Once there were two brothers. One ran away to sea, the other was elected vice president, and nothing was ever heard of either of them again."

William Wheeler, vice president during the presidency of
Rutherford B. Hayes, was happy in his job. When asked if
he was ready to seek the presidency, Wheeler said: "Run
for president? I should say not. The truth alone could beat
me . . . not to mention what the opposition would dig up."

Finley Peter Dunne's "Mr. Dooley" said of the vice presidency: "It's ssthrange about th' vice-prisidincy. Th' prisidincy
is th' highest office in th' gift iv th' people. Th' vice prisidincy
is th' next highest an' th' lowest. It isn't a crime exactly.
Ye can't be sint to jail f'r it, but it's a kind iv a disgrace
. . . it's like writin' anonymous letters . . . at a convintion
nearly all th' dillygtes lave as soon as they've nommynated
th' prisident f'r fear wan iv thim will be nommynated f'r
vice prisident."

Alben Barkley was never president, but this veep left his
mark on Washington, perhaps more than any other vice president, for his style and his warm Kentucky-bred wit.
   Asked about a reported difference he had with the president
and whether he would change his mind, Barkley replied,
"You ask me if I have seen the light? No, but I have felt
the heat."

Barkley once likened the actions of a colleague "to the young
man who slew his mother and father with an ax and then
asked the court for mercy on the grounds that he was an
orphan."

Former Republican senator Kenneth Keating is credited with
first having said, "Roosevelt proved a man could be president
for life; Truman proved anybody could be president; and
Eisenhower proved you don't need to have a president."

Adlai Stevenson said Eisenhower reminded him of an Australian bushman who got a new boomerang and spent the rest of his life trying to throw away the old one.

Like Reagan, Eisenhower, too, had a "Teflon" presidency. A farmer once complained to Stevenson about the Eisenhower administration's farm policy. "Well, then," Stevenson asked, "why aren't the farmers mad as hell at Eisenhower?" The farmer was astonished, "Why, nobody connects Eisenhower with the administration!"

During the 1960 presidential campaign, advance man Maury Maverick was in charge of arrangements for Jack Kennedy's visit to San Antonio. With the Alamo as his backdrop, Kennedy gave a rousing speech to ten thousand people. When he finished, Maverick and other local Democratic leaders took him on a tour inside. After the tour, one of Kennedy's men said, "Maury, let's get Jack out the back door to avoid the crowd."

Maverick replied: "Hell, there's no back door at the Alamo. . . . That's why we had so many dead heroes."

Feisty reporter May Craig loved to outshout the hordes at presidential press conferences. Once during the Kennedy years she bellowed, "Mr. President! Mr. President! What have you done lately for women?"

Kennedy responded, "Obviously, Miss Craig, not enough."

Larry O'Brien quoted JFK: "Mothers may still want their sons to grow up to become presidents—but they do not want them to become politicians in the process."

At a White House dinner honoring Nobel laureates, JFK said, "I think this is the most extraordinary collection of

237

talent, of human knowledge, that has ever been gathered together at the White House—with the possible exception of when Thomas Jefferson dined alone."

As a U.S. senator, Lyndon Johnson displayed a sign in his office: "You ain't learning nothing when you're talking!"

In the key West Virginia primary, Hubert Humphrey had his last chance to defeat Jack Kennedy in 1960. The Humphrey campaign stressed that Kennedy was a millionaire's son who had never done a day's work in his life. These charges were made on radio, in newspaper ads, and on billboards.

One day, as JFK was shaking hands with some coal miners on a shift change, one stopped and said, "Just a minute, Senator Kennedy, is it true that you are a millionaire's son and have never done a day's work in your life?"

Kennedy grinned and said, "Yeah, I guess so."

The old man slapped him on the back and said, "Let me tell you something, Mister, you haven't missed a damned thing."

On a trip to the West Coast, President Kennedy was asked by a little boy, "Mr. President, how did you become a war hero?"

"It was absolutely involuntary," the president replied. "They sank my boat."

On the campaign trail in 1960, Kennedy attempted to rebut Nixon's charge that he was inexperienced in international affairs. "I know something about Mr. Khrushchev, whom I met a year ago in the Senate Foreign Relations Committee, and I know something about the history of his country, which I visited in 1939. Mr. Khrushchev himself, it is said, told a story a few years ago about the Russian who began to run through the Kremlin shouting, 'Khrushchev is a fool. Khrushchev is a fool.' He was sentenced, the premier said, to twenty-three years in prison: 'three for insulting the party secretary, and twenty for revealing a state secret.' "

At a reception at the White House, President Lyndon Johnson came upon Vietnam dove Senator Frank Church. "Where do you get your ideas on Vietnam?" asked LBJ. "From Walter Lippmann," Church replied. Johnson snorted, "Next time you need a dam in Idaho, you just go ask Walter Lippmann."

LBJ told of a college debater who mentioned to his roommate that an upcoming debate would be a real battle of wits. "How courageous of you," his friend said, "to go unarmed."

In his 1964 stump speech, LBJ said it was futile for any country to try to rule the world by ultimatum. LBJ would emphasize his point by adding: "A long time ago I learned that telling a man to go to hell and making him go are two different propositions."

Presidents have constantly been nagged by the political consequences of unemployment. Calvin Coolidge minced no words on the issue: "When a great many people are unable to find work, unemployment results."

Lincoln said, "No country can sustain in idleness more than a small percentage of its numbers. It is the same spirit which says, 'you toil and work and earn bread, and I'll eat it.' "

Jack Kennedy conceded nothing to his critics: "When you have seven percent unemployed, you have ninety-three percent working."

239

TOO FUNNY TO BE PRESIDENT

Speeches and Speakers

Larry L. King tells this story about Lyndon Johnson: One day Johnson—who was not known for his modesty or considerate treatment of his employees—burst out of the Oval Office brandishing a draft copy of a crucial speech. "Now listen, you sons of bitches," Johnson shouted to a group of speech writers. "This just won't do. I want this to be rewritten and I want you to put some stuff in here to make me sound goddamn humble!"

If you listen closely, you will discover that politicians give basically two types of speeches. There is the "Mother Hubbard" speech, which, like the garment, covers everything, but touches nothing; and the "French bikini" speech, which covers only the essential points.

Whenever I hear a politician droning away, oblivious to the fact that he's lost his audience's attention, I am reminded of the cowboy who wandered into church on Sunday and found the minister ready to deliver his sermon. Since the cowboy was the only person in attendance, the minister inquired if he could go ahead with the sermon.

"Sure, when I find only one cow in the field, I feed it," the cowboy said.

The minister began his sermon and continued on for an hour and a half. At the conclusion, he asked the cowboy how he liked it.

"It was all right," the cowboy said. "But when I find just one cow in the field, I don't unload the whole wagon."

A Pennsylvanian known for being a bore drowned in a terrific flash flood. When he reached heaven, he regaled everyone, including St. Peter, with overblown descriptions—this had been the greatest flood of all time, it had done terrible damage, it had terrorized the populace, and on and on.

The bore kept nagging St. Peter to give him twenty minutes to speak of the flood before the celestial body at its weekly assembly. St. Peter finally relented: "All right, I'll give you twenty minutes, but I must advise you that Noah will be in the audience."

An Agriculture Department bureaucrat was invited to address a cattlemen's association in rural Texas. In a high-pitched voice, the bureaucrat rambled on for two hours. Toward the end of his speech, he noticed that some of the men in the audience were unholstering their guns. After he finished, he nervously eyed the surly men and asked the chairman if he was in danger.

"No, you are our guest, so you are safe. But I wouldn't want to be the program chairman."

A professor teaching English told his class that the good story should work into the first paragraph, if possible, a reference to the deity, royalty, sex, and a touch of mystery. A student came back in a few minutes and said, "I think I've got it." His opening paragraph read: "Oh, my God," said the queen, "I'm pregnant again. I wonder who could have done it this time."

Sometimes speech writers get carried away and write florid and eloquent speeches that bear no relation to the way one normally speaks. A Republican friend phoned me one day and said, "I want to read something to you." He proceeded to read a thoughtful and restrained analysis of one of the great issues of the day. When he finished he said, "Well, what do you think of that?"

241

"That's wonderful," I said. "Who said it?"
"You did," he replied.

Sports

The use of sports metaphors is often helpful in making a political point. When Gerry Ford refused to sign my strip-mining bill after I had labored long and hard to secure its passage, I told this story:

Pitcher Don Drysdale of the Los Angeles Dodgers often complained about how little offensive support he and the rest of the Dodgers pitching staff received. After taking a day off, Drysdale returned to the Dodgers' hotel to rejoin the team. As he entered the lobby, an excited fan rushed up to him to tell him that Sandy Koufax had just pitched a no-hitter against the Phillies.

"Did he win?" asked dour Don.

At a troubled point early in JFK's administration, the pundits wrote an endless series of columns offering their advice as to how he could do a better job as president. This prompted JFK to tell this story:

"There was once a legendary baseball player," Kennedy said. "He never failed to hit when at bat; never dropped a ball; grounders hit to him never dribbled between his legs; he had an arm like a bull whip which threw with unerring accuracy. He never had a mental lapse; in the field and on the bases he had the speed and grace of a leopard. Fly balls were judged quickly and accurately on every occasion. He never tired or missed a signal. In fact, he would have been one of the all-time greats except for one thing . . . no one was ever able to get him to put down his beer and hot dog and come out of the press box to play."

Here's another story useful for zinging the pundits: A high school baseball team was in the midst of early season practice, and the left fielder was having a tough time of it. He was dropping fly balls, throwing to the wrong base, and running into other fielders. In disgust, the coach ran out and said, "Give me your glove and I'll show you how to play."

The coach promptly dropped four consecutive flies, ran into the center fielder, tripped, and fell on his face.

He picked himself up and said, "Dooley, you've loused up left field so bad that nobody can play it."

A man was traveling on a train with his elderly mother. When he returned from the diner to find her deathly ill, he rushed off to find a priest. The conductor told him that the Notre Dame football team occupied the last car and that they might have a priest traveling with them. The man went to the car and found a coach. He explained the problem.

"Yes," said the coach, "we have two priests. Which do you want—offensive or defensive?"

Politics is rife with duplicity—and so is the game of golf. I like to tell of the duffer who was approached by a lonely-looking minister waiting to play. The minister asked the duffer if he needed a partner. "Yes, I do," replied the man, "What's your average?" "About eighty-five," said the minister. "Good, that's about mine too," said the duffer.

To make things interesting, the duffer suggested they play for a dollar a hole. The minister accepted, and then was dismayed when he lost eighteen dollars to the obviously expert player.

After the game the minister thanked the hustler for the enjoyable round and then said, "By the way, where do you live?"

"Why do you ask?" said the golfer.

"I thought that I'd go over and perform a marriage ceremony for your mother and father."

To make the point that sometimes in politics things are not what they seem, I tell this story:

A callow Mormon lad was at the racetrack for the first time. He saw a priest in the paddock give a horse a blessing. The boy took the horse's number and placed a small bet. Sure enough, the horse won. For the next several races the boy went to the paddock, saw the priest bless a horse, placed a bet, and won. On the last race of the day he repeated the routine and bet all of his winnings on the anointed horse. Rounding the final turn the horse had a sizable lead, but then he suddenly dropped dead. The young man sought out the priest to complain.

"That's the trouble with you Mormons," said the priest. "You don't know the difference between a simple blessing and the last rites."

When the cards seem stacked against me, I'll tell this yarn:

In Kentucky a race with four horses entered was about to begin. The favorite was named Bluebell. A man walked up to the betting window and placed $100 on Bluebell to win. A minute later he put down another $500 on Bluebell. And then, just a minute later, he returned to put down another $1,000. An observer went up to him and said, "Sir, I couldn't help but notice your bet. I just want to warn you that Bluebell can't win this race."

"Why not?" said the bettor.

"Because," said the observer, "I own Bluebell."

"Well then," said the bettor, "it's going to be a damn slow race because I own all the other horses."

It's often said that the president is the "coach" of the nation, and during the last eight years I've often thought of this story:

A football team, nursing a narrow lead, took possession on its own three-yard line. The coach sent his young quarterback in with instructions to "run play 22-E twice, then punt . . . no matter what happens."

The quarterback called play 22-E and miraculously it gained 45 yards. He called it again and gained 47 more yards. With the ball on the opponent's five-yard line, first down and goal to go, the quarterback called for a punt.

After the punter had kicked the ball virtually out of the stadium, the coach grabbed the quarterback as he came off the field.

"Just what was going through your mind on that last play? First and five to go on the goal line and you call for a punt?" the coach shouted.

"What was going through my mind," answered the player, "was, 'Man, have we ever got a dumb coach.' "

Vices, Including Drinking

Jokes about drunks, vice, sex, and sin are a surefire way to get a laugh. There's a fine line between the tasteful and the tasteless here, however, and I'd advise against using any "vice" jokes unless you are sure of your audience. For example, you obviously wouldn't use jokes about drunks when speaking to a church tea, but they just might work.

LBJ told the story of an old codger by the name of Uncle Ezra who was going deaf, but whose ailment didn't prevent him from pursuing his lifelong enjoyment of hard liquor. "If you ever want to hear again," warned his doctor, "cut out the hootch." But ol' Ezra kept right on drinking because, as he said, "I like what I drink a hell of a lot better than what I hear."

Senator Sam Ervin told the story of a constituent who bought a jug of moonshine liquor and gave a portion to a friend. Later, he asked his friend what he thought of the moonshine.

"Well," the friend said, "it was just right."

"What do you mean, 'just right'?" he retorted.

"I mean that if it had been any better, you wouldn't have given it to me. And if it had been any worse, I couldn't have drunk it."

An old Kentuckian who lay a-dying motioned his wife to his sickbed. "Mary," he whispered, "you remember that old trunk in the basement? There is a quart of bourbon, fine old bourbon, in the trunk. Go down and fetch it."

He then directed her to fill a glass with finely crushed ice, to bruise some mint, and to stir it in the glass with just a pinch of sugar. Next he told her to fill the glass with bourbon and then to set it aside until frost formed on the outside of the glass.

"And then, Mary," gasped the old man, his voice now all but extinguished, "bring it to me and, Mary, no matter what I do or say, make me drink it."

During a mining boom, Mark Twain visited Virginia City, Nevada, a place of rampant sin, abundant booze, and wild women. "It was no place for a Presbyterian," Twain said, "and I did not long remain one."

The desk clerk at a fancy New York hotel got a call in the middle of the night from a man who demanded to know when the bar opened. Told that it opened at 9:00 A.M., the man hung up.

A couple of hours later the man called again to ask the same question. When, a few minutes later, he called a third time, the manager answered and said, "Look, my friend, the bar does not open until nine o'clock. And when it does, I've given instructions that they are not to allow you in!"

"Hey!" the caller protested, "You've got me wrong. I'm not trying to get in—I'm trying to get out!"

Annoyed by numerous complaints of General U.S. Grant's boozing, Abe Lincoln said, "Delegation after delegation has called on me with the same request: 'Recall Grant from command.' One day a delegation headed by a distinguished doctor of divinity from New York called on me and made the familiar protest. After the clergyman had concluded his remarks, I asked if anyone else had anything to add. They replied that they did not. Then, looking as serious as I could, I said, 'Doctor, can you tell me where General Grant gets his liquor?' The doctor seemed quite nonplussed, but replied that he could not. I then said to him, 'I am very sorry, for if you could tell me, I would direct the chief quartermaster of the army to furnish a supply to some of my other generals who have never won a victory.'"

I think it was Speaker Sam Rayburn who said, "Why be stupid and weak when, with one drink, you can feel smart and strong."

A little church was holding a lively prayer meeting and the deacon was warning the congregation of the perils of sin and iniquity. Just then an inebriated gentleman, who had been at a costume party dressed as Satan himself, stumbled into the church. The congregation took one look and spilled out of the chapel from every possible exit, including the windows. One hefty parishioner got herself wedged in the win-

247

dow. As the drunken partygoer approached to help, the lady screamed out, "That's all right, Mr. Devil, I've been on your side all the time!"

Vice president Alben Barkley used to tell a story about a hitchhiker who was picked up by an old moonshiner. They drove along for a while and then the old-timer said, "Son, there's a jug under the seat, get it out." The young man reached under the seat and brought out a jug of freshly made moonshine.

"Take a drink," the man said.

"No, thank you, sir, I really wouldn't care for one," the lad said.

The old man pulled a pistol from his pocket and held it to the boy's temple and said, "Now take a drink."

"Under the circumstances, sir, don't mind if I do," the boy said, taking a healthy swig. His eyes watered, his stomach burned, and he choked as the moonshine hit bottom.

The old man then handed his pistol to the boy, and said, "Now you hold the gun on me and I'll take a drink."

Will Rogers

Everyone has heard something, or read something, that has special meaning, that has given you a path or guiding light. Mine is Will Rogers's admonition: "We are here for just a spell and then pass on. So get a few laughs and do the best you can. Live your life so that whenever you lose, you are ahead."

Of Will Rogers's speech at the Democratic convention of 1932 Heywood Broun said, "It seems ironic that the same convention which thinks Will Rogers is a clown, accepts Huey Long as a statesman."

During the Great Depression, Rogers said he couldn't recall when the country had seemed more united; he explained it by suggesting that "the worse off we get, the louder we laugh, which is a good thing. Every American international banker ought to have printed on his office door: 'Alive today by the grace of a nation that has a sense of humor.' "

Rogers was invited to speak to the board of directors of Standard Oil company. He said, "Your motto is Service. Back on the farm, when I heard that the bull was 'servicing' the cows, I looked behind the barn. And, gentlemen, what that bull was doing to the cow is exactly what you people have been doing to the public all these years."

Rogers had numberless favorite stories. When asked to tell some of the old ones, he told the audience about the prison where all the jokes were so well known that the inmates numbered them to save themselves the trouble of lengthy recitations. Thus they could entertain one another by simply saying, "Number thirty-four," and, after the laughter died down, "Number twenty-eight."

A new inmate came along and thought he'd try his hand. "Number one!" he shouted. No one laughed.

"Why didn't they laugh?" he asked.

"You didn't tell it right."